A Practical Guide to the Memorandum and Articles of Association

2nd edition

**SARA HOLLOWELL AND
MARTHA BRUCE**

ICSA

PUBLISHING

Published by ICSA Information & Training
16 Park Crescent
London W1B 1AH

© ICSA Information & Training Ltd, 2009

Typeset in Sabon with Franklin Gothic by
Hands Fotoset, Nottingham

Printed and bound in Great Britain by
Hobbs the Printers Ltd, Totton, Hampshire

British Library Cataloguing in Publication Data
A catalogue record for this book is available from the British Library.

ISBN: 978-1-86072-431-2

Contents

Preface

This book is intended as a practical resource for anyone wishing to draft, amend or interpret a company's memorandum and articles of association. It will be of interest to company secretaries, company secretarial assistants and anyone with responsibility for or who advises on company secretarial matters, such as finance directors, in-house counsels and other legal advisers.

As the book was being written, much of the Companies Act 2006 had already come into force. The final tranche of provisions is due to be implemented on 1 October 2009 and, where necessary, both the Companies Act 1985 provisions and the Companies Act 2006 provisions yet to be implemented are referred to.

Writing this book in the midst of the most significant revision of company law for two decades and keeping it concise with its focus squarely on providing practical commentary on the memorandum and articles has proved challenging, but it is hoped that the reader finds the book a useful source of reference. Key new areas covered include:

- what action is required to address the change in the status of the memorandum;
- analysis of the new model articles and what they mean for companies;
- guidance on reviewing and revising your articles to take advantage of changes introduced by the Companies Act 2006, such as electronic communications, indemnity clauses, directors' conflicts of interests and provisions relating to the holding of annual general meetings; and
- how to deal with the repeal of authorised share capital requirements.

Many topics of interest and importance relating to the running of a company are referred to in passing as, in practical terms, there are very few matters which can be determined by reference to the articles alone. Forfeiture of shares is one such matter, as it has no statutory basis. However, to ensure the content of the book is considered within context, in addition to the relevant statutory references and model article provisions we have indicated key associated company law topics that are beyond the scope of the book, which the reader might want to address in more detail.

Chapters 2 and 3 of the book discuss the status and content of the memorandum and articles of association. Chapter 4 provides guidance on the amendments companies might wish to make to their articles in light of the changes of law brought into force by the Companies Act 2006. Chapters 5–8 follow the subject headings used in the model articles: directors, shares and distributions, and decision-making by shareholders. Since the constitutional documents are vital right from the start of a company's life, Chapter 9 looks at the procedures for forming a company insofar as they relate to these constitutional documents and key issues to consider, such as restrictions on choosing a company's name. As the book aims to be of practical application, tips and a significant amount of precedent material have been included to assist the reader. Further reference materials can be found at the end of the book in the Appendices.

Whilst every effort has been made to ensure the accuracy of the content of this book, neither the authors nor the publisher can accept responsibility for any loss arsing to anyone relying solely on the information contained herein.

Sara Hollowell LLB FCIS
Martha Bruce FCIS
Both of David Venus & Company Limited

Abbreviations

AGM	Annual general meeting
Articles	Articles of association
CA 1985	Companies Act 1985 (as amended)
CA 2006	Companies Act 2006
DRG	Dematerialisation Reference Group
GC 100	The Association for the General Counsel and Company Secretaries of FTSE 100 companies
ICSA	Institute of Chartered Secretaries and Administrators

Glossary of key terms

Annual general meeting A meeting of the Company's members which must be held in each period of six months beginning with the day following its accounting reference date.

Articles of association A constitutional document setting out the internal regulations of a company. Unless excluded or modified, the default article provisions contained in Table A or the Model Articles, as the case may be, have effect. See also *Table A* and *Model Articles*.

Case law The general term used to describe the principles and rules of law established by judicial opinion and decisions.

Class rights The rights attached to different classes of share.

Companies Acts The Companies Act 1985, the Companies Act 2006 and other companies acts as in force from time to time.

Company secretary An officer of a company who performs a range of duties in relation to the administration and corporate governance of the company, usually with responsibility for legal and sometimes financial compliance. Private companies do not need to have a company secretary unless otherwise stipulated in their articles. The company secretary of a public company must meet specific qualification requirements prescribed by company law.

Corporate representative An individual appointed by a shareholder that is a corporation to act on its behalf at general meetings.

Director An officer of a company responsible for determining policy, supervising the management of the company's business and exercising the powers of the company. Directors must generally carry out their functions collectively as a board.

Dividends Payments made to the members by distributing part of the company's profits in accordance with the members' respective entitlements as determined by the class and number of shares held.

General meeting A meeting which all members are entitled to attend, subject to any restrictions in the articles.

GC 100 A group of senior legal officers of FTSE 100 companies founded in 2005 to provide a forum for members to share ideas on best practice in an increasingly complex regulatory arena and to help influence policy on matters of common interest.

Memorandum of association A constitutional document governing a company's relationship with the outside world. It states a company's name, place of registration, objects, liability, capital and, in the case of a public company, a declaration of that fact.

Model Articles Articles of association in the forms prescribed by the Companies (Model Articles) Regulations 2008 (SI 2008/3229). They replace Table A as the default articles for companies incorporated on or after 1 October 2009 and will automatically apply unless excluded or varied. Table A will continue to apply to limited companies formed before that date until such time as the articles are amended or new articles adopted. We use the term 'Model Articles' when referring to the three sets, whether individually or collectively and where necessary will make clear any distinctions between them.

Officer Includes a director, managers of sufficient seniority and the secretary of a company.

Ordinary resolution A resolution approved by a simple majority of members (or their proxies) at a general meeting.

Ordinary shares The most common form of share in a company, giving holders the right to a share in the company's profits in proportion to their holdings. Generally, ordinary shares also confer the right to vote at general meetings, although it is possible for ordinary shares to be non-voting.

Preference shares Shares carrying the right to a payment of a fixed dividend out of profits before the payment of an ordinary dividend or the preferential return of capital or both.

Proxy An individual appointed by a member to act on their behalf at a general meeting.

Registered office The address at which legal documents may be served on the company and where the statutory books are normally kept. The registered office need not be where the company carries on its business and may be changed provided it remains within the company's place of registration.

Registrar of Companies A government official who is responsible for maintaining the company records that are filed in compliance with statutory requirements.

Special resolution A resolution that is approved by at least 75% of the members voting at a general meeting.

Statutory books The general term applied to the registers and minute books a company is required to keep by the Companies Acts.

Subscriber A person who subscribes to the memorandum and agrees to take up shares in a company when it is formed.

Table A Specimen articles of association for a company limited by shares as set out in the Companies (Tables A to F) (Amendment) Regulations 2007. Unless excluded or modified the version of Table A in force at the time of incorporation automatically becomes a company's articles. From 1 October 2009 Table A will be replaced by the Model Articles although Table A will continue to apply to companies formed prior to that date until amended. See *Model Articles* above.

Written resolution An alternative to passing resolutions at a general meeting which can be used by private companies to transact all business except the removal of directors and auditors. Written resolutions are passed when signed by the requisite majority but lapse 28 days from date of circulation if not yet passed.

1 Introduction

As the basic constitutional documents of a company, the memorandum and articles of association provide the framework within which a company must operate.

Every company registered in England and Wales must have a memorandum and the form of that memorandum is prescribed by legislation. Details on the content of the memorandum are provided in Chapter 2, save to mention here that the memorandum is a written document which essentially sets out any restrictions on what the company can do. In addition, importantly, it contains a statement from the subscribers (being the founder members) that they wish to be formed into a company pursuant to the memorandum.

Every company must also have articles of association. The articles are the regulations governing a company's internal management. As such, there is more freedom about what the articles contain and they can, and in most instances should, be tailored to suit a company's particular circumstances.

Importantly, under the Companies Act 1985 (CA 1985) the articles constitute a contract between each of the members and can be enforced as if signed by each individual member. They set out the relationship between the company and its members and the requirements of the articles must be observed. Under the Companies Act 2006 (CA 2006) the constitutional documents will continue to have a similar binding effect, as section 33(1) states:

'The provisions of a company's constitution bind the company and its members to the same extent as if there were covenants on the part of the company and of each member to observe those provisions.'

The memorandum and articles that are put in place when a company is formed remain that company's memorandum and articles unless amended by resolution of the shareholders. This is explained in more detail at 3.4 and 3.5.

Where there is a conflict between the memorandum and the articles the memorandum prevails (s.17 CA 1985). However, the role of the memorandum is set to change under CA 2006. Traditionally a very important document, in future the memorandum will serve a more limited purpose, i.e. to evidence the intention of the subscribers to form a company and become members on formation. In essence it will be reduced to providing a historical picture of the company at a particular point in time, in much the same way as an annual return.

1.1 Model Articles

The Companies (Model Articles) Regulations 2008 (SI 2008/3229) come into force on 1 October 2009. The Regulations prescribe Model Articles for private companies limited by shares, public companies and guarantee companies. The relevant Model Articles will automatically be the articles for companies formed under CA 2006 from 1 October 2009 which do not register their own articles of association, or which register their own articles but do not exclude the Model Articles in whole or in part as was the case with Table A.

Many companies will have adopted some version of Table A and these Regulations will continue to apply to companies formed prior to the introduction of the Model Articles. When reading a company's articles which incorporate Table A it is essential to establish which version of Table A applies, by reference to the date of adoption of the articles currently in force. It will usually be indicated quite clearly at the start of the articles which version of Table A applies. The wording might for example be:

The regulations contained or incorporated in Table A in the Schedule to the Companies (Tables A to F) Regulations 1985 as amended by the Companies (Tables A to F) (Amendment) Regulations 1985, the Companies Act 1985 (Electronic Communications) Order 2000, the Companies (Tables A to F) (Amendment) Regulations 2007 and the Companies (Tables A to F) (Amendment) (No. 2) Regulations 2007 (such Table being hereinafter called 'Table A') shall apply to the Company save in so far as they are excluded or varied hereby and such regulations (save as so excluded or varied) and the Articles hereinafter contained shall be the regulations of the Company.

Alternatively, individual regulations are sometimes excluded, as can be seen from the following example taken from some articles which, although very old, were still in use at time of writing:

> Subject as hereinafter provided, the regulations contained in Table A in the First Schedule to the Companies Act 1929 (hereinafter referred to as 'Table A') shall apply to the Company.
>
> Clauses 7, 11, 19, 45, 47, 48, 50, 64, 66, 69, 72, 82, 90, 101 and 104 of Table A shall not apply to the Company, but the clauses hereinafter contained, and the remaining clauses of Table A, subject to the modifications hereinafter expressed, shall constitute the regulations of the Company.

1.2 Relationship between the constitutional documents and statutory provisions

As mentioned in the preface, the constitutional documents can only very rarely be said to constitute the last word on any particular issue. They must generally be viewed against a broader framework of company law. Given that law is always evolving, it is quite usual for the articles to refer to the legislation in force at the time of their adoption, but also to encompass any later changes, as in the following example:

> In these Articles the term 'the Act' shall mean the Companies Act 1985, including any statutory modification or re-enactment of it for the time being in force.

Unhappily for those who wish to know what rules apply on a particular point, there is no magic formula for determining whether the constitutional documents or the statutory provisions take precedence. In very broad terms, the articles cannot stipulate requirements or procedures that are less stringent than the statutory position where this would or could result in some loss of rights for the shareholders. Sometimes the Companies Acts permit the articles to contain more detailed or challenging requirements than are prescribed by law, such as allowing the delivery of proxies up to the time scheduled for a general meeting, or requiring longer notice to be given of a general meeting than is required by company law. Sometimes statute does not conceive of this possibility at all. While this may seem a little confusing, the exact position should become clear by detailed review of the relevant clauses of the Companies Acts.

Further, as will be seen in Chapter 4, many of the statutory provisions which have come into force recently cannot automatically be read into a company's articles. In such cases the articles need to be amended before the new provisions can be made use of.

1.3 Shareholder agreements

Increasingly, companies are putting some rules of internal management into shareholder agreements rather than into articles. Shareholder agreements are simple contracts. As such they are completely distinct from the articles. Articles are automatically a contract between a company and its members. However, a shareholder agreement is merely a contract between those persons who are parties to it. It is therefore essential that any person joining the company as a member agrees to become a party to the shareholder agreement, because failure to do so means that they are neither bound by the agreement, nor can they enforce it against a party to it. Shareholder agreements commonly include a clause which stipulates that allottees, transferees and transmittees agree to be bound by the terms of the agreement. The following example deals with a member wishing to transfer shares:

Before transferring any of its shares in the Company, the Shareholder proposing to make the transfer shall procure that the transferee executes a deed in favour of the other Shareholders by which the transferee agrees to be bound by terms identical, *mutatis mutandis*, to the terms of this agreement (including the terms of this clause as regards any subsequent transfer of the shares).

While articles of association constitute a public document, shareholder agreements are generally viewed as being confidential. It is arguable that certain provisions of a shareholder agreement (such as anything which purports to vary a provision stated in the company's articles) should be filed at Companies House. Sections 29 and 30 of CA 2006 provide that copies of all agreements agreed to by all the members that would not otherwise have been effective unless passed by a special resolution should be filed at Companies House within 15 days of being made. In the absence of any judicial authority on this point it is likely that shareholder agreements will continue to be treated as purely private documents.

While a shareholder agreement may contain a number of provisions that also appear in the articles, there are a number of other matters that shareholders might prefer to include only in the shareholder agreement so that they are not available on the public record. Examples of such matters include: transferability of shares in a range of different circumstances including circumstances that are to be regarded as 'permitted transfers', e.g. transfers from or to founder members of the company or their family members; and restrictive covenants on the company and the parties or the company's distribution policy.

Under section 21(1) of CA 2006, unless the provisions in the articles are more stringent, a company can change its articles by passing a special resolution (see 3.4 for details). A shareholder agreement, however, can only be changed in accordance with the manner set out in the contract itself, or, if the contract is silent, by obtaining the agreement of all parties to it. As hinted at above, a company can choose a higher threshold of approval that needs to be obtained before its articles can be amended, for example by requiring unanimity, but this could be restrictive from a practical perspective on a day-to-day basis, especially if the company's shareholder base is large. It is also quite common to find provisions in the shareholder agreement that impose some additional requirements with regard to amendment of the articles, for example that approval must be given by a particular shareholder (often an institutional investor) as well as the 75 per cent majority being met.

1.4 Subsequent changes

Sometimes, as in regulation 64 of the 1985 version of Table A, which deals with the number of directors, a requirement begins 'unless otherwise determined by ordinary resolution . . .'. It is therefore also important to identify whether there have been any amendments to the articles that may not be immediately apparent. Another example of where this could occur is regulation 89 of the 1985 version of Table A, which fixes the quorum for directors' meetings at two 'unless so fixed at any other number'. There is an obvious risk of board meetings not being properly convened if a quorum requirement has been increased but no one has picked up on the change.

To minimise confusion it is a good idea for any amending resolutions to be attached to the articles so that anyone looking at them can tell straight away which rules apply.

CHAPTER

2 The memorandum

Every company must have a memorandum of association, which should closely follow the prescribed statutory form of memorandum (Table B for private companies and Table F for public companies). In this chapter we look at what needs to be contained in the memorandum and the changes that can be made to it, both deliberate changes for example to the objects clause and so-called consequential changes which automatically apply to and require a change in the memorandum, such as a change of company name or an increase in share capital.

When this book was being written, the applicable statutory provisions affecting the memorandum were all still under CA 1985. However, the last phase of implementation of CA 2006, effective from 1 October 2009, brings with it significant changes to the content and role of the memorandum. What these changes mean is examined at the end of the chapter.

2.1 Current content of the memorandum

Section 2 of CA 1985 provides that the memorandum of a company must contain the following clauses:

- the name of the company;
- where the registered office is situated – England, Wales or Scotland;
- the company's objects;
- where applicable, a statement that the liability of the members is limited;
- where the company is limited by shares, the amount of share capital,

together with details of how the capital is divided (e.g. £1,000 of authorised capital divided into 1,000 ordinary shares of £1 each); and

- where relevant, a statement that the company is incorporated as a public company.

In addition, the memorandum must end with a subscription clause in which the subscribers agree to form a company in accordance with the terms of the memorandum. The name and address of each subscriber and the number of shares they are to take up on incorporation must be shown. This clause has to be signed by each subscriber in the presence of at least one witness who attests the signature.

For electronic incorporations the provisions concerning authentication of electronic documents introduced by the Companies Act 1985 (Electronic Communications) Order 2000 (SI 2000/3373) apply. This means that for electronic incorporations the memorandum must be authenticated by way of a six-digit authentication code obtained from Companies House, which must be specified when incorporation details are submitted for companies being formed electronically.

2.1.1 Name of the company

Every company must be registered with a unique name. Details about the restrictions affecting the choice of company name are given in Chapter 9.

While it is required at present, from 1 October 2009 the name of the company will no longer need to appear as a separate clause in the memorandum but will still need to appear in the title of the document for identification purposes.

A company's name may be changed by special resolution (s.28 CA 1985). The same rules on choice of name on incorporation that are set out in Chapter 9 apply when changing a company's name. Once the special resolution approving the change of name has been passed, as well as a certified copy of the special resolution and the filing fee (currently £10 for the application to be processed on a 'normal course of business' basis or £50 for a 'same day' service), an updated version of the memorandum and articles must be submitted to Companies House showing the new company name, including full details of the company's name history shown as a footnote.

Sample minutes and resolutions to support a change of name are given as Precedents 1 and 2 for a change of name by way of general meeting and written resolution respectively.

2.1.2 Registered office clause

The registered office or domicile clause states the law under which the company has been incorporated. In the case of an English company the clause will state that the registered office is situated in England and Wales. This determines the law to which a company is subject, i.e. English law for a company registered in England and Wales.

Form 10, which is filed as part of the formation process, states the location of a company's first registered office. Any subsequent change of registered office address must be approved by the directors of the company and notified to the Registrar by using Form 287. When changing the registered office address, it should be remembered that the address cannot be changed from the jurisdiction specified in the memorandum on incorporation. For example, if the company is registered in England and Wales, as stated in the memorandum, it cannot move its registered office to somewhere in Scotland.

2.1.3 Objects clause

This clause sets out the main activities of the company and defines what the company may do. Although it was originally intended that the objects clause would be a short statement stating the precise purpose for which the company was formed, the practice has evolved of making objects clauses very long and wordy. The objects can usually be divided into three categories: main activities, ancillary activities or supporting activities and 'catch all' activities.

Often written in quite archaic language, objects clauses increased in length over time in order to protect a company from being found to have acted outside its powers, or *ultra vires*. Eventually legislation was enacted to try to deal with this problem.

In February 1991, the Companies Act 1989 introduced two important provisions to CA 1985. The first provision (s.35 CA 1985) states that 'the validity of an act done by a company cannot be called into question on the ground of lack of capacity because of anything in the company's memorandum.' Secondly, section 3A of CA 1985 makes provision for a company's memorandum merely to state that the object of the company is to carry on business as a general commercial company. Where a company's objects are so stated the company can carry on any trade or business it likes and it has the power to do anything that is incidental and conducive to the carrying-on of any trade or business by it. Since this time it has therefore been usual to see companies incorporated with the objects clause simply stated as:

> The object of the company is to carry on business as a general commercial company.

While this is obviously simple and easy to understand, many companies still choose to include specific objects in addition to a general commercial objects clause because of commercial and funding considerations. They might, for example, add the words:

Without prejudice to the generality of the foregoing and the powers of the company derived from section 3A of the Companies Act 1985 the company has power to do all or any of the following things:

Thereafter sub-clauses may be added setting out the company's main activities, stipulating that it can act as a holding company, hold investments, take loans and mortgage property etc.

At the time of writing a company can change its objects clause by special resolution (s.4 CA 1985). Suggested wording is included in Precedent 3. A company formed before the provisions allowing a general commercial objects clause came into effect can therefore amend the objects clause in its memorandum to take advantage of the wider provisions.

A period of 21 days must be allowed to elapse after the passing of the special resolution to permit any dissenting members to object. The holders of 15 per cent of the shares of the company may raise such objection provided they did not vote for the resolution in the first place. When an objection is raised the matter must go to court for the alteration to be sanctioned. In so doing, the court may make such order as it thinks fit to meet the objection. In particular, it may order the shares of the objecting members to be purchased by the company.

If no objection is raised a copy of the special resolution and the amended memorandum must be filed within 15 days of expiry of the 21 day objection period.

2.1.4 Limited liability clause

Where the liability of the members is limited this must be stated in the memorandum. This is a simple statement that:

The liability of the members is limited.

The liability of members of a company limited by shares will be limited to any amounts paid up or owed but unpaid on their shares. So, for example, although now relatively rare, where partly paid shares have been issued the holder of those shares would be required to pay up the unpaid balance.

For a company limited by guarantee, the comparable clause in the memorandum is one which states how much the members will each contribute to the assets of the company in the event of it being wound up.

2.1.5 Share capital clause

This clause states the amount of authorised capital with which the company is incorporated and the nominal value of each share, for example that the capital is £1,000 divided into 1,000 ordinary shares of £1 each. It is required for any company limited by shares.

For private companies there is no minimum capital requirement and there are no restrictions on the amount of authorised capital the company has on incorporation. In practice the amount will either be the standard amount the formation agent usually incorporates companies with, or some other amount specifically determined to be sufficient for issue, plus allowing some headroom to meet the company's short to medium term funding requirements.

For a public company to be able to begin trading it must meet the 'authorised minimum' share capital. Currently this is £50,000 of authorised and allotted capital when denominated in sterling (or €65,000 when denominated in Euros), of which at least a quarter of the nominal value must be paid up.

A company can usually increase its authorised share capital by ordinary resolution, unless a more stringent and onerous procedure is required by the articles. A copy of the resolution and Form 123 must be sent to the Registrar within 15 days of the resolution being passed.

Currently it is usual practice for an updated print of the memorandum to be filed with the Registrar (and the articles if the share capital details were stated therein) when changes are made to a company's authorised share capital by, for example, an increase, re-designation or consolidation of shares etc. As set out in 2.2 below, this will not be of continuing relevance when the status of the memorandum changes.

2.1.6 Public company clause

If the company is a public company, a clause of the following kind must be included in the memorandum:

The Company is to be a public company.

2.1.7 Subscriber clause

As described at 2.1 above, the memorandum must end with a subscriber clause. For a private company limited by shares it will take a form similar to the following:

We, the subscriber to this memorandum of association, wish to be formed into a company pursuant to this memorandum; and we agree to take the number of shares shown opposite our name.

Name and address of subscriber	Number of shares taken
	One
Total shares taken	One
Dated [WitnessDate]	
WITNESS to the above signature:	[Witness Name] Address

2.2 Future of the memorandum

Under CA 2006 the role of the memorandum will be significantly different than under previous legislation. Historically the memorandum has been a superior document to the articles, taking precedence where there is a conflict in the provisions of the two documents.

However, from 1 October 2009 (as detailed in s.8(1) CA 2006) much of the content of the memorandum will be stripped out and it will merely comprise a statement from the subscribers that they:

(a) wish to form a company under CA 2006; and
(b) agree to become members of the company and, in the case of a company that is to have a share capital, to take at least one share each.

No other information than the above will be contained in the memorandum. The memorandum will remain an important document in that it evidences the intention of the members to form a company, but its scope will be limited, in effect only providing a summary of the company at the point of incorporation.

In addition, from 1 October 2009 a company's objects will be unrestricted unless the articles of association specifically restrict them [s.31 CA 2006]. This provision applies equally to existing companies and those formed after the legislation comes into force. After 1 October 2009 any existing objects clause in a company's memorandum will be treated as being a provision of a company's articles, pursuant to section 28 of CA 2006.

If an existing company wishes to ensure that its objects are unrestricted, it can do so by amending the articles to remove the objects clause. Any such amendment will have to be notified to the Registrar and the amendment only takes effect when entry of the notice has been made on the register. New charity companies will need to make sure that appropriate restrictions on their objects are contained in their articles in future.

3 Articles of association

As mentioned in Chapter 1, all companies are required to adopt articles of association on incorporation and the articles contain the basic rules for the internal management of the company. No decisions should be taken without first consulting the articles of association to establish whether a particular course of action is permitted and what approvals need to be obtained.

The articles commonly cover such matters as: the rights of shareholders; allotments; transfer and transmission of shares; pre-emption rights on allotments and share transfers, the power and conduct of directors and requirements for how they are appointed, re-elected, resign or removed; dividends and distributions; and the procedural aspects of convening and holding directors' and shareholders' meetings.

The articles cannot, however, be read in isolation. In Chapter 1 we looked at the relationship between the articles and statutory provisions and between the articles and shareholder agreements. We now consider the relationship between bespoke, or tailored, articles that a company may choose to adopt and the various sets of default regulations that may apply.

3.1 The articles and default regulations

Tables A to F of the Companies (Tables A to F) Regulations 1985 (SI 1985/805), as amended, provide default articles of association. Table A provides standard sets of articles for private and public companies limited by shares and is the most commonly used of the Tables. Table A will apply by default to any company incorporated before 1 October 2009 that does not register its own articles of association.

3.1.1 Table A

Companies do not have to use Table A and are free to write their own articles but it is quite rare for companies other than publicly listed companies to have an entirely bespoke set of articles. Even where Table A is disapplied entirely, the bespoke articles will often draw heavily on the provisions of Table A. More commonly a company will adopt Table A with modifications. One of the most frequent modifications for a private company is to exclude the regulations in Table A that require directors to retire by rotation, particularly now as a private company is no longer required to hold an annual general meeting unless its articles state otherwise. Another common amendment is the addition of requirements on pre-emption on transfer of shares.

The relationship between the articles and Table A is usually set out as the first clause of the articles. It is therefore made clear at the start whether Table A is being adopted, with or without modification, or whether it is disapplied completely. Since Table A has been through many different versions care needs to be taken to ensure that the correct version is disapplied.

> TIP: When checking the articles for the rules on a particular point always make sure you are consulting the correct version of Table A. If a company's articles have not been updated for some time it may even be the 1948 version that is applicable.

A copy of Table A of the Companies (Tables A to F) Regulations 1985 (as amended by the Companies Act 1985 (Electronic Communications) Order 2000 (SI 2000/3373)) is included as Appendix 1. This is the version of Table A referred to when regulations of the 1985 version of Table A are cited in this book. This version has been included in preference to the transitional version of Table A as it is applicable to significantly more companies and the changes between the two versions are not extensive.

3.1.2 Model Articles

From 1 October 2009 the default set of articles for companies being incorporated on or after that date will be the new streamlined Model Articles contained in the Companies (Model Articles) Regulations 2008 (SI 2008/3229) (the 'Regulations'). Tables of destinations and origins comparing Table A and the Model Articles for a private company limited by shares can be found at Appendices 2 and 3 respectively.

The Regulations provide for three sets of Model Articles:

- private companies limited by shares;
- private companies limited by guarantee;
- public companies.

Copies of the Model Articles for private companies limited by shares, private companies limited by guarantee and public companies are included as Appendices 4, 5 and 6 respectively.

The Model Articles are structured to follow as far as possible the order of the corresponding parts of CA 2006. Where procedural matters are set out clearly in CA 2006, the provisions are not duplicated in the Model Articles. Consequently, the Model Articles for private companies are shorter than Table A, comprising only 53 clauses, compared to the 118 regulations in Table A. In addition, certain assumptions have been made, for example that the directors of private companies will not wish to appoint alternates. The Model Articles for private companies limited by guarantee closely follow the Model Articles for private companies limited by shares, but without the provisions relating to shares.

The Model Articles for public companies are far longer and cover all the matters previously dealt with by Table A. Examples of additional provisions which can be found in the Model Articles for public companies include:

- provisions relating to the holding of AGMs, including provisions for retirement of directors by rotation;
- provisions for the appointment of alternate directors;
- rules concerning uncertificated holdings; and
- detailed provisions regarding partly paid shares.

As mentioned at 3.1.1 above, public companies, especially those with some sort of listing, are less likely to accept default provisions without modification. It is therefore envisaged that public companies will wish to use the Model Articles as a useful source of information when they are drafting their articles, rather than adopting them in their entirety.

3.2 Format of the articles

The articles must be divided into paragraphs numbered consecutively (s.7 CA 1985) [s.18 CA 2006]. CA 1985 also requires that the articles are printed, whilst section 18 of CA 2006 stipulates that the articles be contained in a single document. Beyond these requirements, a company is free to tailor the content of the articles, subject to any statutory provisions, common law considerations or any provisions of the company's memorandum.

3.3 Existing companies and the Model Articles

As detailed in Chapter 1, the version of default articles in force at the time of incorporation, or as specifically amended or adopted by resolution of the shareholders, continue to apply to a company. Therefore existing companies which have adopted 1985 Table A, the transitional Table A, or an earlier form of Table A will not be affected by the introduction of the new Model Articles in October 2009 unless they specifically choose to make a change to their articles.

3.4 Amending the articles

A company may amend its articles by special resolution (s.9 CA 1985) [s.21 CA 2006] unless a higher percentage approval requirement is specified in the articles or a shareholder agreement. A copy of the updated articles must be filed with the Registrar within 15 days of amendment. A checklist for amending the articles is included at Appendix 7, and Precedents 4–7 deal with the adoption of new articles and the amendment of existing articles by written resolution and general meeting.

> **TIP:** If external advisers are engaged to help update your articles of association make sure they give you a soft copy of the revised articles as this will make it easier to make changes when the articles are next updated.

While a company is generally free to amend its articles at any time, subject to obtaining approval from the members, this freedom is fettered in a number of ways:

- The memorandum of association is, for the time being at least, a superior document to the articles. Therefore, if there is any conflict between the provisions of the memorandum and the provisions of the articles, the memorandum prevails. Any amendment is therefore subject to the memorandum.
- The proposed amendment must be lawful and cannot therefore conflict with any provisions of the Companies Acts or any other rule of law.
- When the court deals with an unfair prejudice application under section 994 of CA 2006, it is open to the court to alter the company's articles and to prohibit any alteration of that amended article without its consent. When any such order is made, subsequent alterations must be with the consent of the court.

- An amendment to the articles cannot increase the liability of any member unless the member agrees in writing, before or after the amendment has taken place (s.16 CA 1985) [s.25 CA 2006].
- If the amendment seeks to vary class rights, members holding shares in the class in question have a right under section 127 of CA 19850 [s.633 CA 2006] to object. Members who voted against the resolution and who hold between them at least 15 per cent of the shares of the class in question have 21 days to object to the court.
- Any amendment must be bona fide for the benefit of the company and not a potential fraud on minority shareholders. A recent case which illustrates this point is that of *Constable v Executive Connections Ltd* [2005] EWHC 3 (Ch) which concerned a purported amendment to a company's articles by the 95 per cent shareholder to compel members to sell their shares where an offer to buy the company was approved by 75 per cent of the members. The claimant owned 5 per cent of the shares and sought a declaration that the amendment was invalid and an injunction prohibiting the company from enforcing the amendment. Rejecting the argument that there was no serious issue to be tried, the court granted the injunction and made clear that a change which compelled a minority holder to sell their shares could only be effective if the alteration was made in good faith for the benefit of the company as a whole.

Many companies will wish to amend their articles to take advantage of provisions of CA 2006. While many have already made changes, further amendment will be necessary when CA 2006 has come fully into force in full on 1 October 2009. Key amendments for private and public companies are considered in Chapter 4.

A copy of the amended articles must be filed at Companies House within 15 days. This is something that many companies forget to do and, to date, this has not usually resulted in any adverse consequences, although default is a criminal offence. However, from 1 October 2009, there is a new civil penalty of £200 for failure to comply. The penalty is triggered if a company receives notice from the Registrar requiring it to deliver a copy of its amended articles and fails to comply within 28 days.

3.5 Entrenchment

Section 22 of CA 2006 is a new provision. From 1 October 2009 it replaces the rules under section 17(2)(c) of CA 1985 which enable a company to entrench certain parts of its constitution in its memorandum and provide that it cannot be amended.

Under section 22 of CA 2006 a company can provide in its articles that certain provisions can only be changed if conditions are met that are more restrictive than in the case of a special resolution. Such a provision is known as a 'provision for entrenchment'. As a consequence companies will no longer be able to provide that a certain provision can never be repealed or amended. For example, a company with charitable aims might use entrenchment to ensure that profits cannot be distributed to its members, rather than relying on charity law or using the community interest company vehicle. However, following consultation by the then DTI (now BERR), the Government has decided that existing absolute entrenchment provisions should be preserved.

Section 23 of CA 2006 provides that a company must give notice to the Registrar when an entrenching provision is included in its articles (whether on formation or subsequently) or where the company's articles are altered by order of a court or other authority so as to restrict or exclude the power of the company to amend its articles. Correspondingly, a company must also notify the Registrar when an entrenching provision is removed.

Where a company's articles contain provision for entrenchment or where the articles are subject to an order of a court or other authority restricting or excluding the company's power to amend its articles and the company subsequently amends its articles, it is required to send to the Registrar the document making or evidencing the amendment (s.24 CA 2006). This document must be accompanied by a 'statement of compliance'.

The statement of compliance must certify that the amendment has been made in accordance with the company's articles (including any provision for entrenchment) or, where relevant, in accordance with any order of the court or other authority that is in force at the time of the amendment.

The purpose of the provisions in sections 23 and 24 of CA 2006 is to ensure that the Registrar and anyone searching the register is aware of the special rules that apply to the company's articles.

4

Companies Act 2006 amendments

One of the main aims behind the introduction of CA 2006 was to ease the regulatory burden faced by companies, especially smaller private companies. The legislation contains a number of deregulatory measures and seeks to bring the procedural requirements into line with modern business practice to make administration easier and more flexible.

Despite this, many changes do not apply automatically to companies upon implementation and companies have to take some form of positive action, whether by resolution or amendment to the memorandum and articles, to take advantage of the changes. An obvious example is the much-touted dispensation with the requirement for private companies to appoint a company secretary. Provided the articles of association only contain provisions which imply a company secretary will be in office, there is no longer a requirement to have a company secretary (although it would be tidier to remove any such provisions if the office is to cease). However, any provision in the articles which specifically requires the company to appoint a secretary will override the statutory position and the articles will need to be amended before the dispensation provisions of CA 2006 can be taken advantage of.

In this chapter we consider the most common amendments to the articles that companies may wish to make. Companies that have not already undertaken a review of their articles would be well advised to do so this year to assess whether changes which would be beneficial to the company are required. For those who have already made changes to their articles, this chapter and the checklist at Appendix 8 will serve as a reminder in case there are still further changes that need to be dealt with the next time a review of articles is being considered.

4.1 Officers

Changes affecting both public and private companies have already come into force. Of these, the new provisions on conflicts of interest are by far the most significant as their potential reach is extensive.

4.1.1 Restrictions affecting appointment of directors

A number of new restrictions about who can be appointed a director mean that companies should review their articles and remove any clauses that permit a greater degree of leniency than permitted by statute.

Section 157 of CA 2006 introduces a requirement that only persons who have attained the age of 16 may be appointed as directors. Any appointments which contravene this requirement are void (s.157(4) CA 2006). Under-age directors in office at the time of enactment cease to be directors (s.159(2) CA 2006) and a company's register of directors should be updated accordingly. Interestingly, there is no requirement for notification to be made to the Registrar, but if it appears to the Registrar from other information that the appointment has ceased he may make a note to that effect on the public record.

It has been suggested that the introduction of a minimum age is a response to concern about the use of child directors as a way of escaping liability. Concern about companies avoiding liability by having corporate directors was behind another new requirement, namely that at least one director must be a natural person. Previously all directors of a company could be companies or other corporations.

The final provisions on this subject which should be removed are age-dependent provisions which could contravene the Employment Equality (Age) Regulations 2006 (SI 2006/1031). This includes provisions which prevent the appointment of directors above a certain age (commonly 70) or which require resignation from office once a prescribed age has been attained. If a company retains such provisions in its articles it risks a claim of age discrimination.

4.1.2 Indemnity provisions

CA 2006 has largely widened the scope for a company to indemnify directors and to fund expenditure incurred in connection with certain actions against directors. Existing provisions should be reviewed and, where thought appropriate, amended to ensure that directors are afforded the widest protection permitted by statute.

In particular, a company that is a trustee of an occupational pension scheme can now indemnify a director against liability incurred in connection with the company's activities as trustee of the scheme. Further, the existing exemption allowing a company to fund a director's defence in court proceedings has been extended to apply to associated companies and can now cover regulatory proceedings.

The Model Articles provide a general authority for directors to be indemnified out of the company's assets against all liabilities, including any incurred in connection with the activities of an associated company or in a company's capacity as a trustee of an occupational pension scheme. However, companies may wish to include more specific provisions in their articles, such as a clause dealing with the funding of expenditure in defending proceedings. An example of such a clause might be as follows:

> The company may also provide funds to any director or other officer (excluding the auditors) of the company or any associated company to meet, or do anything to enable a director or other officer of the company or any other officer of the company to avoid incurring expenditure of the nature described in sections 205(1) or 206 of CA 2006.

4.1.3 Conflicts of interest

Given the impracticability, cost and logistical difficulties presented by the need to convene general meetings frequently, if they have not done so already, most companies will wish to amend their articles of association to enable directors to authorise any situational conflicts of interest held by directors and to set out the procedure to be followed when such conflicts are being considered and approved.

4.1.3.1 Duty

Section 175(1) of CA 2006 requires a director to avoid a situation in which he has, or can have, a direct or indirect interest that conflicts, or possibly may conflict, with the interests of the company. The duty applies particularly in respect of the exploitation of property, information or opportunity whether or not the company could take advantage of it (s.175(2)). While there is no definition of 'interest' or 'conflict of interest', it is made clear in section 175(7) that it includes both a conflict of interest and of duty so, for example, could include a situation where involvement with another organisation restricts the time the director has to devote to the company's affairs.

It should be noted that the duty for the director to disclose the interest and for it to be sanctioned applies to the actual or potential situation rather than the actual conflict. Further, the duty does not apply to a conflict of interest arising in relation to a transaction or arrangement with the company (s.175(3)). These types of conflict are covered by sections 177 and 182 of CA 2006 and the requirements are addressed in Chapter 5. However, directors should be aware that situations which initially fall within the scope of section 175 can change over time so that they fall within section 177, at which point the requirements of section 175 cease to apply. The example given in the GC100 guidance is where a director of one company is also on the company's list of preferred suppliers. The general relationship is likely to fall within section 175, but if a supply contract was entered into by the company an additional duty for the director to disclose an interest under section 177 would apply.

4.1.3.2 Authorisation of conflicts by the directors

Section 175(4)(b) provides that the duty to avoid conflicts of interest is not infringed if the matter has been authorised by the directors. For public companies such authorisation can only be given where its articles contain an enabling provision permitting authorisation of the matter by the directors and where a situational conflict is proposed to the directors and authorised by them in accordance with the rules set out in the articles.

For private companies incorporated on or after 1 October 2008, the directors can authorise situational conflicts provided there is nothing in the articles to prevent this (s.175(5)(a)). For private companies incorporated before 1 October 2008 it is also possible for the directors to authorise conflicts, but an enabling shareholders' resolution that authority may be given in accordance with section 175(5)(a) is required first. We would, however, suggest that the authority is embodied in the articles to ensure that it is clear and can be easily found and referred to in future years.

4.1.3.3 Key provisions for inclusion in the articles of association

While the key provision that should be included in the articles is undoubtedly the power for the directors to authorise conflicts of interest, there are a number of other provisions that should be covered in the articles, as follows:

- the procedures for proposing conflicts to the board for consideration and for authorising the matter proposed;
- the quorum requirements for approving a conflict, preferably including a reiteration of the provisions of section 175(6) which state that authorisation

is only effective if the quorum requirements are met without counting the director in question or any other interested directors and that the matter was agreed to without their voting or would have been agreed to if their votes had not been counted;

■ provisions designed to take advantage of the so-called safe harbour provision contained in section 180(4)(b). This section provides that the general duties of directors are not breached by anything done (or omitted) by the directors acting in accordance with article provisions for authorising conflicts of interest. There is at present no consensus about how companies should approach the matter in their articles. One approach is to set out the circumstances in which the general duty is not breached, whilst the other is for the articles to grant the directors authority, when authorising a conflict, to specify how the director should treat the conflict;

■ separate provisions dealing with interests in proposed transactions and arrangements.

Suggested wording for a clause permitting the directors to authorise conflicts of interest is provided in Precedent 8.

4.2 Shares

4.2.1 Transfer of shares

Existing article provisions concerning the procedure to be followed when a transfer is lodged with the company should be checked. In particular, the commonly included authority for the directors to refuse to register a transfer without giving any reasons no longer has any effect as it is overridden by the new requirements contained in section 771(1) of CA 2006. This subject is also dealt with in Chapter 7.

Section 771(1) of CA 2006 provides that as soon as practicable, and at most within two months of the transfer being lodged, a company must either register the transfer or notify the transferor of the refusal to register the transfer and provide the reasons for this. Section 771(2) imposes a requirement on the directors to provide the transferor with such further information as he or she may reasonably request, but this does not confer a right on the transferor to see copies of minutes of meetings of directors.

It is worth mentioning that further changes regarding share transfers may be made, although these are likely to be some years off. Chapter 2 of Part 21 of CA 2006 contains powers for the Secretary of State to make regulations to replace the existing paper-based system for certificated holders with an electronic system.

This project for dematerialisation has been developed with support of the

Institute of Chartered Secretaries and Administrators (ICSA) and detailed proposals for the extension of electronic share transfers are being developed by the Dematerialisation Reference Group (DRG). In September 2008 the Chairman of the DRG wrote to the Government to seek confirmation that the Government remained committed to the dematerialisation of shares and was prepared to proceed with the necessary legislation, and the response from the Treasury indicated that the most appropriate timescale for implementation would be during 2012. Further consultation on proposals for legislation is likely to follow and this will have an important bearing on clauses in a company's articles.

4.2.2 Authorised capital

From 1 October 2009 the requirement for companies to have an authorised share capital will be abolished, but pre-existing authorised capital details contained in a company's constitutional documents will continue to operate as a restriction after that date. Therefore companies wishing to remove the deemed restriction from the articles will need to amend their articles accordingly. It is expected that transitional provisions will enable this to happen by way of ordinary resolution rather than a special resolution being required. For more on authorised capital see Chapter 6.

4.2.3 Variation of class rights

The procedural and quorum rights that will apply to any meeting convened to vary class rights are set out in section 334 of CA 2006. The required quorum for a meeting other than an adjourned meeting is two persons present holding at least one-third in nominal value of the issued shares of the class in question (excluding any shares of that class held in treasury), while for an adjourned meeting the quorum is one person present holding shares of the class in question. To minimise confusion, we recommend that any article provisions which differ from these requirements should be removed.

4.3 Meetings and resolutions

For both private and public companies the introduction of CA 2006 has ushered in significant changes to the rules about how decisions are taken by shareholders. Some changes, for example enhanced rights for proxies, are common to both kinds of company. Many changes affect private companies only. This section provides a summary of the article changes that should be considered. More detail on all the topics raised here can be found in Chapter 8.

4.3.1 Redundant terminology

Some long-standing concepts have been dropped in the new legislation. For example, extraordinary general meetings and extraordinary resolutions are no longer referred to. In future shareholder meetings other than the AGM should be termed simply as general meetings, and resolutions will be either ordinary or special. The articles should be checked so that any obsolete references are removed and, where appropriate, replaced with the current terminology.

4.3.2 Written resolutions

Written resolutions are only available to private companies. The provisions contained in Part 13 of CA 2006 are far more detailed than were the provisions under the 1985 Act and have clarified many of the procedural uncertainties that existed under the old regime. For example, the introduction of a 28-day lapse date is designed to combat the old uncertainty about what happens if a resolution has been in circulation for a long time without being passed. Given the comprehensive nature of the new regime, companies would be well-advised to remove any non-statutory procedures pertaining to written resolutions to avoid confusion.

4.3.3 Reduced requirements

Two key areas in which the procedural requirements have been eased under CA 2006 are considered below.

4.3.3.1 Notice of special resolutions

For all companies the notice required to convene a general meeting at which a special resolution is to be considered has been reduced from 21 days to 14 days. This is subject to a caveat for fully listed companies, which must have passed an enabling resolution at an AGM before the shorter notice period can be taken advantage of. This requirement stems from implementation of the EU Shareholder Rights Directive rather than being a requirement under CA 2006. Generally, however, companies should check their articles of association to see whether they contain any notice requirements regarding special resolutions so that any clauses requiring more than 14 days' notice can be removed.

4.3.3.2 Consent to short notice

For private companies the percentage majority required for the members to consent to a general meeting being held on shorter notice than prescribed by statute has been reduced. Sections 307(5) and (6) stipulate that the shorter notice may be agreed to by a majority in number of the members having a right to attend and vote at the meeting, being a majority who together hold not less than the requisite percentage in nominal value of the shares giving a right to attend and vote at the meeting (excluding any shares held in treasury). The requisite percentage for private companies is 90 per cent or such higher percentage (not exceeding 95 per cent) as may be specified in the company's articles. Companies wishing to take advantage of this reduced requirement will need to amend their articles. The requisite percentage for public companies remains 95 per cent.

4.3.4 Shareholder meetings and voting

Article changes to consider with regard to shareholder meetings are set out in the following four sections.

4.3.4.1 Annual General Meetings

The concept of the AGM no longer exists for private companies. Assuming private companies wish to take advantage of this, any provisions contained in their articles which require an AGM to be held should be removed. Without such action, an AGM will need to be held each year as the articles override statute on this point. However, the requirement to hold an AGM is not triggered by ancillary article provisions, such as procedures for retirement of the directors by rotation, which assume that AGMs will be held. Of course, companies may wish to retain a mechanism by which the term of appointment for directors is limited or subject to shareholder scrutiny. Either way it will generally be more satisfactory for any provisions which link rotation to AGMs to be removed, to be replaced by an alternative procedure where deemed necessary.

4.3.4.2 Enhanced proxy rights

Proxy rights have been extended so that members of both private and public companies are entitled to appoint more than one proxy and all appointed proxies have the right to attend, speak and vote at general meetings, on a show of hands as well as a poll. These rights may be extended by the articles (s.331) but cannot be lessened except where expressly permitted by the Act. Therefore, the best approach would be for any existing article provisions concerning the rights of proxies to be removed and for the articles to be silent on the subject unless a company wishes to afford proxies greater rights than conferred by statute.

For more detailed information on proxies please refer to Chapter 8.

4.3.4.3 Calculation of proxy receipt deadline

Section 327(2) prevents companies from stipulating a proxy return deadline in their articles that is more than 48 hours before the meeting, which has always been the case. However, under section 327(3) weekends and bank holidays can now be ignored when determining the deadline. The new exclusion of non-working days does not apply automatically and companies will need to amend their articles if they wish to make use of this provision.

4.3.4.4 Proxies and corporate representatives

The provisions on corporate representatives are contained in section 323 and cannot be overridden by a company's articles. In contrast to the position regarding the appointment of proxies, there is nothing in CA 2006 which permits the articles to give greater powers to corporate representatives than conferred by statute. Existing article provisions should therefore be removed. Commentary on the new rules concerning the appointment of corporate representatives can be found in Chapter 8.

4.4 Electronic and web communications

Companies are now permitted to communicate with members by electronic and/or website communications instead of sending documents in hard copy. The new provisions have significant potential benefits for companies in terms of streamlining administration processes and cost savings. Therefore companies, whether private or public, with a large shareholder base will wish to consider amending their articles to take advantage of these provisions. Sample wording for such a clause is included at Precedent 9.

In its guidance note (ref. 160207) on electronic communications, the ICSA states that not all companies will need to change their articles if they wish to communicate with shareholders by means of the company's website as the provisions introduced by section 1143 and Schedule 5 apply irrespective of the provisions in a company's articles. Therefore if a company had been communicating with its shareholders by electronic means prior to the introduction of CA 2006 (even without authority in the articles), or wants to start using electronic communications, with no default to website, no article changes or resolutions are required. However, for those companies subject to the Disclosure and Transparency Rules, electronic communications may only be used where an enabling resolution has been passed by members in general meeting, unless it would have been lawful under CA 1985.

The new provisions also allow a company to change its default method of communication from hard copy to website communication. Initially a person must agree or be deemed to have agreed to receive communications in this way. CA 2006 introduces a new concept of deemed agreement to website communication. This means that where shareholders have either resolved, or the articles state, that a company may communicate via its website, and a shareholder has not responded within 28 days of an invitation to say that they do not wish to receive communications in that way, they can be deemed to have agreed to it. It is recommended that amending the articles to permit website communication is preferable to passing an authorising resolution as it will be more transparent for future shareholders.

TIP: Although it is technically possible to issue individual invitations along with the notice of the meeting at which a change is to be proposed, it might be preferable from an investor relations perspective to explain the proposals in a memorandum accompanying the notice and wait until later on to issue the individual invitations.

5 Directors

Section 250 of CA 2006 defines a director as including 'any person occupying the position of director, by whatever name called'. In legal terms, the use of the word 'person' means that the definition encompasses corporate bodies with a legal persona as well as individuals. However, all companies are now required to have at least one director who is a natural person (s.155 CA 2006).

In this chapter we consider in detail directors' powers and responsibilities, decision-making by directors and the appointment and termination of directors. References in this chapter to article numbers are to articles of the Model Articles. Where the article number is not the same for private and public companies, the private company article number is given first.

5.1 Directors' powers and responsibilities

5.1.1 Directors' powers

The directors are generally charged with the management of the company's business and given the right to exercise all the powers of the company (article 3). While this authority is fairly wide, it is subject to provisions in the articles directing how the directors must regulate the company's affairs. This requirement corresponds with the provisions of section 171 of CA 2006 which exhort directors to 'act in accordance with the company's constitution and only exercise their powers for the purposes for which they are conferred'.

It is important to note that the powers are conferred on the board of the company rather than on directors individually. However, the Model Articles provide that the directors may delegate their powers to any person or committee and in such manner as they think fit and further delegation is also permitted where it has been authorised by the directors (article 5).

In a change from the position under regulations 71 and 72 of Table A, no specific reference is made in the Model Articles to the right to delegate to a managing director or other executive officer, but in practice directors remain free to do so provided the directors collectively decide such delegation is appropriate.

5.1.2 Committees

Where directors have delegated powers to a committee the committee must follow, as far as possible, the article provisions governing the taking of decisions by the directors (article 6(1)). However, article 6(2) does give the directors the discretion and authority to make additional or different rules for the committee to follow where considered appropriate in the circumstances. This, in practice, would involve the board deciding terms of reference for the committee at the same time as the committee is formed and its composition approved.

5.1.3 Shareholders' reserve power

The Model Articles now contain a specific provision that shareholders may, by special resolution, direct how the directors should act in relation to particular matters. This provision was not in Table A and it serves to clarify the position with regard to the manner in which shareholders can control how directors manage the company.

In the past it was not uncommon to see certain restrictions on directors' powers set out in a company's articles and this practice may still continue. Such clauses might specify the requirement for decisions on certain matters to be referred to the company's members where, for example, the decision involves sale of the company's freehold property or particular assets, a significant change in trading activity, obtaining loans over a certain amount or the giving of guarantees etc.

5.2 Meetings of directors and committees

Nothing is prescribed under CA 2006 about how directors should conduct their meetings. Therefore, the directors have a fairly unrestricted freedom to regulate their own affairs. However, the Model Articles (article 9 for private companies and article 8 for public companies are slightly more prescriptive about the way in which notice of meetings should be given and companies will wish to consider whether to modify such provisions to ensure their directors' meetings can operate efficiently and appropriately, while retaining the maximum flexibility.

5.2.1 Calling a directors' meeting

The Model Articles preserve the position under regulation 88 of Table A that any director may call a meeting. The directors of private companies may authorise the company secretary (if any) to give the notice. For public companies the company secretary is compelled to call a directors' meeting if requested by a director to do so (article 8(2)).

In terms of the form that such notice takes, a number of changes have been made to the Model Articles to reflect current commercial practices, advancements in communications and the international nature of many companies and their directors. This being the case, notice must be given to all directors, but need not be in writing (article 9(3)/ article 8(5)). In addition, the old provision of regulation 88 of Table A which meant that notice need not be given to directors outside the UK is not included in the Model Articles.

The minimum requirements for the content of notice given to directors are set out in article 9(2) for private companies and article 8(4) for public companies. The notice must specify the proposed date, time and location of the meeting and, if the directors will not all be present at the same location, how it is proposed they communicate with each other.

Unlike general meetings, there is still no requirement in the Model Articles for the business of the board meeting to be set out in the notice convening it and the length of notice required is still not specified. However case law (*Browne v La Trinidad* (1887) 37 ChD 1) has previously established that 'reasonable' notice must be given and what is reasonable will depend on the precise facts of each case. In *Browne v La Trinidad* five minutes' notice was found to be sufficient as the complaining director was on the premises and had no other appointments at the time of the meeting. When deciding what is reasonable, a company's usual practice for calling meetings is likely to be taken into account.

The Model Articles permit directors to waive their right to receive notice of a board meeting up to seven days after the meeting has been held without invalidating the meeting or business conducted (article 9(4)/article 8(6)). This might be important if key decisions have been made and it is subsequently discovered that one or more directors were not sent notice of the meeting.

In practice, directors' meetings for smaller, usually private, companies will be held on an ad hoc basis when matters arise that need to be formally recorded. However, this is not always the case and some smaller companies hold regular board meetings at fixed intervals, usually quarterly or monthly.

Where meetings are held regularly in accordance with a scheduled timetable it is usual for a 'board pack' to be issued to all directors at least a few days prior to the meeting which includes the agenda setting out the business of the meeting and any papers that are to be discussed. Even if such practice is normally followed, it will generally be preferable that detailed requirements are not specified in the articles so that directors are able to call a meeting informally and quickly should a matter arise that needs to be discussed and resolved upon as a matter of urgency.

5.2.2 Meetings where directors are not all present in the same place

In order for meetings to be held when it is not possible for the directors to be physically present in the same place, a company's articles need to include specific provision for participation by electronic means, for example by telephone or via video conferencing. Given the fast pace of modern life and that many companies' directors are based in a wide range of locations and travel extensively, this is something that the majority of companies will wish to include in their articles. The Model Articles recognise this and allow the directors to participate in a meeting provided 'they can each communicate to the others any information or opinions they have on any particular item of the business of the meeting' (article 10/article 9). At first sight this would seem to extend the scope of what constitutes valid participation in a directors' meeting as it appears to include such methods as instant messaging, although this would seem to stretch the definition of a 'meeting' too far and could hardly be deemed to be the method of choice, especially where complex matters are being discussed. It is envisaged that it may be used more to support a telephone meeting and provide a means of giving presentation rather than being used on its own. The most usual method would be meetings held by telephone where all directors are able simultaneously to hear the comments of others and express their own opinions.

Companies whose articles were adopted many years ago should review their articles to see whether they include provision for meetings to be held by electronic means to ensure they are not inadvertently operating in breach of requirements.

5.2.3 Quorum

The Model Articles fix the quorum for directors' meetings for both private and public companies as two (article 11/article 10), unless the directors decide otherwise. This is slightly at odds with the statutory position of allowing private companies to have a sole director (s.154 CA 2006) and if the company only has one director this provision will need to be changed. There is no anomaly with public companies, as they are required by section 154 of CA 2006 to have at least two directors anyway.

Companies are free to specify alternative quorum requirements in their articles and frequently do when the company is, for example, a joint venture or where an outside investor has the right to appoint one or more directors. In such cases, the company's share capital will often be made up of different classes, in which case the quorum could, for example, be expressed as being '3 directors, comprising at least one 'A' and one 'B' director', the titles corresponding to the holders of the A and B ordinary shares who each have a right set out in the articles to nominate a director.

When determining the quorum provisions that are suitable for a particular company, as well as taking into account the rights of the different board factions involved, it is important that any exclusions that may make it difficult to convene a meeting validly are considered and taken into account. In particular, the introduction of the new rules on directors' conflicts of interest may cause difficulties for companies with a small number of directors to achieve the necessary quorum for meetings at which a director's conflict of interest is to be authorised by the directors, for example where all the directors are similarly conflicted and cannot be counted in the quorum or vote on the matter. Further commentary on this point can be found at 5.2.7.

If the number of directors falls below that required for a quorum, for example if a director resigns or dies, the Model Articles specify that the continuing directors may act only to appoint another director or to call a general meeting so that the shareholders can appoint another director (article 11). For public companies article 11 provides two procedures: one for when only one director remains and another for when there is more than one director still in office, in which case a meeting of the directors must be held to appoint additional directors or convene a general meeting to do so. In practice many private companies adopt articles which allow the remaining director or directors to exercise all the normal powers of a director even where the number of directors has fallen below the minimum required. Sometimes this is expressed as a general authority but more often the directors will only be permitted to act for the purpose of rectifying the situation.

5.2.4 Chairing the meeting

The directors may appoint one of their number to chair their meetings (article 12). Article 12(3) of the Model Articles for public companies also makes provision for the appointment of a deputy chairman who will chair meetings in the chairman's absence. If the chairman (or usual alternative chairman in the case of public companies) is not present within 10 minutes of the scheduled start time, article 12 gives the directors present the right to appoint one of themselves to chair the meeting.

Companies may wish to vary these rules, for example to permit greater lassitude about the point at which an alternative chairman is to be appointed. This could be of relevance if directors travel fairly long distances to meetings and are often delayed in traffic, in which case it might be preferable to allow half an hour's leeway rather than 10 minutes.

Arguably, the 10-minute rule contained in article 12 also addresses the issue of what happens if the chairman is prevented from chairing the meeting, or part of it, because of a conflict of interests. Strictly speaking, this might only be considered to be the case if the chairman is not participating within 10 minutes of the meeting's scheduled start time, but by extension and by reference to the default conflicts of interest provisions (article 14/article 16) it should be possible for non-interested directors to appoint one of them to chair either the whole meeting or just the affected section of it. Companies adopting their own tailor-made articles concerning the chairing of meetings may wish to address this point specifically.

As detailed at 8.1.6, the chairman of the board will usually also act as the chairman at general meetings and this is stated elsewhere in the Model Articles as being the default position (article 39(1)/ article 31(1)). If the articles are silent, any member (s.319 CA 2006) or any proxy (s.328 CA 2006) may be elected by the meeting to act as chair.

5.2.5 Voting

Decisions taken at board meetings must be passed by a majority (article 7/article 13). For companies with a sole director in office and no higher minimum number requirement, the provisions of articles 7 and 8 of the Model Articles for private companies will not apply as there are no others with whom consensus needs to be reached.

Article 13 in the Model Articles for private companies and article 14 in the Model Articles for public companies give the chairman a casting vote at directors' meetings where there is an equality of votes for and against a resolution. Where the chairman exercises this right, it is usually to preserve the status quo on the grounds that the meeting has not formed a positive intention to make a change. There is no right under CA 2006 for the chairman to have a casting vote and there is no need for the articles to confer a second or casting vote on the chairman. In practice, where agreement cannot be reached on a particular matter one or more directors are charged with undertaking certain actions before the next meeting so that the matter can be discussed again when the directors are possessed of more detailed information upon which to base their decision.

5.2.6 Resolutions in writing

For private companies article 8 provides an alternative process for decision-making by directors. The provisions go further than the written resolution procedure under regulation 93 of Table A as they permit decisions to be taken 'when all directors indicate to each other by any means that they share a common view on a matter'. While this does give more flexibility, it is still necessary, and in any event advisable, to record decisions reached in writing to ensure there are no misunderstandings or disputes, and article 8(2) permits such decisions to be by way of written resolution signed by all 'eligible' directors or to which all directors have agreed in writing. Eligible in this context means directors who would have been allowed to vote on the matter had it been considered at a directors' meeting (article 8(3)). If the eligible directors are not capable of forming a quorum at a meeting, no decision may be taken under the written resolution procedure.

Although written resolutions are specifically cited as a way of reaching and recording a unanimous decision under article 8, the clause can also be interpreted as permitting more informal decision-making, such as by way of a series of emails or even text messages. However, article 15 of the Model Articles for private companies contains a requirement that a written record of all directors' decisions is kept for at least 10 years from the date of decision.

If the relevant model article provisions or regulation 93 of Table A are not part of a company's articles, decisions will have to be taken at directors' meetings. The best way of ensuring compliance with article 15 will usually be to prepare written resolutions which are then signed and placed with the company's minutes. If article 15 is excluded and there are no similar provisions in the company's articles, the only written records of decisions that need to be kept are minutes of board meetings, which is required under section 248 of CA 2006. However, it is always a good idea to ensure that there is a written record of decisions taken.

5.2.7 Transactional conflicts of interest

Companies will need to consider very carefully how to address this issue in their articles of association. Detailed commentary about situational conflicts is provided in Chapter 4, together with the amendments that can be made to a company's articles of association to give non-conflicted directors the ability to authorise such conflicts. Chapter 4 does not, however, consider transactional conflicts in any detail.

Section 177 of CA 2006 requires directors, subject to certain limited exceptions, to declare the nature and extent of any interest they have in a proposed transaction or arrangement with the company. This declaration can be made:

- at a board meeting; or
- by giving written notice to the directors pursuant to section 184 of CA 2006; or
- by giving general notice at a meeting in accordance with the requirements of section 185 of CA 2006.

Such notice or declaration can be in relation to a specific transaction or arrangement or can be more general notice of an interest in any transaction or arrangement, for example with a particular company or individual. Section 182 of CA 2006 sets out the disclosure requirements in relation to existing conflicts and the requirements can be discharged by any of the three methods outlined above. Section 182 does not apply if disclosure has already been made under section 177.

The Model Articles for both private and public companies deal only with transactional conflicts (article 14/article 16). They provide that interested directors cannot be counted in the quorum or vote on any matter that concerns an actual or proposed transaction or arrangement with the company. There are certain exceptions to this rule which permit interested directors to be counted in the quorum and to vote notwithstanding their interest, where:

- an ordinary resolution has been passed which disapplies the provisions of the articles which would otherwise prevent the director from being counted or from voting; or
- the director's interest cannot reasonably be regarded as likely to give rise to a conflict of interest; or
- the director's conflict of interest arises from a permitted cause.

A permitted cause includes inter-group guarantees and subscription agreements relating to any group companies.

The Model Articles are more restrictive than was the case under section 317 of CA 1985 and regulation 85 of Table A. Under the old rules a director could be personally interested in a transaction with the company, vote on the matter and be counted in the quorum for that part of the meeting during which the matter was under consideration provided proper disclosure of the interest had been made by the director, including full disclosure of the amount of profit or reward the director would, or is expected to, obtain from it.

However, under the Model Articles full disclosure in itself is not sufficient to permit the interested director to participate in the decision-making process. This is only possible where the interest falls under one of the categories of exemption set out above. Therefore, if the interest does not arise from a permitted cause and is adjudged by the directors as being likely to give rise to a conflict of interest, a director will only be permitted to take part in the business of the meeting that considers the interest where such participation has been authorised by the shareholders in the form of an ordinary resolution (see Chapter 4).

CA 2006 does not prevent directors from participating in a meeting when a transactional interest exists and companies are likely, therefore, to wish to exclude the Model Articles or at least to amend them so that the directors can permit a director to participate fully in a meeting once he has made proper disclosure of an interest in a proposed transaction or arrangement. Sample wording for such an article is included within Precedent 5.

5.3 Appointment of directors

5.3.1 Appointment

The Model Articles of both private and public companies state that any person who is willing to act as a director, and is permitted to do so by law, may be appointed to be a director by ordinary resolution of the members or by the directors (article 17/article 20).

Articles 17(2) and 17(3) of the Model Articles for a private company also set out what will happen where, as a result of death, the company has no shareholders and no directors. This is important for many private companies which have only one or two directors and in many cases they are also the only shareholders. In these instances the Model Articles provide for the personal representatives of the last surviving shareholder to appoint a director by giving notice in writing. This is an important addition for many companies' articles, without which they would have to resort to the courts and legal process to resolve the situation.

Companies may wish to specify alternative or additional appointment mechanisms in their articles. One very common provision is a clause which gives the holding company power to appoint (and remove) directors for as long as the company is a subsidiary of it, as follows:

> The immediate holding company (if any) for the time being of the company may appoint any person to be a director or remove any director from office. Every such appointment or removal shall be in writing and signed by or on behalf of the said holding company and shall take effect upon receipt at the registered office of the company or by the secretary.

5.3.2 Retirement by rotation

Companies will need to take care that they follow the right procedures for retirement of directors by rotation because the regime under Table A is quite different from the new rules under article 21 of the Model Articles for public companies.

The procedures under Table A are as follows:

- All directors retire from office at a company's first AGM (regulation 73).
- At each subsequent AGM one-third of the directors who are subject to retirement by rotation shall retire from office. If the number of directors is not divisible by three the nearest number to one-third shall retire (regulation 73). Some companies' articles vary on this point and provide that the number to retire shall not exceed one-third.
- The directors to retire by rotation are those who have been longest in office since their appointment or last reappointment. Where there is no difference in the dates of reappointment, for example at the second AGM if all directors who retired and were reappointed at the first AGM are still in office, those to retire are to be determined by lot. Directors who are retiring at the next AGM after their appointment by the directors under regulation 79 are not to be counted when determining who is to retire by rotation.
- Directors who retire by rotation are eligible for re-election but the members may decide to appoint someone else in accordance with the provisions of regulation 76. This gives both directors and members the right to recommend someone else for appointment, subject only to the requirement that at least 14 and not more than 35 clear days must be given for member-recommended appointments.

The provisions on retirement by rotation contained in the Model Articles for public companies are considerably simpler:

- All directors retire from office at the company's first AGM (article 21(1)).
- At subsequent AGMs directors who have been appointed by the directors since the last AGM or who were not appointed or reappointed at one of the preceding two AGMs must retire from office and may offer themselves for reappointment by the members (article 21(2)).

Where a private company's articles do not contain a positive requirement for an AGM to be held, but still state that the directors are to retire by rotation at an AGM, the provisions fall away as there is no longer any provision in CA 2006 for an AGM to be held. To avoid confusion companies should consider amending their articles to remove any such redundant provisions, replacing them with alternative rotation provisions if appropriate.

5.3.3 Alternate directors

The practice of allowing directors to appoint alternate directors has no statutory basis beyond inclusion of alternate directors in the definition of 'director' in section 250 of CA 2006. Therefore, alternate directors may only be appointed if this is allowed by the articles.

The Model Articles of a private company do not provide for alternate directors to be appointed and it must therefore be specifically added if required.

Articles 25–27 of the Model Articles for public companies contain provisions for the appointment and removal of alternate directors, the rights and responsibilities of alternates and termination of alternate directorships. The provisions contained in the Model Articles are similar to the provisions under regulations 65–69 of Table A, but the circumstances in which an alternate director's appointment terminates (article 27) are more detailed. In addition to the situation envisaged by regulation 67 of Table A that the appointment ceases when the appointor ceases to be a director, the appointment will also cease when revoked by the appointer in writing, if the alternate does something which, if done by the appointor, would result in termination of the appointor's directorship and on the death of the appointor.

For appointments of alternate directors under either regime it is necessary for the relevant particulars to be entered in the register of directors and for a Form 288a to be filed at Companies House.

5.3.4 Minimum number of directors

Section 154 of CA 2006 requires a private company to have at least one director and a public company to have at least two directors. As mentioned in Chapter 4, at least one director must be an individual rather than a corporation (s.155 CA 2006).

Regulation 64 of Table A provides that unless the shareholders otherwise decide by ordinary resolution, the minimum number of directors shall be two and there shall be no maximum. There is no equivalent regulation in the Model Articles for either private or public companies. Companies may choose to adopt different requirements in the articles if required.

As with the quorum requirements set out at 5.2.3 above, where the number of directors has fallen below the required minimum, Table A only permits the directors to meet to appoint the required additional directors, or to call a general meeting so that the members can do so. The articles can provide a greater power than this, so that the continuing directors may act generally for an indefinite period notwithstanding any vacancy in their number.

> **TIP: Always check the articles when you are given details of an appointment or resignation of a director. Even if the matter seems very straightforward, problems could arise later if the action will cause director number or quorum requirements to be breached.**

Sometimes it is not realised until later that the number of directors has fallen below the required minimum. For example, where a director resigns without the articles of association being checked there is a risk of the number of directors falling below the minimum required and acts taken by the remaining directors being considered invalid. In such cases it may be several months or more until the problem is discovered. However, if the actions taken and decisions made are within the scope of the board's authority, they can be ratified by the board. If not, ratification will need to be by the members of the company.

5.3.5 Executive positions

The articles may provide for the appointment of directors to various executive offices, such as managing director or chief executive officer. Under such provisions the directors are usually given the power to make the appointments, determine the terms of appointment and delegate powers. Such provisions are contained in regulation 84 of Table A. It is also usual for the articles to authorise the directors to revoke any such executive appointment without reference to the members, although this will be subject to anything contained in the director's service agreement. There are no specific provisions in the Model Articles concerning appointment to executive positions and, although the provisions on delegation of powers are sufficient to enable this, if specific mention is required, it will need to be added.

5.3.6 Termination of appointment

Article 18 of the Model Articles for private companies sets out the circumstances in which a director's appointment will terminate. The equivalent provision in the public company articles is article 22. Under these provisions a person ceases to be a director as soon as:

- they cease to be a director by virtue of any provision of CA 2006 or are prohibited by law from being a director;
- a bankruptcy order is made against them;

- a composition is made with their creditors in satisfaction of debts;
- a doctor's written opinion states that they are physically or mentally incapable of acting as a director and will remain so for more than three months;
- they are subject to a court order concerning their mental health which prevents them from personally exercising any powers or rights they would otherwise have;
- they resign.

The equivalent provisions of Table A are contained in regulation 81 which also provides that the office of director shall be vacated if a director has, without permission, failed to attend board meetings for more than six consecutive months and the directors resolve that his office be vacated. With regard to this provision the period of absence for determining the six months begins on the date of the last meeting the director attended, rather than the date of the first meeting missed. The article applies even where the absence is involuntary, such as where the director is prevented from attending owing to ill-health.

Additional reasons for disqualification may be inserted into the articles and these might include such things as no longer satisfying a shareholding qualification or ceasing to be an employee.

5.3.7 Removal of directors

Regardless of anything contained in the articles, section 168 of CA 2006 gives the members the right to remove directors by ordinary resolution provided certain procedural requirements, such as the giving of special notice, are observed. These statutory provisions cannot be excluded by the articles but additional provisions may be made, such as giving the holding company the right to remove a director by notice in writing (see 5.3.1 for an example of such wording) or permitting removal to be effected by a unanimous decision of the other directors.

5.3.8 Remuneration and expenses

Regulations 82 and 83 of Table A deal with remuneration and expenses respectively. Regulation 82 states that the directors are entitled to such remuneration as the company may by ordinary resolution determine. The Model Articles of both private and public companies give the directors rather than the shareholders the power to determine remuneration. The Model Articles concerning entitlement to be paid expenses are largely the same as the Table A provisions. They permit the payment of any reasonable expenses which the directors properly incur in connection with their attendance at board, committee, class and general meetings or otherwise in connection with the exercise of their powers and the discharge of their responsibilities in relation to the company.

Although it is open to companies to make any provision they see fit in the articles in connection with the payment of expenses, this will tend to be limited to an overall statement of what maximum remuneration can be paid to directors. In practice the more detailed requirements relating to expenses, including specific limitations, a definition of what constitutes reasonable expenses, and the procedure for claiming expenses, tend to be set out in a director's service agreement and/or a company's employment handbook.

5.4 Indemnity and insurance

As mentioned in Chapter 4, a company's articles will often contain provisions pertaining to the indemnification of directors against liabilities and may also contain an express right to purchase insurance for directors.

Section 232(2) of CA 2006 states that any provision by which a company provides an indemnity for a director against any liability, whether as a result of negligence, default, breach of duty or breach of trust, is invalid, subject to some limited exceptions, one of which is the purchase of insurance in accordance with section 233 of CA 2006. A sample clause detailing indemnity provisions including a company's right to provide insurance can be found in Precedent 10.

6

Share capital

In this chapter we look at the rules concerning share capital and how it can be changed, focusing on those aspects that are relevant to a company's memorandum and articles. At the time of writing the laws that define how these matters have to be dealt with are for the most part to be found in CA 1985, pending implementation of the remaining parts of CA 2006 in October 2009. The position under both pieces of legislation is therefore considered and it should be clear from the text which provisions apply.

A company's share capital is that part of its capital which derives from the shares issued to the members. Under CA 1985 companies limited by shares must have an authorised capital, which is the maximum amount of share capital that can be issued. This is distinct from the issued share capital, which is the amount of share capital that has actually been issued to the members. As we saw in Chapter 4 the concept of authorised share capital is set to disappear once the remaining provisions of CA 2006 come into force on 1 October 2009.

6.1 Authorised capital

As mentioned above, a company's authorised share capital and issued share capital are two different things and another name for authorised capital is 'nominal capital'. The authorised or nominal capital is usually expressed as a total amount and by the number and value of the shares of which it is comprised, and it is the maximum nominal amount of share capital that the directors can issue, as prescribed in the company's memorandum. This amount acts as a ceiling on the number of shares that can be issued.

TIP: The market value of a company's shares is different from the nominal value. The market value changes to reflect the company's trading performance and public perception of its prospects, whereas the nominal value remains the same unless the members formally resolve to change it.

As mentioned in Chapter 2, the memorandum of a company with a share capital must state the amount of share capital with which the company proposes to be registered and the division of the shares into so many shares of a fixed nominal value. The authorised capital can be increased by passing an ordinary resolution to that effect (unless the articles require a special resolution). For more on possible changes to a company's capital, please refer to 6.3 below.

When all the provisions of CA 2006 have come into force in October 2009, there will be no requirement for a company to have an authorised share capital. For companies with a share capital that were formed prior to 1 October 2009, the existing authorised capital details will continue to restrict the number of shares that can be issued and any provisions relating to authorised share capital will automatically become part of the company's articles. However, while a special resolution is normally required to amend the articles, it will be possible for the clause detailing the authorised capital, and therefore the limit on how many shares can be issued, to be removed by ordinary resolution. Companies may pass an ordinary resolution to remove or amend their authorised capital provision before the new rules have come into force but the resolution will only take effect from 1 October 2009.

A company will still be required to ascribe a fixed nominal value to its shares after 1 October 2009 (s.542(1) CA 2006). Article 21 of the Model Articles for private companies requires that shares are not issued for less than the aggregate nominal value and any premium to be paid and the allotment of any shares that do not have a nominal value will be void (s.542(2)).

Under section 542(3) of CA 2006 companies are still permitted to denominate their shares in any currency and may denominate different classes of share in different currencies. Neither the Model Articles nor Table A set out any requirements on these points and, if particular provisions are required, such as restricting the currencies into which shares may be denominated or limiting the number of different classes of capital, they will need to be added.

6.2 Classes of share

A company may issue different classes of shares, each with their own rights and restrictions. While details of the different classes and their rights may historically have been set out in the memorandum, this is not the most flexible approach from a company's perspective. Including the information in the articles or setting out the rights in a shareholders' resolution when changes to the company's capital are made will generally be preferable as it makes the details easier to amend in future.

For companies formed on or after 1 October 2009, given the limited content of the memorandum, this information will usually be included in the company's articles.

6.2.1 Authority in articles to issue different classes of share

The Model Articles of both private and public companies (article 22(1)/ article 43(1)) permit companies to issue shares with such rights or restrictions as may be determined by ordinary resolution. This authority is also contained in regulation 2 of Table A. Companies may vary these default provisions to permit the directors rather than the members to issue shares and determine the rights and restrictions attached to them, subject to them having obtained the required authority from the members to do so.

Prior to 1 October 2009 a company could only issue redeemable shares if there was a provision allowing this in the articles. While after 1 October 2009 this requirement will remain the same for public companies, a private company will be able to issue redeemable shares unless any restriction or prohibition has been added to its articles.

6.2.2 Rights for different classes of share

A company can create classes of shares with such rights and restrictions as it deems appropriate. Most of these rights can be altered whether or not shares of that class have been issued, save only that shares which have been issued that were not redeemable cannot be converted into redeemable shares.

Some examples of the different rights commonly attached to shares include the following:

- right to vote at general meetings;
- right to receive a dividend: some classes of share may carry a preferential right to receive a dividend ahead of the holders of shares in another class, or some classes of shareholder may not be entitled to receive any dividend at all;
- right to capital on a winding-up or a return of capital: this is often linked to the right to a dividend;
- pre-emption rights on the transfer or allotment of shares;
- right of redemption: these allow investors to realise their investment on a specified future date or in accordance with a prescribed formula;

- right to conversion: usually given to holders of a class of shares with enhanced dividend rights but no other rights.

These rights will usually be stated in the company's articles.

6.2.3 Variation of class rights

Under section 125 of CA 1985 class rights can only be varied with the written consent of the holders of three-quarters in nominal value of the issued shares of that class, or by the passing of a special resolution to approve the variation at a meeting of the relevant class. More stringent requirements than this, such as requiring unanimous consent, may be specified in a company's articles, in which case they must be observed. The Model Articles and Table A do not contain any procedures for the variation of class rights.

Sections 630–640 of CA 2006 specify provisions concerning the variation of class rights that are largely the same as the equivalent provisions of CA 1985. A couple of points of difference are worth noting. The first difference is the extension of the principles to cover companies that do not have a share capital so that, for example, there is a mechanism for dealing with the variation of the rights of different categories of member of a company limited by guarantee. Another difference is that companies will be able to make the provisions about variation of class rights in their articles less demanding than the procedures specified by CA 2006.

Under both pieces of legislation shareholders may object to a variation. To do so, members amounting to not less than 15 per cent of the members of the relevant class who did not consent to or vote in favour of the variation may apply to the court to have the variation cancelled. The court may cancel a variation where it is satisfied that the variation would unfairly prejudice the members in the affected class. The company must submit a copy of the order to Companies House within 15 days of the date on which it is made.

Sometimes shares are allotted that have special rights attached to them that do not match exactly the rights attached to previous shares allotted in that class. If details of these special rights are not provided in the memorandum or articles or in any agreement that has already been submitted to Companies House, a statement of the special rights must be filed (at the time of writing using a Form G128(1)) within one month of the allotment).

6.3 Changes to capital

There are a variety of changes a company may make to its share capital. These are set out in Parts 4 and 5 of CA 1985 and in Chapter 8 of Part 17 of CA

2006. A fundamental difference between the position under CA 1985 and the stance taken by CA 2006 is the relationship between statute and the articles in determining whether a proposed alteration is permitted.

Under CA 1985, although procedures for several different types of alteration are given a company may only use those procedures where a specific authority to that effect is contained in its articles. Conversely, under CA 2006 silence in the articles is no bar to altering a company's share capital in one of the ways stipulated by statute. A method may not be used only where there is a specific prohibition in the articles. Consequently from 1 October 2009 there is no need for a company's articles to contain specific authority for the company to reduce its share capital, subdivide or consolidate its capital, redeem shares or purchase its own shares.

Types of alteration to share capital permitted by law include:

- increase of capital;
- consolidation or subdivision of shares;
- reduction of share capital;
- purchase of own shares;
- redenomination of share capital;
- redemption of shares.

Each of these is considered in more detail below and it is important to note that if a company wants to place any restrictions on changes being made to its share capital in any of the ways described above then from 1 October 2009 such restrictions must be specifically added to the articles.

6.3.1 Increase of capital

Until 30 September 2009 a company may increase its authorised capital by passing an ordinary resolution, unless a more onerous procedure, such as the need for a special resolution, is stated in its articles. A copy of the resolution must be sent to Companies House, together with a Form 123 within 15 days of passing the resolution. No filing fee is payable. Any references in the company's constitutional documents to the authorised capital should be updated and reprints filed at Companies House. However, many companies merely attach a copy of the resolution to the company's constitutional documents.

> TIP: When increasing a company's authorised capital the directors' authority to allot shares should be renewed.

The rationale behind renewing the directors' authority to allot shares is that the directors' authority to allot is only in respect of the shares that were unissued at the time the authority was last given. Consideration should also be given to whether pre-emption rights on allotment need to be waived. For more on pre-emption rights see Chapter 7.

Once the remaining provisions of CA 2006 have been implemented, companies should consider amending their articles to remove any limits on share capital that have become 'deemed restrictions' in accordance with the transitional provisions. Companies formed on or after 1 October 2009 will not be limited as to the number of shares they can issue and an increase in share capital will merely mean an increase in issued capital by way of an allotment. Share allotments are considered in detail in Chapter 7.

6.3.2 Consolidation and subdivision of shares

Under CA 1985 a company may consolidate or subdivide its shares by ordinary resolution if authorised to do so by its articles of association. Consolidation occurs where the company's shares are changed so that they are divided into fewer shares each with a larger nominal value. For example, 100 shares with a nominal value of 1p are consolidated into 1 share with a nominal value of £1. When shares are subdivided the opposite process occurs with the result that the company has more shares in number but these each have a lower nominal value. However, with both consolidation and subdivision the total value of the share capital remains the same.

Notice of a consolidation or subdivision must be sent to Companies House together with a revised copy of the company's memorandum showing the change to the share capital clause within one month of approval by the members.

The main change that will result from implementation of section 618 of CA 2006 is that companies will be able to do a consolidation or subdivision irrespective of whether the company's articles contain specific permission to this effect. Under CA 2006 a consolidation or subdivision needs to be approved by ordinary resolution (s.618(3) CA 2006), unless the articles provide otherwise, for example, requiring approval by special resolution. Notice of the event must still be submitted to Companies House, but a statement of capital needs to be filed along with the prescribed form rather than a reprint of the memorandum with the share capital clause amended.

6.3.3 Reduction of share capital

Both private and public companies may apply to the court to reduce their share capital. Since 1 October 2008, private companies limited by shares have also had the option of reducing their capital by passing a special resolution supported by a solvency statement.

Until 1 October 2009 CA 1985 is the governing law for court-approved reductions. In common with the other share capital changes we have looked at, CA 1985 requires that a company's articles contain authority for the proposed reduction of capital before it can be carried out. After 1 October 2009 a court-approved reduction can be undertaken by special resolution provided there is nothing in the articles which prohibit it (s.641(6) CA 2006).

A public company cannot do business unless the Registrar has issued it with a trading certificate. In turn, a trading certificate will only be issued if the company has an allotted share capital of at least the authorised minimum (s.761(1), (2) CA 2006). The authorised minimum is specified in section 763(1) of CA 2006 as £50,000 or the prescribed Euro equivalent of 65,600. If a proposed reduction in share capital will cause the company's issued capital to fall below the authorised minimum, the Registrar will only register the court order if directed to do so by the court, or if the company re-registers as a private company. Section 651 of CA 2006 provides an expedited procedure for re-registration as a private company which allows the court to authorise the re-registration of a company as a private company without a special resolution being passed. When the court does so, it must specify in the order any changes to the company's name and articles that need to be made in connection with the re-registration. A copy of the revised articles needs to be filed along with a copy of the court order and notice of the company's name when applying for the re-registration.

6.3.4 Re-denomination of share capital

Under CA 1985 there is no simple mechanism for re-denominating shares from one class to another. Public companies wishing to change the currency in which their shares are denominated are constrained by the authorised minimum requirements and must consequently keep at least £50,000 of their capital in sterling. Subject to this requirement, however, public companies may bring about a re-denomination by cancelling existing shares and creating a new class of shares in the desired currency. Private companies may use this method and can also achieve a re-denomination by way of a purchase of own shares. For details about a purchase of own shares see 7.1.6.

From 1 October 2009 private companies limited by shares will be able to re-denominate their share capital by ordinary resolution alone as long as the articles do not specifically prohibit this. The rules concerning the maintenance of a public company's authorised minimum capital are also being relaxed so that once the initial capital requirements have been satisfied a public company is fee to re-denominate its entire share capital into another currency, provided this is the equivalent of £50,000.

6.4 Minors as members

While neither Table A nor the Model Articles address the matter, the issue of whether minors should be accepted as members of a company merits consideration.

It is not considered good practice to accept minors (i.e. in England, Wales and Northern Ireland those below the age of 18) as members of a company. The rationale for this is that becoming a member may lead to the member assuming liabilities in respect of their shares. Some articles contain express provisions giving the directors the power to refuse to process allotments or transfers in the name of a minor. Even where the articles do not contain such a provision, there is an implied power in common law. A member who transfers shares, however unwittingly, to a minor remains liable for any calls on those shares insofar as they are only partly paid until such time as the registered holder comes of age.

6.5 Share certificates

Share certificates are *prima facie* evidence of title but do not constitute a document of title in the same way as share warrants do. It is therefore important that share certificates are prepared and issued correctly. Both the Model Articles and Table A contain provisions regarding share certificates.

6.5.1 Model Articles for private companies

Articles 24 and 25 of the Model Articles for private companies limited by shares set out the requirements relating to share certificates. Under these articles each shareholder is entitled to one or more certificates in respect of the shares they hold and the certificate(s) must be provided free of charge. The minimum basic information to be shown on the share certificate is as follows:

- how many shares the certificate is for and what class they are;
- the nominal value of the shares;
- that the shares are fully paid up; and
- any distinguishing numbers assigned to the shares.

Under article 24(3) a share certificate may not cover holdings in more than one class. Joint holders are only entitled to one share certificate between them. Certificates must be sealed or executed in any other way provided for by law (i.e signed by one director and witnessed or signed by two officers).

A shareholder is entitled to a replacement certificate where the original is damaged, defaced, lost, stolen or destroyed (article 25(1)). Where a certificate is damaged or defaced, the certificate should be returned to the company. Where the certificate cannot be found, the shareholder will usually be asked to sign an indemnity. Often such indemnity has to be joined in by a bank or insurance company, but sometimes the requirement is waived. While it is generally good practice for replacement certificates to be clearly marked as such, there is no such requirement in the Model Articles that this be done.

6.5.2 Model Articles for public companies

The requirements pertaining to share certificates can be found in articles 46–51. The general requirements as to the contents of share certificates are the same as for private companies save for the fact that shares can be partly paid. The Model Articles also deal with uncertificated shares and warrants, which are not mentioned in the private company articles.

Under article 50(4) shares may be transferred wholly or partly without a share certificate. Article 50(5) gives the directors the discretion to take whatever steps they think fit regarding the evidencing of title and the records related to the uncertificated shares. Article 51 deals with share warrants; under its provisions the directors may issue share warrants in respect of fully paid shares and have complete discretion over the form of the warrants.

6.5.3 Table A

Regulation 6 of Table A allows for shares to be partly paid, whereas the Model Articles for private companies require the share certificate to state that the shares are fully paid (article 24(2)(c)). This stems from article 21 which requires that all shares be fully paid up. When drafting or amending private company articles to which the Model Articles apply, articles 21 and 24(2)(c) should therefore be viewed in conjunction, with article 24(2)(c) also being disapplied.

As we saw at 6.5.2 above, the Model Articles for public companies contain detailed provisions about consolidated share certificates and uncertificated holdings, which do not feature in Table A.

Allotments, transfers and distributions

In this chapter we examine the rights and restrictions concerning allotments, transfers and distributions that may be contained in a company's articles of association.

7.1 Allotments

The words 'allot' and 'issue' and all variants thereof are used here to mean the same thing, i.e. the process by which members acquire new shares in a company. In fact there is a fine distinction to be made between the terms, which are two parts of the same process. Shares are 'allotted' when the company enters into a contract with a person who thereby acquires an unconditional right to be issued the shares in question. Shares are 'issued' when a person is registered as a member in the company's register of members. While the provisions of Chapter 2 of Part 17 of CA 2006 which deal with the allotment of shares consistently use the term 'allot', the Model Article provisions give the company a general right to 'issue' shares.

The directors must be authorised to allot shares, either by ordinary resolution or by authority contained in the articles of association. In addition, before an allotment proceeds, consideration needs also to be given as to whether any pre-emption provisions on allotment need to be observed (or waived).

7.1.1 Authority to allot shares

7.1.1.1 CA 1985 position

Shares can be allotted provided the directors are authorised to do so by either an ordinary resolution of the members or by an authority contained in the company's articles of association (s.80(1) CA 1985). Such authority can be general or may be made subject to certain conditions (s.80(3) CA 1985). The authority must state the maximum number of shares over which the power is exercisable and the date on which the authority will expire (which cannot be more than five years from the date on which the resolution giving the authority was passed save for private companies that had passed an elective resolution to make the period unlimited).

7.1.1.2 What happens in practice?

Private companies will usually seek to renew this authority only when needed, whereas public companies may routinely renew the authority on an annual basis. The current guidance from the Association of British Insurers (ABI) recommends that public companies limit the authority sought to one-third of the existing issued capital, but that the authority can last for the maximum five years. However, where authority is sought to allot a further one-third for use with fully pre-emptive rights issues, the ABI recommends that the authority be renewed at the next AGM. While such guidance is not binding, many AIM and fully listed companies will tend to accept and adhere to such limits in the interests of 'best practice' and to obtain market approval concerning their proposed allotments. It should be noted that authority may only be granted in respect of shares authorised but unissued at the time the authority is sought. For that reason it is always a good idea to renew the directors, authority under section 80 of CA 1985 when a company's share capital is increased (see Chapter 6).

A sample resolution for the general power to allot under section 80 of CA 1985 is included as Precedent 11.

7.1.1.3 CA 2006 position

From 1 October 2009 the directors of private companies with only one class of shares are unconditionally authorised by section 550 of CA 2006 to allot shares unless prevented from doing so by a prohibition in the company's articles. Therefore if the shareholders wish to restrict the directors' ability to allot new shares they will need to do so by including a suitable limiting clause in the articles.

For both private companies with more than one class of shares and for public companies section 551 requires that authority is obtained from the members before new shares are allotted. As with CA 1985 the authority must state the maximum number of shares over which the authority is granted and the date on which the authority is to expire. This date cannot be more than five years from the date of grant of authority. However, elective resolutions passed before 1 October 2008 by private companies under section 80A of CA 1985 to extend the directors' authority to allot shares for an indefinite period, or for a fixed period that ends after 1 October 2009, continue to have effect indefinitely in accordance with the Companies Act 2006 (Commencement No. 8, Transitional Provisions and Savings) Order 2008.

7.1.2 Pre-emption rights

Pre-emption rights give existing shareholders the right to be offered any new shares to be allotted in proportion to their holding before the shares are offered to anyone else. Pre-emption rights are contained in sections 89–94 of CA 1985 but may also be contained in a company's articles. If a company chooses to make specific provisions in its articles, the following points will normally be addressed:

- what is required to waive the right, for example the passing of a special resolution or obtaining consent from all members;
- the manner in which an offer shall be made and the details to be contained in it, such as in writing specifying the number of shares involved;
- the period in which the offer must be accepted, after which an offer can be deemed to have been declined;
- what happens to shares that have been declined, for example it is usual that shares declined must be offered to accepting shareholders before they can be allotted freely.

Private companies may choose to exclude the statutory pre-emption rights via their articles, and the provisions contained in the articles will take precedence over the statutory provisions even where they are inconsistent with them. In addition, both private and public companies may disapply pre-emption rights by special resolution. If a company's articles are silent, the statutory rights of pre-emption on allotment will still apply and will need to be excluded before an allotment can be made to someone without the shares being offered to the existing members. An alternative to passing a special resolution would be to obtain individual waivers from all the members who were entitled to be offered the shares.

> TIP: Make sure your resolution disapplies the right provisions. It is no good disapplying statutory pre-emption rights if the rights in the articles still need to be observed.

The ABI's guidance recommends that companies seeking authority to allot shares as if the statutory pre-emption provisions did not apply should limit their request to 5 per cent of the company's issued ordinary capital. A sample resolution for the disapplication of statutory pre-emption rights is included as Precedent 12.

The regime under CA 2006 is largely the same and no pre-emption provisions on allotment are contained in the Model Articles or Table A.

7.1.3 Nominee shareholders

Usually a nominee shareholding is used when the beneficial owner does not wish to have the company's shares registered in their own name. Sometimes, though, the use of a nominee shareholding may be due to a clause of the company's articles, for example a requirement that the company have at least two members. In this case, the company or person who would otherwise hold all the shares in their own name has one share held in trust for them by the nominee or they become a joint holder of a share with the nominee. As it is the nominee or joint holder's name that will appear on the register, the nominee should execute an appropriate stock transfer form so that the shares can easily be transferred when necessary. It is usual for this to be supported by a declaration of trust, but this need not be disclosed to the company. The nominee should provide a dividend mandate so that the dividends can be paid to the beneficial owner.

For private companies any provisions requiring the company to have more than one member can be removed when the articles are next amended and the share held by a nominee can be transferred.

7.1.4 Calls on shares

Calls on shares occur when only part of the nominal value has to be paid on the shares at the time of their allotment and no fixed terms have been stipulated as to when the balance on the partly paid shares must be paid.

Directors are often authorised by the company's articles to make calls on partly paid shares. Regulations 12–17 of Table A contain provisions relating to calls, under which the directors can make calls on the shares provided they give members at least 14 clear days' notice specifying when and where payment of the unpaid sums is to be made. Regulations 18–22 detail what happens if the terms of the call are not observed, including disenfranchisement of rights and, ultimately, the possible forfeiture of the shares.

Unless the transferee has expressly agreed to assume the liability and evidence of this is provided in writing, directors should refuse to register the transfer of a share which is partly paid because liability to pay the amount owing on the shares remains with the shareholder who was registered at the time of the call.

7.1.5 Forfeiture of shares

Shares can be forfeited for non-payment of calls where a procedure for this is specified in the articles. Regulations 18–22 of Table A and articles 57–62 of the Model Articles for public companies contain forfeiture provisions.

It is vital that the forfeiture procedure specified in the articles is adhered to properly as the forfeiture may otherwise be held to be invalid. The person ceases to be a member of the company when the forfeiture is entered in the register of members. However, they remain liable for any sums outstanding in respect of the shares unless the shares are reissued and paid up in full.

Often the forfeiture procedure specified in the articles will permit the directors to cancel the forfeiture if payment of the call is subsequently received in full, provided that the shares have not already been sold.

Although directors will generally have discretion about the way in which forfeited shares are sold, the sale price cannot be less than the amount needed to make them fully paid once the amount already paid has been taken into account.

Regulation 22 of Table A provides for a director or the secretary to make a statutory declaration that a share has been forfeited and that such declaration is conclusive evidence against anyone who claims to be entitled to the shares in question.

An alternative to following a formal forfeiture procedure is for the member to surrender their shares. Article 62 of the Model Articles for public companies provides that a member may surrender their shares in the following circumstances:

- where the directors may issue a notice of intended forfeiture;
- when the directors are able to forfeit the shares; and
- when the shares have been forfeited.

Shares that have been voluntarily surrendered can be sold in the same way as if they had been forfeited.

For public companies there are additional, statutory provisions that apply when shares have been forfeited pursuant to the company's articles. At the time of writing the provisions of ssections 146–149 of CA 1985 were still in force, to be replaced by sections 662–669 of CA 2006 with effect from 1 October 2009. Under these new provisions any shares which have been forfeited or surrendered and remain unsold after three years from the date of forfeiture or surrender must be cancelled by the company and the company's share capital must be reduced by the corresponding nominal value.

If a public company's reduction of share capital has the effect of taking the issued capital below the authorised minimum (£50,000 or the prescribed Euro equivalent) the company is obliged to re-register as a private company. Under the provisions of both CA 1985 and CA 2006 the re-registration can be done on an expedited basis without the need for the usual formalities connected with a reduction in capital being followed. To apply for re-registration as a private company a Form 147 must be submitted together with a reprint of the memorandum and articles altered to reflect the new private company status.

7.1.6 Purchase of own shares

At present a company may purchase its own shares provided it is authorised to do so by its articles of association (s.162 CA 1985). Such authority may be found, for example, in regulation 35 of Table A, which also makes the necessary provision (s.171 CA 1985) to enable a private company to make a payment in respect of a purchase of own shares otherwise than out of its distributable profits or from the proceeds of a fresh issue of shares.

There are three ways in which a purchase of own shares may be effected:

- out of the distributable profits of the company;
- out of the proceeds of a fresh issue of shares made for the purpose of the purchase; and
- out of capital (only available to private companies).

The procedures for making a purchase of own shares may be split further according to whether the purchase is made 'on' or 'off' market, as defined in section 163 of CA 1985. A market purchase is one which is made on a recognised investment exchange, while an off-market purchase is one made other than on a recognised investment exchange or which is made on a recognised investment exchange but the shares are not subject to a marketing arrangement on the exchange concerned. A market purchase of own shares requires the approval of a company's members by ordinary resolution, while an off-market purchase needs to be authorised by a company's members passing a special resolution. A copy of the relevant resolution should be attached to the company's constitutional documents.

For more details on the procedural requirements for market and off-market purchases readers are referred to section 7 of the ICSA's publication *Company Secretarial Practice*.

From 1 October 2009 purchases of own shares will be governed by the rules set out in Part 18 of CA 2006. Under the new rules companies will still be able to purchase their own shares and private companies can make purchases out of capital. From the perspective of the articles, the most important change brought in by CA 2006 is that companies will be able to purchase their own shares provided there is nothing in their articles expressly forbidding this. Consequently it will no longer be necessary for a company's articles to include specific authority for a company to purchase its own shares before the statutory procedures can be followed. In line with this approach, the Model Articles are silent on the subject of purchases of own shares.

7.1.7 Bonus issues

A bonus issue is also known as a capitalisation issue or scrip issue and is a process whereby shareholders are issued with additional shares in proportion to their existing holdings. The shareholders do not have to pay anything for the shares as they are already fully paid by the company. Although it may appear that shareholders are getting something for nothing, in reality bonus issues are often used by companies to reduce the market value of their shares so the value of each member's holding is unlikely to increase.

A company's articles will usually contain a provision enabling the company to carry out a bonus issue, subject to an ordinary resolution being passed. This is the case with regulation 110 of Table A which allows for the capitalisation of profits.

The Model Articles for private and public companies contain provisions relating to the capitalisation of profits (article 36/article 78 respectively). The only difference between the two sets of articles is that the public company articles make provision (article 78(4)(a)) for a capitalised sum to be used in paying up any unpaid amounts on existing shares. This difference merely reflects the assumption that the shares of public companies will not be issued partly paid.

7.1.8 Redeemable shares

Under sections 159–161 of CA 1985 a company limited by shares or limited by guarantee may issue shares which are to be redeemed or which may be redeemed at the option of either the company or the shareholder provided this is allowed by the company's articles. When redeemable shares are issued, the company must also have other issued capital comprised of shares which are not redeemable. By section 160(3) the terms of redemption and the manner in which the redemption is to be effected must be set out in the articles.

When sections 684–689 of CA 2006 come into force on 1 October 2009, private companies will be able to issue redeemable shares without any enabling provision in their articles. However, by section 684(2) private companies may use their articles to exclude or restrict the issue of redeemable shares. Public companies will still need express authority in their articles to permit the issue of redeemable shares (s.684(3) CA 2006)). The directors of both private and public limited companies may determine the terms, conditions and manner of redemption of shares where they are authorised to do so by the company's articles or by a resolution of the company. If the directors are not authorised in either of these ways, the terms, conditions and manner of redemption must be stated in the company's articles.

7.2 Transfers

The procedures a company must observe in respect of the transfer of shares depend on both statute and what requirements are contained in the company's articles.

7.2.1 Transfer of shares

7.2.1.1 Form of transfer

Article 26(1) of the Model Articles for private companies provides for shares to be transferred by means of an instrument of transfer in any usual form or any other form approved by the directors, which is executed by or on behalf of the transferor. The corresponding provision in the Model Articles for public companies is article 63(1) which relates to certificated shares. For private companies the usual form of transfer will be a stock transfer form of the kind included as Precedent 13, which is in accordance with the form of transfer prescribed by the Stock Transfer Act 1963.

7.2.1.2 Refusal to register a transfer

When presented with an acceptable instrument of transfer, the directors must either register the transfer or notify the intending transferor of the refusal to register the transfer (s.771 CA 2006). This notification must be made within two months of the transfer form being lodged with the company (s.771(1)). This is also the position under regulation 25 of Table A. However, it is usual for companies to have excluded this Regulation, including instead permission for the directors to refuse to register transfers without giving any reason. Any such provisions have now ceased to have effect as they are overridden by the statutory provisions and should be removed the next time the company's articles are altered. Interestingly, while the Model Articles require the directors to return a refused instrument of transfer to the would-be transferor along with the notice of refusal, no reference is made to a time limit.

Regulation 24 of Table A sets out certain grounds on which the directors may refuse to register a transfer. A company's articles may make additional provisions, such as giving the directors the right to make approval of a transfer of partly paid shares conditional on the shares being fully paid before registration of the transfer which could be useful if the directors have any doubts about the intended transferee's ability to pay for the shares.

The directors may only refuse to register the transfer of fully paid shares if the articles of the company expressly provide for this. Many companies adopt a very broad approach which gives the directors the power to refuse a transfer to anyone of whom they do not approve. In light of the new statutory requirement to give reasons for the refusal to register a transfer it is hard to envisage a scenario in which this kind of provisions can be justified.

The shares of public companies that are listed on a recognised exchange must be freely transferable and consequently it is not appropriate to include any restrictions on transfers of shares in the articles.

7.2.2 Pre-emption rights

As with an allotment of shares, the articles may contain pre-emption provisions which necessitate that any shares to be transferred are first offered to the other members of that class before they can be offered to a third party. Clauses concerning pre-emption rights on transfer will commonly include the following:

- the manner in which a transfer notice must be given, usually in writing specifying the number of shares to be transferred and the price sought;
- the period in which the offer must be accepted, after which an offer can be deemed to have been declined;
- what happens to shares that have been declined, often that any unsold shares are offered to accepting shareholders. With this in mind, it is helpful if the members are asked to specify the maximum number of additional shares they would be interested in buying when they accept the original offer. It is possible for the company to specify that it has the first right to buy any shares not taken up rather than them being offered to the accepting shareholders, and a provision of this kind can be a good idea if preserving the existing dilution of shares (i.e. the percentages held by each member) is a primary concern.

The final part of the process is usually that any shares that remain unsold after the various rounds of offers can be freely transferred.

Pre-emption provisions can be waived by the members by execution of a waiver or by the passing of a special resolution. If a transfer is processed without pre-emption provisions being properly observed, the members can object. If some procedural deficiency subsequently comes to light it would be good practice to have the transfer ratified. This point is not addressed in either

Table A or the Model Articles and companies may therefore wish to specify the procedures to be followed if the matter should arise.

7.2.3 Tag-along rights

Tag-along rights do not feature in Table A or the Model Articles and therefore need to be specifically included in a company's articles or shareholder agreements if they are considered necessary and appropriate. The inclusion of tag-along rights in a company's articles or in a shareholder agreement gives minority shareholders a measure of comfort about what will happen when the majority shareholder wishes to sell shares in circumstances which would lead to a change of control of the company.

In such circumstances tag-along rights ensure that the shares can only be sold if the proposed buyer offers to buy all the other shares in the company on the same (or better) terms as the original offer. The articles also need to include a clause which prevents completion of the sale in the event that the seller fails to comply with the provisions of the tag-along clause. The company will also be empowered to refuse to register the transfer in the buyer's name unless a compliant offer has been made to the minority shareholders.

7.2.4 Drag-along rights

Drag-along rights may also be included in a company's articles or in a shareholders' agreement and, as with tag-along rights, since they are not dealt with in Table A or the Model Articles inclusion of such rights in a shareholder agreement or the company's articles is the only way of ensuring they apply.

Drag-along rights compel a majority shareholder to bring all the other shareholders with them when they accept an offer to buy their shares which would result in a change of control of the company. This ensures that the prospective buyer can acquire the entire company. Inclusion of these rights is generally at the behest of the majority shareholder keen to ensure they do not miss out on an opportunity to sell their investment because the buyer refuses to proceed with a transaction that would see minority shareholders remaining in situ. When drafting such clauses consideration should be given as to whether there should be any exclusions to the general rule as there may be circumstances in which minority shareholders need not be compelled to sell their holdings.

7.2.5 CREST

CREST is an electronic system that allows shares to be transferred by making changes to computerised records of share ownership. These computer records provide shareholders with evidence of title in place of a share certificate. In order for a company to make use of CREST, its articles must include an enabling provision. As discussed below, the Model Articles for public companies include such a clause, but existing companies wishing to use CREST will need to amend their articles to allow for shares to be held in uncertificated form. A company that is seeking a listing for the first time will usually need to amend its articles to enable the transfer of shares via CREST.

The Model Articles for public companies provide for shares to be held in uncertificated form (article 50) and deal with the transfer of uncertificated shares. By article 64 a transfer of an uncertificated share must not be registered if it is in favour of more than four transferees. This requirement is driven by the capabilities of the CREST system.

7.2.6 Transmission of shares

Ownership of shares is sometimes 'transmitted' rather than 'transferred'. This occurs by operation of law, most commonly on the death of a registered shareholder or when a registered shareholder is made bankrupt.

When someone dies, any shares held in their name vest in their personal representative or executor. Evidence of the death must be provided to the company by the executor so that the personal representative can receive all notices and dividends relating to the shares. The evidence required is the same evidence as would suffice for grant of probate (s.774 CA 2006). The articles often provide that a personal representative cannot exercise the voting rights attached to the shares until the representative has been registered as the holder of the shares.

The position is similar with regard to bankruptcy, with the rights attached to the shares vesting in the trustee in bankruptcy until such time as the shares are registered in the name of the new member. It is usual for the articles to confer a right on the trustee to apply to be a member in respect of the bankrupt's shares.

Articles 27–29 of the Model Articles for private companies deal with transmission of shares. The corresponding provisions in the Model Articles for public companies are articles 65–68.

According to the defined terms contained in the first clause to the Model Articles, a 'transmittee' is 'a person entitled to a share by reason of the death or bankruptcy of a shareholder or otherwise by operation of law'. Under both Table A and the Model Articles a transmittee can choose to be registered as the holder of the shares or can nominate another person to become the registered holder.

The provisions concerning transmittees' rights are expressed to be subject to a company's articles. Therefore other clauses of the articles may take precedence, for example where there is a requirement that shares be transferred on the death of a member.

7.3 Dividends and other distributions

Subject to the provisions of the Companies Acts and to the provisions of a company's memorandum and articles, there is an implied power for companies to distribute their profits to the members in proportion to the number of shares they hold. The most usual way in which this is done is by way of a dividend.

7.3.1 Procedure for declaring dividends

Although there is a common law right for companies to make distributions, a company's articles will usually make specific provision for interim dividends to be declared and paid by decision of the directors, whereas final dividends require shareholder approval. This is the case with both the Model Articles (article 30(1)/article 70(1)) and Table A. Regulation 102 of Table A provides for dividends to be declared by ordinary resolution provided the dividend does not exceed the amount recommended by the directors. Although not specified in regulation 102, these dividends are usually known as final dividends. The members can reduce the amount of a final dividend to be paid, but cannot increase the sum recommended by the directors. Regulation 103 of Table A permits the directors to pay interim dividends without shareholder approval, provided the payment of a dividend is justified by the company's profits available for distribution.

Despite the different practices described above being followed generally, there is nothing to prevent a company from excluding the default provisions concerning the declaration of dividends. Indeed, some companies change their articles to permit the directors to declare and pay final dividends without the need for shareholder approval. However, the payment of dividends remains subject to it being permissible by reference to the company's financial position.

7.3.2 Payment of dividends and other distributions

The Model Article provisions concerning the payment of dividends and other distributions (article 31/article 72) extend the ways in which dividends can be paid when compared with regulation 106 of Table A which stipulates that payment be made by cheque. In line with usual bank and commercial practice, the Model Articles also permit payment by bank transfer or any other method agreed with the distribution recipient.

Regulation 106 of Table A also provides that dividends for joint share-holders are paid to the person whose name appears first in the register. Regulation 107 of Table A and the Model Articles both stipulate that interest is not payable on dividends. This has been a constant feature of successive versions of default articles but can be varied. If the default articles are excluded there will be little practical effect since the mere exclusion of the provision does not give rise to an implied right to receive interest. However, companies may choose to provide a positive right to interest in their articles, which approach might arguably be more consistent with the fact that an unpaid dividend amounts to a debt.

7.3.3 Unclaimed distributions

The Model Articles (article 33/article 75) and regulation 108 give share-holders 12 years in which to claim an unpaid dividend. This reflects the fact that unpaid dividends amount to a speciality debt enforceable within 12 years of declaration. Twelve years is also the minimum period that listed companies must allow in order to fulfil the UKLA's requirements in this respect.

The UKLA permits listed companies to make provision in their articles for unclaimed dividends to be forfeited after 12 years and for the directors to sell the shares of any shareholders it cannot trace. However, these powers are subject to two further conditions being fulfilled and these conditions must be made part of the procedures specified in the articles of listed companies. The first is that during the 12-year period at least three dividends on the shares in question must have been declared and no dividend claimed. Secondly, after the 12-year period has elapsed, the company has to place an advertisement in two national newspapers notifying that it plans to sell the shares and it must also advise the UKLA of this intention.

7.3.4 Non-cash distributions

If non-cash distributions are to be made, the articles must specifically confer the right to do so. The articles may permit the members to approve a distribution *in specie*, as in regulation 105 of Table A, article 34 of the Model Articles for private companies and article 76 of the Model Articles for public companies. This power is subject to the terms of issue of the relevant shares, if recommended by the directors, being approved by the shareholders by ordinary resolution. Non-cash distributions are also subject to section 845 of CA 2006 which details the rules for determining the amount where a distribution is made in kind.

7.3.5 Waiver of distributions

Shareholders may choose to waive a specified or future dividend payment by giving the company written notice to that effect (article 35/article 77). To be effective, such waiver must be received by the company before the declaration or payment of an interim dividend and before a final dividend has been approved by the members in general meeting. In addition, all holders or persons otherwise entitled to the share must sign the notice for it to be effective.

8

Decision-making by shareholders

The shareholders of both private and public companies can take decisions at general meetings. Private companies may also, with a couple of specific exceptions, take decisions by way of written resolutions.

While many of the rules that govern the way in which general meetings are convened and held are to be found in CA 2006, procedural requirements will also be contained in a company's articles. As in other areas, the provisions in the articles cannot overrule the statutory provisions where this would lessen shareholders' rights.

8.1 Organisation of general meetings

8.1.1 Notice of general meetings

Section 307 of CA 2006 specifies the minimum notice periods required for general meetings. A company is not permitted to provide for shorter notice periods than these in its articles, but can specify a longer notice period. If Table A applies to a company's articles and the articles have not been reviewed and amended in light of CA 2006, slightly different notice requirements may apply. It is therefore very important that the articles are checked to make sure that the correct period of notice is given. In the interests of not duplicating the requirements in the CA 2006, the Model Articles are silent concerning the notice period.

Companies are now permitted to use electronic and website communications to circulate the notice and other documents to shareholders where shareholders have consented to this method of communication. This topic is covered in detail at 4.4 and sample wording for a clause on electronic communications for inclusion in a company's articles of association can be found in Precedent 9.

Notice requirements under CA 2006 and regulation 38 of Table A.

Meeting type	CA 2006 s.307	Table A Reg. 38
Public company AGM	21 days	21 days
General meeting to consider special resolutions or the appointment of a director	14 days	21 days
Other general meetings	14 days	14 days

In addition, where a resolution requiring special notice is to be considered, 28 days' notice must be given.

For listed companies, as a matter of best practice, the provisions of the Combined Code should be followed where possible. The Combined Code recommends that the period of notice given for an AGM is 20 working days.

> TIP: When calculating the last day of posting you also need to consider whether the notice period is expressed as 'clear days' *and* how long after posting the notice is deemed to be received.

The notice periods stated in CA 2006 and in regulation 38 of Table A are expressed as 'clear days'. This means that two days need to be added to the figures given in the table above because the day of posting and the day of the meeting cannot be counted as part of the 14 or 21 days. Further, the date on which the notice is deemed to have been received will vary from company to company depending on what is stated in the articles. Under regulation 115 of Table A, notice is deemed to have been received 48 hours after being sent, whether by post or electronically. Care needs to be taken as the articles may contain different provisions depending on the method of sending, e.g. 48 hours for posting first class or 72 hours where sent second class.

8.1.1.1 Postal strikes

A common modification made to the default articles provides for notice of meetings to be given by way of an advertisement in one or more national newspapers in the event of a postal strike that prevents the notice being sent in the usual manner. This kind of modification is likely to be of less relevance in the future as companies embrace the use of electronic means as their method of choice for circulating notices and associated documents.

8.1.2 Entitlement to notice of general meetings

Generally every member entitled to attend and vote at a meeting is entitled to receive notice of that meeting. A common exception to this position is shareholders who live outside the UK. Regulation 112 of Table A, and many bespoke article clauses, provides that notice need not be served on members residing outside the UK. Given the speed of modern international communications, it no longer seems reasonable for this to be the case and we would recommend that any such existing provisions be excluded or amended so that shareholders living outside the UK have a right to receive notice, but not necessarily by post.

Regulation 116 of Table A gives the executors or administrators of a deceased shareholder or trustee a right to receive notice of a meeting, even though they may not be entitled to vote at the meeting. Regulation 38 of Table A also extends the right to notice to a company's directors and auditors.

The Model Articles do not contain any provisions concerning entitlement to notice.

8.1.3 Content of notice

Requirements about the content of the notice are set out in section 311 of CA 2006. In line with the general approach followed in the Model Articles of not duplicating procedural provisions where they are set out clearly in CA 2006, the Model Articles do not stipulate anything about the form or content of the notice.

According to section 311 of CA 2006 the notice is required to state the time, date and place of the meeting, together with a statement of the general nature of the business to be transacted at the meeting. This is very similar to the requirements of regulation 38 of Table A, which states that the notice shall specify the time and place of the meeting and the general nature of the business to be transacted, and in the case of an AGM, shall specify the meeting as such. The notice of a public company AGM must state that the meeting is to be an annual general meeting (s.337 CA 2006).

Section 311 of CA 2006 has effect subject to any provision of the company's articles, so companies are free to specify additional requirements as to the content of the notice. While what the general nature of the business to be transacted at the meeting is will be a question of fact, the notice must be sufficiently detailed to enable to shareholder to understand what each resolution is about so that they can form a view on the matter under consideration.

8.1.3.1 Statement of right to appoint proxies

Section 325 of CA 2006 provides that the notice should contain a statement of rights. This relates to the rights to appoint proxies under section 324. Each notice must therefore also contain, with reasonable prominence, a statement informing the member of their right under section 324 to appoint one or more proxies to attend, speak and vote on their behalf. Any more extensive rights to appoint multiple proxies conferred by the articles must also be stated.

The right to appoint multiple proxies is a new right and it is important to note that any article provisions seeking to limit this right will have no effect and should be ignored until such time as the articles can be amended to remove them.

8.1.4 Agreement to short notice

8.1.4.1 Private companies

A general meeting can be called on less notice than required by section 307 provided a majority in number of the members holding a sufficient percentage of the shares having the right to attend and vote at the meeting agree. For private companies section 307(5) and (6) of CA 2006 set the required level of agreement at 90 per cent. A higher percentage can be specified in the articles but the requirement cannot exceed 95 per cent.

The percentage required under CA 1985 was 95 per cent. The articles of many companies may still contain this higher requirement and this will need to be removed or amended before a private company can take advantage of the reduced level of consent. For more on amendments to take into account CA 2006 see Chapter 4.

8.1.4.2 Public companies

For a public company an AGM may only be held on shorter notice than required by section 307(2)(a) if all the members with a right to attend and vote at the meeting agree. For other public company general meetings the required level of consent is a majority in number of the members together holding no less than 95 per cent of the shares giving entitlement to attend and vote at the meeting. The provisions are mirrored by the requirements of regulation 38 of Table A.

8.1.4.3 Relationship with articles

As well as the overall percentage being attained, the agreement must be given by a 'majority in number' of the shareholders (see, for example, regulation 38 of Table A). This is important as it can operate to protect minority share-holders who might otherwise be overridden by a shareholder owing sufficient shares to meet the percentage requirement on their own. The articles cannot override this provision.

Neither Table A nor the Model Articles contain any provisions relating to consent to short notice beyond the inclusion of a catch-all clause in regulation 39 of Table A which states that the accidental omission to give notice shall not invalidate the proceedings of the meeting.

8.1.5 Quorum

8.1.5.1 Required number

Section 318 of CA 2006 sets the quorum for general meetings as one member present in person or by proxy where the company has a sole member or two members present in person or by proxy in all other cases. However, where a company has more than one member the statutory requirement is subject to the company's articles and the company can therefore choose to stipulate a higher requirement. Regulation 40 of Table A states the quorum as two persons present in person or by proxy who are entitled to vote upon the business to be transacted. The Model Articles merely state that no business other than the appointment of the chairman of the meeting is to be transacted where the quorum is not met.

A company may choose to adopt provisions which set the quorum at a higher number. For example, where two members hold a very significant proportion of the company's shares between them it may be desirable, from the perspective of protecting the minority shareholders, that these two parties cannot meet without others present to drive through decisions that would benefit them alone.

8.1.5.2 What happens when a meeting is inquorate?

It is common for the articles to specify what happens if a quorum is not present within a certain period after the scheduled start of the meeting, or if a quorum ceases to be present part way through the meeting because of members leaving. Regulation 41 of Table A makes provision for the automatic adjournment of a meeting that is not quorate within 30 minutes of the scheduled start time, or which subsequently becomes inquorate. In such cases, the meeting is adjourned to the same day, time and place the following week or to such time and place as the directors may determine. Under regulation 41 of Table A the adjourned meeting must be quorate, but this provision is frequently amended so that the shareholders who are present at an adjourned meeting constitute a quorum even though they may be fewer than the number required to constitute a quorum in usual circumstances.

8.1.6 Chairing general meetings

The role of the chairman at a shareholders' meeting is to ensure the meeting is properly and fairly conducted. Procedures for determining who will chair a company's general meeting are normally specified in the articles.

8.1.6.1 Who chairs the meeting?

Section 319(1) gives the members present at a general meeting the right to pass a resolution to elect one of their number as chair of the meeting. This right is subject by section 319(2) to any provisions of the company's articles that state who may and may not be chairman.

Under both regulation 42 of Table A and the provisions of the Model Articles (article39/article 31) the starting position is that the chairman of the board of directors will act as chairman of general meetings.

According to regulations 42 and 43 of Table A, if neither the chairman nor their usual deputy is at the meeting within 15 minutes of the time appointed for holding the meeting, the directors present may nominate one of their number to act as chair. If no director present wishes to act as chair, or if no directors are present, the members present are entitled to choose one of their number to be chairman. Under the Model Articles the usual chairman has even less leeway in terms of getting to the meeting on time. They prescribe that if the directors have not appointed a chairman, or if the chairman is not present within 10 minutes of the time at which the meeting was due to start, the directors present or, if no directors are present, the meeting must appoint a director or member to chair the meeting and the appointment of the chairman must be the first business of the meeting. Any person so appointed must be referred to as 'the chairman of the meeting'.

There is no requirement that the person chairing the meeting be a shareholder.

8.1.6.2 Chairman's powers

Table A gives certain powers to the chairman in regard to the conduct of the meeting, particularly with regard to voting and the conduct of polls. For more on voting see 8.3.

8.1.7 Attendance and speaking at general meetings

As mentioned in **6.2.2**, different classes of share will have different rights attached to them and these rights will be detailed in the company's articles. For example, the holders of ordinary shares will generally be entitled to attend and speak at general meetings, whereas the holders of certain types of preferred share may be entitled to receive notice of the meeting but not to attend and speak.

The Model Articles provide (article 40/article 32) that directors do not need to be members to attend and speak at general meetings. The Model Articles also give the chairman the discretion to allow others who are not members or otherwise entitled to exercise the rights of members to attend and speak at a general meeting. When exercising this discretion the chairman will have regard to their duty to make sure that the meeting is properly and fairly conducted. This will mean allowing a range of opinions to be expressed about the matter under consideration, but the chairman will also need to ensure the meeting does not get out of control.

8.1.8 Adjournment

8.1.8.1 The right to adjourn

The chairman may adjourn a general meeting with the consent of the members and must adjourn a meeting if directed to do so by the members. This position is reflected in both regulation 45 of Table A and in the Model Articles (article 41/article 33).

In addition, the chairman has a common law power to adjourn a meeting which becomes disorderly. The chairman must take care to use this power properly and should not be too hasty about adjourning a meeting for disorder as a premature adjournment without time being allowed for order to be resumed may be invalid. This common law power has been incorporated into the Model Articles and somewhat extended. Under the Model Articles the chairman has the power to adjourn a quorate meeting when it appears to him that an adjournment is necessary to protect the safety of any person attending the meeting or to ensure that the business of the meeting is conducted in an orderly manner.

8.1.8.2 Procedural aspects of adjournment

Under the Model Articles the chairman must either specify the time and place to which the meeting is adjourned or state that it is to continue at a time and placed to be fixed by the directors. Where a meeting is adjourned for more than 14 days the company must give at least seven clear days' notice of the new date. The same requirements as to entitlement to notice and content of notice apply as with the original meeting.

No business may be transacted at an adjourned general meeting which could not have been transacted at the original meeting if the adjournment had not taken place. By section 332 of CA 2006 it is made clear that a resolution passed at an adjourned meeting is to be treated as having been passed on the date on which it was actually passed, rather than on the date of the original meeting that was adjourned.

8.2 AGMs

8.2.1 The business of the AGM

The business to be conducted at an AGM derives for the most part from provisions of CA 2006 or from corporate governance requirements that apply to listed companies. However, it is not uncommon for specific requirements to be included in a company's tailored articles although absent from Table A and the Model Articles.

The following items can be considered to be routine business at an AGM and the requirement for them to be addressed at the AGM might be specified in the articles:

- laying the annual accounts and reports before the members pursuant to section 437 of CA 2006;
- declaring a final dividend;
- election of directors;
- reappointing auditors and giving authority to the directors to determine their remuneration.

Other business which is commonly transacted at an AGM includes:

- renewal of the directors' authority pursuant to section 80 of CA 1985 to allot shares;
- giving authority to the directors to allot shares as if the statutory pre-emption rights did not apply;
- where considered necessary, amending the articles of association.

Of these different types of business, it is really only the election of directors and declaration of a final dividend that are of particular relevance in terms of drafting and interpreting the articles of association.

8.2.1.1 Election of directors

Retirement of directors by rotation is considered in some detail in Chapter 5. For the purposes of the business of the meeting, both the election of directors who have been appointed mid-year and the re-election of directors who are retiring pursuant to a requirement of the company's articles will be dealt with as part of the routine business of an AGM.

It has long been the case that it is best practice to vote on resolutions for the election or re-election of directors individually rather than grouping several appointments together in one resolution. For public companies it is now mandatory unless the meeting has previously agreed unanimously that motions for more than one appointment can be dealt with as a single resolution.

8.2.1.2 Declaration of a dividend

Subject to the financial position of the company dividends may be declared:

- by ordinary resolution, the amount of dividend not to exceed the amount recommended by the directors. This is the position under both the Model Articles (article 30/ article 70) and regulation 102 of Table A; or
- by the directors (Model Articles and regulation 103 of Table A). This applies to interim dividends only.

Companies may make different arrangements in their articles in terms of who can declare and pay dividends, for example to permit directors to pay final dividends without approval from the members or to provide for the automatic payment of dividends without a decision from either the directors or the members. Whatever provisions are made, the right to declare and pay dividends will always be subject to the requirements of Part 23 of CA 2006 and dividends can only therefore be paid when the profits of the company available for distribution justify this. For more on this topic refer to Chapter 7.

8.3 Voting at general meetings

8.3.1 Voting

8.3.1.1 Voting on a show of hands

The Model Articles for both private and public companies provide (article 42/ article 34) that a resolution put to the vote of a general meeting must be decided on a show of hands unless a poll is duly demanded in accordance with the articles. The position is the same under regulation 46 of Table A.

8.3.1.2 Chairman's casting vote

Companies need to be careful to make sure that they follow the correct procedures in the event of an equality of votes as the position has changed under CA 2006. Section 282 of CA 2006 provides that an ordinary resolution is passed when a simple majority of members votes in favour of the resolution. To bring the default article provisions into line with this, the Model Articles do not give the chairman the right to a casting vote in general meeting. However, many existing companies have a provision in their articles which gives the chairman a casting vote in the case of an equality of votes. Where such a provision was contained in the articles prior to 1 October 2008 the provision can be relied on and used. Companies incorporated after 30 September 2008, or amending or adopting articles, cannot make provision for the chairman to have a casting vote.

8.3.1.3 Declaration of result

The chairman's declaration that a resolution has or has not been passed or that it has been passed with a particular majority is conclusive proof of the fact, without the need for the number or proportion of votes cast to be recorded. An entry in respect of such declaration in the minutes of the meeting is also conclusive evidence.

8.3.2 Proxies

Under CA 2006 proxies have enhanced rights in relation to voting at general meetings and nothing in a company's articles can deprive them of these additional rights.

Under section 324 of CA 2006 a shareholder may appoint one or more proxies to attend, speak and vote on their behalf, on both a show of hands and on a poll (s.284). The person appointed as a proxy need not themselves be a member of the company.

Every notice must contain a statement informing the member of their rights with regard to the appointment of proxies under section 324. Although only listed companies are obliged to send proxy forms to members along with the notice of the meeting, most companies would do so.

8.3.2.1 Content of proxies

According to the Model Articles for private and public companies (article 45/ article 38) proxies may only be validly appointed in writing. The Model Articles specify that the proxy notice must:

- state the name and address of the shareholder appointing the proxy;
- give the identity of the person appointed as proxy and the general meeting in relation to which they are appointed;
- be signed by or on behalf of the shareholder appointing the proxy; and
- be delivered to the company in accordance with the articles and any instructions contained in the notice of the meeting to which they relate.

This is very similar to the requirements set out in regulation 60 of Table A which also requires the appointment to be made in writing and to be executed by or on behalf of the appointor. However, Table A also provides a suggested format by the inclusion of a model form of proxy for use by private companies and unlisted public companies.

A company's articles may simply provide that the appointment of a proxy can take any form which is usual or approved by the directors. The precise requirements will vary from company to company and although, for example, a properly executed letter from a shareholder might suffice, in practice the form of proxy is likely to be drafted by the company and provided to share-holders along with the notice of the meeting, even where this goes beyond what is strictly required. It is increasingly common for companies to accept proxies in electronic form. The ICSA has included a proforma proxy form which complies with the requirements of CA 2006 in its 'Guidance on Proxies & Corporate Representatives at General Meetings' (Reference No. 080122). Two alternative forms of proxy based on this but adapted for intended use by private and unlisted public companies are included as Precedents 14 and 15.

As well as containing boxes for shareholders to vote for or against a partic-ular resolution, the form of proxy should also have a 'vote withheld' option. This allows members to register reservations about the resolution concerned without having to vote against it. This approach is endorsed by the NAPF in its corporate governance policy and voting guidelines. A vote withheld, or an abstention, is not a vote in law and will not generally be counted when calcu-lating the proportion of votes for and against a resolution.

8.3.2.2 Delivery of proxy forms

The Model Articles for private and public companies (article 46/article 39) set out the provisions that apply in respect of the delivery of proxy forms. The Model Articles for public companies are more detailed and reflect the use of registrars to co-ordinate the receipt and evaluation of proxy forms.

The address specified for the return of proxies will usually be the com-pany's registered office or the address of a third party such as the company's registrars or its company secretarial advisers who are co-ordinating the AGM mailing. The company or its registrar will check proxy forms to make sure that they have been completed properly. If there is time, proxy forms that have not been completed correctly can be returned to the member for amendment and re-submission. A running total of the voting should be kept. Where this is done by the registrars, online access to proxy voting figure reports is often provided to the company to enable it to monitor how much support for each resolution there is.

Article 46(1) of the Model Articles for private company echoes the position at common law that the member remains entitled to attend, speak and vote at a general meeting even when a proxy has been validly appointed and the member's vote will take precedence over that of their proxy. Article 46(2) states that a proxy notice may be revoked by notice in writing by or on behalf of the person by whom or on whose behalf the proxy form was submitted. In practice any such revocation will usually be made by lodging another proxy form, for example if the member has changed their mind about how they wish their votes to be cast. This is acceptable provided the new proxy form is lodged before the deadline specified for the receipt of proxies (article 46(3)).

The company's articles should be checked to ascertain how the deadline for the return of proxy forms is to be calculated. While it is still not possible for a company to require the return of proxies more than 48 hours before the appointed start time of the meeting, the way in which 48 hours is calculated has changed as non-working days, such as weekends and bank holidays, can now be excluded when determining the deadline (s.327(3) CA 2006). However, the possibility of excluding non-working days cannot be relied on by companies who already had article provisions under the old legislation which requires weekends and bank holidays to be counted. Companies wishing to take advantage of the new provisions will need to amend their articles.

The Model Articles also provide that if a proxy form is not executed by the member themselves, it must be accompanied by written evidence of the authority of the person who did execute it to do so on behalf of the member.

8.3.3 Corporate representatives

8.3.3.1 Difference between corporate representatives and proxies

Corporate shareholders can be represented at general meetings by appointing a person to act as their representative (s.323 CA 2006). The extension to proxies' rights that has been brought into effect by CA 2006 has blurred the distinction between proxies and corporate representatives so that now the most fundamental difference between them is that proxies must be submitted by the specified deadline (not more than 48 hours before the meeting) whereas a letter of appointment of a corporate representative does not need to be submitted to the company in advance of the meeting. This distinction is not even especially significant since the directors retain the discretion to accept proxy forms after the receipt deadline has passed.

8.3.3.2 Article provisions

The rules on corporate representatives contained in s.323 of CA 2006 cannot be overridden by a company's articles. In contrast to the position with proxies, CA 2006 does not allow companies to give corporate representatives greater rights in their articles than are provided by statute.

8.3.4 Problems with section 323(4) of CA 2006

Although not strictly relevant to drafting and interpreting a company's articles of association, it is worth mentioning that the interpretation of section 323(4) of CA 2006 has caused some difficulties. The problem centres on what happens when multiple corporate representatives are appointed by a member and those representatives do not all vote in the same way.

Section 323(4) reads as follows:

(4)   Where the corporation authorises more than one person, and more than one of them purport to exercise a power under sub-section (3) –

   (a)   if they purport to exercise the power in the same way, the power is treated as exercised in that way,
   (b)   if they do not purport to exercise the power in the same way, the power is treated as not exercised.

Some commentators do not think this section raises any difficulties and consider that multiple corporate representatives can vote in different ways without any risk of the votes being deemed to be invalid. However, a fairly significant body of legal opinion takes a divergent view and cannot see any way for different votes of multiple corporate representatives to be validly exercised. Concerned about the uncertainty over the interpretation of section 323(4), the ICSA has included detailed commentary on the point in its Guidance (Reference No. 080122) and recommends that wherever possible proxies are appointed in preference to corporate representatives. Where exceptional circumstances mean that the only option is to appoint multiple corporate representatives, the so-called designated corporate representative (DCR) method should be employed. This method involves one corporate representative acting as the DCR on a poll. All the other corporate representatives give instructions to the DCR and only the DCR completes a poll card. For more details on this see the ICSA's Guidance note.

8.3.5 Polls

The procedures for demanding and conducting a poll will largely be set out in a company's articles, although sections 321 and 329 of CA 2006 must also be taken into account.

8.3.5.1 Demanding a poll

Section 321(1) prevents a company from having an article provision which would exclude the right to demand a poll at a general meeting on any question other than the election of the chairman of the meeting or the adjournment of the meeting.

The Model Articles (article 44/article 36) provide that a poll can be demanded by:

- the chairman; or
- the directors; or
- two or more members who have the right to vote on the resolution; or
- a person or persons representing not less than one-tenth of the total voting rights of all the shareholders entitled to vote on the resolution.

The corresponding provisions in Table A are contained in regulation 46. The only differences between the two clauses are that regulation 46 does not give directors the right to demand a poll but gives the right to demand a poll to 'a member or members holding shares conferring a right to vote at the meeting being shares on which an aggregate sum has been paid up equal to not less than one-tenth of the total sum paid up on all the shares conferring that right'. In practical terms the omission of the latter does not make any difference because a corresponding provision can be found in section 321(2)(c) of CA 2006 which will apply irrespective of the articles.

On the other hand, the Model Article provision permitting two or more members with the right to vote on the resolution to demand a poll makes it easier for members to demand a poll than under section 321(2)(a) of CA 2006, which stipulates five members. This issue was considered during the consultation period for the Model Articles as some respondents expressed concern that the proposed number was too low. BERR concluded that any number chosen would be arbitrary and as only article provisions requiring more than five members to demand a poll would be void, the number of two has remained.

8.3.5.2 Procedure on a poll

The Model Articles for private companies state that a poll must be taken immediately (unless withdrawn in accordance with article 44(3)) and in such manner as directed by the chairman. The Model Articles for public companies provide (article 37(1)), subject to the articles, that the chairman has complete discretion as to when, where and how a poll at a general meeting is taken. The public company Model Articles also contain further provisions on poll procedure, requiring a poll on the election of the chairman of the meeting or on a question of adjournment to be taken immediately. All other polls are to be taken within 30 days of being demanded. The provisions also permit the appointment of poll scrutineers. This corresponds with the provisions of regulations 49 and 51 of Table A.

8.3.6 Amendments to resolutions

Articles 47 and 40 of the Model Articles for private and public companies respectively set out the circumstances in which resolutions may be amended. The provisions are identical and there are no corresponding provisions in Table A.

8.3.6.1 Ordinary resolutions

Ordinary resolutions can be proposed by anyone who is entitled to vote on the resolution in question provided that written details of the proposed amendment are received by the company at least 48 hours before the appointed time of the meeting (or later if the chairman permits) and the amendment does not materially alter the scope of the resolution.

8.3.6.2 Special resolutions

Special resolutions can only be amended where an amendment is proposed by the chairman at the actual meeting and the amendment must be restricted to correcting a grammatical or other non-substantive error in the resolution.

8.4 Written resolutions

Private companies may use the written resolution procedure specified in CA 2006 to do most things, save for removing a director under section 168 of CA 2006 and removing an auditor. To avoid confusion it is recommended that companies remove any alternative written resolution procedures from their articles.

Public companies may not make decisions by written resolution even where there is express provision to the contrary in the articles.

Key features of the statutory procedure are as follows:

- Written resolutions can be proposed by the directors or the members (s.288).
- A copy of the resolutions must be sent to all the members who are entitled to attend and vote at a general meeting. This can be done electronically if members have agreed to this (s.289).
- Members signify their consent by returning the document in hard copy or electronically (s.296).
- In a change to the position under Table A, which required unanimity, written resolutions are passed when approved by the requisite majority for the particular type of resolution, i.e. a simple majority for ordinary resolutions and a three-fourths majority for special resolutions.
- If the resolutions are not passed within 28 days of being circulated they are deemed to have lapsed and consent given after the lapse date is ineffective. An alternative lapse date can be provided in the articles.

Various examples of written resolutions in a format suitable for use under CA 2006 can be found in the precedents section of this book.

Considerations when forming or re-registering a company

The memorandum and articles of association are basic constitutional documents that need to be registered when forming a company. They are therefore key documents right from the start of a company's life. Forming a company gives it a distinct legal persona separate from its members. This chapter provides an overview of forming a company insofar as it has implications for the form and content of a company's memorandum and articles of association.

The decision to form a company and determination of which type of company is most suitable will involve the detailed consideration of many factors. To name but a few, such factors are likely to include tax and accounting implications, whether privacy of financial information is desired, whether profit is to be generated, potential exposure to liability and the desire for this to be limited, whether working capital is needed on incorporation and requirements for further fundraising in the future etc. Evaluation of these factors will help determine which type of company is most suitable and, as shown below, the type of company will have an important bearing on the content of a company's memorandum and articles of association.

9.1 Types of company

The most common types of company and the effect they have on the memorandum and articles are set out below:

- **Private company limited by shares** – this type of company has a share capital and each member's liability is limited to the amount paid and owed but unpaid on their shares.

- **Private company limited by guarantee** – members of this type of company do not hold shares; rather, they agree to contribute a certain amount of money to the company's assets if the company is wound up. Consequently the constitutional documents of a company of this type will not contain clauses relating to shares and will use the term 'member' rather than 'shareholder' throughout. The Model Articles for companies limited by guarantee are very similar to the Model Articles for private companies limited by shares, but all references to shares and shareholders have been omitted or modified as appropriate.
- **Private unlimited company** – members' liability is unlimited and the company may or may not have a share capital. The memorandum for this type of company does not therefore have a limited liability clause and the clause containing the company's name will not contain the word 'limited'.
- **Public limited company** – this type of company has a share capital and each member's liability is limited to the amount paid and owed but unpaid on their shares. Unlike a private limited company, a company of this type may offer its shares to the general public and may be quoted on a stock exchange. As mentioned in Chapter 3, companies of this type will often adopt entirely bespoke articles which take account of the various additional regulatory requirements to which public companies are subject. At the most basic level, one difference (which is also referred to in Chapter 2) is that the memorandum of a public company must contain a clause stating that the company is a public limited company. Examples of other effects on the constitutional documents include the need to satisfy minimum authorised capital requirements, the fact that shares in a listed public company must be freely transferable, which means that no restrictions on transfer, such a pre-emption rights, can be included in the articles, and the ability of public companies to offer their shares to the public. All these matters will affect the content of the company's memorandum and articles.

9.2 Choosing a name

A necessary first step when forming a company is to decide what it is going to be called and, once the name has been decided, it must be added to the memorandum and articles and all forms submitted to Companies House to facilitate incorporation. It is important to note that every company must have a unique name and there are a number of restrictions which govern the choice of name. Key requirements include:

1. The name may not be 'the same as' one already registered

In deciding whether a proposed name is 'the same as' one already registered, the Registrar ignores the following:

- punctuation;
- the word at the end of the company's name which shows what sort of company it is, e.g. 'limited' or 'plc';
- 'the' at the start of the name and words like 'company'.

> **TIP:** To help make sure your chosen name is suitable a search should be carried out on the Index of Company Names at: www.companieshouse. gov.uk before an application to form a company is made to see if any similar company names are already registered. It does not cost anything to search the Index. Alternatively, Companies House staff can give advice on whether a proposed name is registerable (telephone: 0303 123 4500). If using a formation agent to carry out the incorporation they should advise on the suitability of the proposed name as a matter of course.

Anyone forming a company should also be aware of the possibility of facing an action for 'passing-off'. Passing-off occurs where a name is so similar to that of an existing business that it is likely to mislead people into thinking that the new business is the existing one, possibly leading to a loss of revenue for the existing business.

> **TIP:** Before forming a company it is a good idea to check the Trade Marks Register to check that the proposed company name is not the same as or similar to a registered trade mark.

New provisions of CA 2006 were introduced from 1 October 2008 which allow a person to object to a company name for 'opportunistic registration' if the company's name is:

- the same as the name associated with the complainant in which he has goodwill; or
- so similar that its use in the UK would be likely to mislead by suggesting a connection between the company and the complainant.

Objections concerning opportunistic registration are dealt with by the Company Names Tribunal (also known as the Adjudicator) which is attached to the UK Intellectual Property Office.

2. The correct company name ending must be used

The proposed name must end with the word 'limited', 'public limited company' or the Welsh equivalents 'Cyfyngedig' and 'Cwmni Cyfyngedig Cyhoeddus', or the abbreviated versions of either. These words may not be used anywhere other than at the end of the name and the Welsh versions may only be used for a company that is to have its registered office in Wales.

3. The name must not be offensive

A company may not be formed with a name which, in the opinion of the Secretary of State, is offensive.

4. The name must not constitute a criminal offence

The proposed name may not be one which, in the opinion of the Secretary of State, constitutes a criminal offence. An example of this is that it is a criminal offence for a company to use a name which suggests that it carries on the business of banking, unless the Bank of England has recognised it as a bank under the Banking Act 1979.

> TIP: Companies House will register company names that include the words 'bank', 'banking' or 'deposit'. If the company is engaged in banking activities it will require authorisation from the Financial Services Authority (FSA). The FSA's website www.fsa.gov.uk should be consulted for more information on this point.

5. Sensitive words and expressions

Some names which need to be approved by the Secretary of State before they can be registered. These include names containing words prescribed by the Companies and Business Names Regulations 1981 (SI 1981/1685), as amended, and words which suggest a connection with Her Majesty's Government or local government. Full details of all such 'sensitive words and expressions' can be found in Appendix 9.

All of these issues concerning the choice of company name and the need to satisfy any special requirements will need to be resolved prior to submitting formation documents, including the memorandum and articles, to Companies House.

9.3 How to form a company

A company is formed by sending the following documents to Companies House together with the applicable registration fee:

- a memorandum of association;

- articles of association (except where the applicable default regulations are adopted without modification);
- Form 10 giving details about the officers and the situation of the registered office; and
- Form 12, which is a statutory declaration of compliance with all the legal requirements of forming a company.

Commentary about the status and content of the memorandum and articles can be found in Chapters 2 and 3 respectively.

The required documents can be submitted on paper or electronically. The monthly workload figures published by Companies House indicate that the overwhelming majority of formations are now carried out electronically. For example, 91.7 per cent of incorporations were filed electronically during April 2009.

In order to be able to submit formations electronically you need to have access to a software package which is compatible with the system used by Companies House. The process followed is very similar, but Form 12 does not need to be sworn before a solicitor. The documents submitted are verified by way of an electronic PIN and three pieces of security information relating to a director and based on information provided from the following seven options act as a signature:

- place of birth;
- telephone number;
- national Insurance number;
- passport number;
- mother's maiden name;
- eye colour;
- father's first forename.

Sections 9 and 10 of CA 2006 set out the rules concerning the statement of capital that must be submitted when forming a company on or after 1 October 2009. The statement of capital must contain the following information:

- the total number of shares of the company to be taken by the subscribers on formation;
- the aggregate nominal value of those shares;
- for each class of shares –

  □ particulars of the rights attached to the shares,
  □ the total number of shares of that class,
  □ the aggregate nominal value of shares of that class;

- the amount to be paid up and the amount (if any) to be unpaid on each share.

Private companies no longer need to appoint a company secretary, but can do so if they wish and must do so if the company's articles of association require it. Public companies still have to have a qualified company secretary, as detailed in sections 271 and 273 of CA 2006. Since detailed requirements about the manner of appointment are not included in either CA 2006 or the Model Articles for public companies, companies may choose to include an appointment procedure in their articles on incorporation where this is considered desirable.

9.4 Registered office

Every company must have a registered office (s.287 CA 1985) [s.86 CA 2006 from 1 October 2009]. The registered office is a company's official address, which can be used for serving formal documents. It is the address Companies House uses when sending notices, letters and reminders. It is also the place where a number of records must be kept for statutory purposes such as the register of members and the register of charges unless they are held at an alternative 'place of inspection' which has been duly notified to Companies House on the prescribed form.

The chosen address must be somewhere in the company's country of incorporation, i.e. in England and Wales for companies registered in that jurisdiction or in Scotland for Scottish-registered companies.

As mentioned above, details of a company's first registered office are provided on Form 10 when forming the company. After formation any change of registered office address must be notified to Companies House using the prescribed form within 14 days. The change takes effect when the public record is updated.

9.5 Director restrictions

All private companies must have at least one director. A public company must have at least two directors (and a suitably qualified secretary). The articles of association may require more directors to be appointed, in which case this requirement must be specifically stated. Whatever the number of directors appointed, at least one of them must be a natural person, i.e. an individual rather than a legal person, such as another company.

No director may be appointed if they have been disqualified from acting as a company director and they must not be an undischarged bankrupt. Directors may act in these instances where they have been given permission by the court to act for a particular company. A director must not be under the age of 16.

For more details on additional provisions concerning directors that are often included in a company's articles, refer to Chapter 5.

9.6 Getting the memorandum and articles right from the start

Whether you are forming a company yourself or using a solicitor or formation agent to carry out the process for you it is important that, from the outset, you think about what sort of provisions you need in the company's articles (and whether to enter into a shareholder agreement).

If you order a company through a solicitor or formation agent, you will almost certainly have to complete an order form providing limited information about the type of company you want formed and the basic details as to preferred company name, officers to be appointed and share capital. You will rarely be asked many questions about the content of the articles, for example whether you require any special provisions relating to how further directors can be appointed, or whether shares to be transferred must be offered to existing members before being offered to others ('pre-emption rights'). In most instances, unless you specify otherwise, the formation agent will simply use its standard form of memorandum and articlesit would usually put in place for that type of company.

It is important that you think about whether the memorandum and articles need to be changed to make them more suitable for your company's own particular circumstances and set up. More information on changing the memorandum and articles can be found in Chapters 2, 3 and 4.

However, it is worth mentioning here that a company's articles may be changed either by amendment of individual clauses that are no longer appropriate, for example if a company becomes a sole member company and wishes to tidy up its articles by removing pre-emption provisions on transfer, or by the wholesale adoption of a new set of articles. Which route is preferred is based largely on practical considerations. From a drafting perspective it can be easier to adopt a whole new set of articles save in those instances where the changes being made are minimal, since to do otherwise can result in very unwieldy resolutions as the full text of the new clauses needs to be set out. On the other hand, it can be costly for companies to adopt an entirely new set of articles if they have to provide a copy of the new articles to each member along with notice of the meeting or the proposed written resolutions.

With regard to the memorandum, the only change that can actively be made is a change to the objects clause, although consequential changes to the clauses detailing the company's name and authorised capital may also arise (see Chapter 2). From 1 October 2009, the introduction of the remaining provisions of CA 2006 means that any existing restrictions on a company's objects contained in its memorandum will become part of the company's articles and, if a company wishes to remove any such restrictions on what it is permitted to do, the articles will need to be amended accordingly.

9.7 Re-registration

When re-registering a company, whether from private to public, public to private, or from limited to unlimited or vice versa, the company's constitutional documents will need to be reviewed and amended to ensure they are appropriate for the re-registered entity.

9.7.1 Private to public

At the time of writing, section 43(2) of CA 1985 requires that the special resolution approving re-registration of a company from private to public must also alter the company's memorandum so that it states that the company is to be a public company and to make such other changes to the memorandum and articles as are necessary and appropriate to its new status, such as changing the company's name so that it ends with 'plc' rather than 'limited' (or, where applicable, the Welsh equivalents), amending the share capital clause where the authorised capital has been increased, and including any new clauses appropriate to public companies, such as provisions for the rotation of directors at the AGM or adding clauses permitting shares to be held in uncertificated form and removing any restrictions on transfer if the company is planning to seek a listing.

The same considerations will apply from 1 October 2009 once the procedure is governed by CA 2006, save that the only change that needs to be made to the memorandum is the change of company name to include 'plc' at the end. Section 90(3) provides that a company seeking re-registration as a public company limited by shares must make such changes to its name and articles as are necessary in connection with it becoming a public company. If the company was previously unlimited, changes to the articles must also be made to take account of its new limited status.

9.7.2 Public to private

Under section 53(2) of CA 1985, a public company seeking re-registration as a private company must alter the company's memorandum so that it no longer states that it is a public company and must make such other changes to the memorandum and articles 'as are requisite in the circumstances'. Such changes might include reflecting the new status in the company's name, removing article provisions that no longer apply, such as a requirement to hold AGMs and ancillary clauses which assume that AGMs will be held, or reference to any minimum capital requirements

As with re-registration as a public company, a company wishing to re-register as private under CA 2006 must make suitable changes to its name and articles to reflect its new status (s.97(3)).

9.7.3 Limited to unlimited

Section 49 of CA 1985 governs the procedure for re-registering a private company as unlimited. Section 49(5) stipulates that the application for re-registration must set out such alterations to the company's memorandum as are needed, depending on whether or not it is to have a share capital. The articles must also be altered to take into account whether or not there is a share capital (s.49(6)).

The position is the same under CA 2006, as detailed in section 102(3).

9.7.4 Unlimited to limited

When re-registering an unlimited company as a limited company, the prime consideration when thinking about the effect on the memorandum and articles is whether the re-registered company will have a share capital or whether it will be limited by guarantee. As set out at 9.1 above, the constitutional documents of a company limited by guarantee have no references to shares and will use the term 'member' instead of shareholder. In such a case it is likely to be necessary to adopt a new set of articles specific to a company limited by guarantee rather than merely making changes to the company's existing articles.

Under CA 1985 the requirement to make suitable changes to the memorandum and articles is set out in section 51(3). Under CA 2006 the equivalent rules can be found in section 105(4).

Irrespective of the type of re-registration being carried out, a reprint of the amended or new memorandum and articles must be filed at Companies House as part of the application for re-registration.

Precedent materials

This section contains suggested wording for minutes, resolutions, notices and other documents that may be required from time to time in connection with the adoption or amendment of a company's memorandum and articles of association. While they cannot attempt to cover every possible scenario, it is hoped they will provide a useful starting point.

Several complete document sets have been provided as well as some stock phrases. Much of the wording is fairly standard, but amendments will still need to be made, especially for precedents dealing with amendments to the memorandum or articles as it is usual practice for the full text of the amended clauses to be included in the resolution.

Detailed commentary on the requirements for written resolutions is given in Chapter 8, but it is worth mentioning here that a copy will be needed for the filing with the Registrar. This can be achieved either by having two copies of any members' written resolutions signed so that there is one 'copy' for the company's minute book and one for filing with the Registrar, or by preparing a separate 'conformed' copy of the resolution for signature by a director or the company secretary.

Precedents

Change of company name by board meeting and general meeting

[●] LIMITED
("the Company")
Company Number: [●]

Minutes of a Meeting of the Board of Directors of the Company
held at [●]
on [●] 200[●] at [●] am/pm

Present:

Attending:

Chairman
It was noted that [●] was chairman of the meeting.

Notice and Quorum
The chairman reported that notice of the meeting had been given to all of the directors and noted that the quorum necessary for a meeting of the board of directors was present.

Change of Name
The chairman reported the proposal to change the name of the Company to [●]. It was noted that the change of name would require the approval of the shareholders by special resolution.

General Meeting
The meeting considered the matter and **IT WAS RESOLVED THAT** a general meeting of the Company be convened and held on [[●] 200[●]/on short notice immediately following this meeting] to consider and if deemed fit approve a special resolution changing the name of the Company **AND THAT** the company secretary be and is hereby authorised to sign and issue to the members a notice convening the said meeting.

Close of Meeting
There being no further business the chairman declared the meeting closed.

_____

CHAIRMAN

[●] LIMITED
("the Company")
Company Number: [●]

Agreement to Short Notice

We, the undersigned, being a majority in number of the members together holding not less than 90%[1] of the issued share capital of [●] Limited having a right to attend and vote at the meeting referred to below, hereby agree to an extraordinary general meeting of the Company being held on [●] 200[●] notwithstanding that shorter notice has been given of the said meeting than the period of notice prescribed by Section 307(1) of the Companies Act 2006.

Dated this [●] day of [●] 200[●].

_____
[name]
Sole Member

_____   _____
[name of shareholder]   [name of shareholder]

---

[1] Articles must be checked for short notice requirements; if silent it is necessary to check whether Article 38 of Table A is applicable.

[●] LIMITED
("the Company")
Company Number: [●]

Notice of General Meeting

NOTICE IS HEREBY GIVEN THAT a General Meeting of the Company will be held at [●] on [●] 200[●] at [●]am/pm to transact, consider and, if deemed fit, to approve the following resolution being proposed as a special resolution:

Special Resolution
IT WAS RESOLVED THAT the name of the Company be changed to:

[●]

Date: [●] 200[●] BY ORDER OF THE BOARD

Registered Office:

COMPANY SECRETARY

Notes:

1. A member entitled to attend and vote at the meeting is entitled to appoint more than one proxy, to exercise all or any of his rights to attend, speak and vote in his place on a show of hands or on a poll provided that each proxy is appointed to a different share or shares, or to a different £10.00 or multiple of £10.00 of stock. Such proxy need not be a member of the Company.

2. To be valid, the completed and signed form of proxy must be returned to [●] not less than 48 hours (excluding weekends, Christmas Day, Good Friday or recognised public and bank holidays) before the time fixed for the meeting. Lodging a form of proxy does not preclude a member from attending and voting at the meeting.[1]

Explanatory notes on the resolution

Resolution 1

The directors are proposing to change the company name to more accurately reflect the Company's brand. The change of name requires approval of a special resolution of the shareholders.

---

[1] Articles must be checked; if Table A 1985 is applicable 48 hours includes weekends, bank holidays etc.

95

[●] LIMITED
("the Company")
Company Number: [●]

Minutes of a General Meeting of the Company
held at [●]
on [●] 200[●] at [●]am/pm

Present:

Attending:

Chairman
It was noted that [●] was chairman of the meeting.

Notice and Quorum
The chairman reported that all of the Company's members had consented to the meeting being held on short notice and that the quorum necessary for a general meeting of the Company was present. The notice convening the meeting was taken as read.

Change of Name
IT WAS RESOLVED THAT the name of the Company be changed to [●] Limited and that the company secretary be and is hereby authorised and instructed to file a copy of the special resolution with the Registrar of Companies.

Close of Meeting
There being no further business the chairman declared the meeting closed.

_____

CHAIRMAN

Company Number: [●]

THE COMPANIES ACT 1985 TO 2006

SPECIAL RESOLUTION

OF

[●] LIMITED

COMPANY LIMITED BY SHARES

At a general meeting of the above-named Company, duly convened and held at [●] on the [●] day of 200[●], the following **SPECIAL RESOLUTION** was duly passed:

IT WAS RESOLVED THAT the name of the Company be changed to:

[●]

DIRECTOR/ SECRETARY

2

Change of company name by written resolution

[●] LIMITED
("the Company")
Company Number: [●]

Resolution in writing of the [sole] director[s] of the Company in accordance with [Article [●] of the Articles of Association of the Company] or [Regulation 93 of Table A of the Companies Act 1985 that forms part of the Articles of Association of the Company]

[●] 200[●]

IT WAS RESOLVED THAT the [sole] member[s] be requested to approve a special resolution to change the name of the Company to

[●]

[name]
Sole Director

[name of director]

[name of director]

Company Number:

The Companies Acts 1985 and 2006

PRIVATE COMPANY LIMITED BY SHARES

WRITTEN RESOLUTION

[•] LIMITED
("the Company")

We, the undersigned, being members of the Company eligible to attend and vote at general meetings of the Company, hereby pass the following resolution designated as a special resolution and agree that the said resolution shall be as valid and effective as if it had been passed at a general meeting the Company duly convened and held.

IT WAS RESOLVED THAT the name of the Company be changed to:
[•]

Signed:

....   Date:...................200[•].
[Name]

....   Date:...................200[•].
[Name]

Notes:
1.   This written resolution has been proposed by the directors of the Company. The purpose of the resolution is to change the name of the Company.

2.   The circulation date of this written resolution is _____ 200[•].

3.   Please signify your agreement to the resolution by signing against your name where indicated, enter the date on which you signed the document. Please then return the document to the Company.

4.   If you sign the document and return it to the Company without indicating whether you agree to the resolution, it will be assumed by the Company that you agree to the resolution being passed.

5.   If you return the document signed, but un-dated, it will be assumed by the Company that you signed the document on the day immediately preceding the day on which it was received by the Company.

6.   If not passed by the requisite majority of the total voting rights of eligible members, this written resolution shall lapse on the _____ 200[•].

7.   As the resolution is a special resolution, the requisite majority needed to pass the resolution is three-fourths of the total voting rights of eligible members.

8.   Once this resolution has been signed and returned to the Company, your agreement to it may not be revoked.

Company Number:

The Companies Acts 1985 and 2006

PRIVATE COMPANY LIMITED BY SHARES

WRITTEN RESOLUTION

[●] LIMITED
("the Company")

On the [●] day of 200[●], the following resolution designated as a special resolution, was duly passed by the [sole] shareholder[s]:

IT WAS RESOLVED THAT the name of the Company be changed to:

[●]

DIRECTOR/COMPANY SECRETARY

3

Resolution to amend objects clause

THAT the Company's memorandum of association be amended by the adoption of a new clause [•] in substitution for and to the exclusion of the existing clause [•].

4 Adopt new articles by written resolution

[●] LIMITED
("the Company")
Company Number: [●]

Resolutions in writing of the [sole] director[s] of the Company in accordance with [Article [●] of the Articles of Association of the Company] or [Regulation [●] of [*enter details of applicable version of Table A]* that forms part of the Articles of Association of the Company]

_____

[Date]

_____

IT IS RESOLVED THAT the [sole] member[s] be requested to approve a special resolution to adopt the regulations contained in the draft articles of association attached hereto as the Company's articles of association in substitution for, and to the exclusion of, all existing articles of association.

_____
[name]
Sole Director

_____   _____
[name of director]   [name of director]

Company Number: [●]

The Companies Acts 1985 and 2006

PRIVATE COMPANY LIMITED BY SHARES

WRITTEN RESOLUTION

[●] LIMITED
("the Company")

We, the undersigned, being members of the Company eligible to attend and vote at general meetings of the Company, hereby pass the following resolution designated as a special resolution and agree that the said resolution shall be as valid and effective as if it had been passed at a general meeting the Company duly convened and held.

IT IS RESOLVED THAT the regulations contained in the draft articles of association attached hereto be approved and adopted as the Company's articles of association in substitution for, and to the exclusion of, all existing articles of association.

Signed:

.... Date:...................
[Name]

.... Date:...................
[Name]

Notes:

1. This written resolution has been proposed by the directors of the Company. The purpose of this resolution is to adopt new articles of association to replace the existing articles of association in their entirety.

2. The circulation date of this written resolution is [●].

3. Please signify your agreement to the resolution by signing against your name where indicated and enter the date on which you signed the document. Please then return the document to the Company.

4. If you do not date your signature we will assume you signed the document on the day immediately preceding the day on which the document was received by the Company.

5. If not passed by the requisite majority of the total voting rights of eligible members, these written resolutions shall lapse on [●].

6. As the resolution is a special resolution, the majority needed to pass the resolution is three-fourths of the total voting rights of eligible members.

7. Once the resolution has been signed and returned to the Company, your agreement to it may not be revoked.

Adopt new articles by board meeting and general meeting

[●] LIMITED
("the Company")
Company Number: [●]

Minutes of a Meeting of the Board of Directors of the Company
held at [●]
on [*date*] at [*time*]

Present:

In attendance:

Chairman
It was noted that [●] was chairman of the meeting.

Notice and Quorum
The chairman reported that notice of the meeting had been given to all of the directors and noted that the quorum necessary for a meeting of the board of directors was present.

Adoption of Articles of Association
The chairman reported that the Company wished to adopt new articles of association in the form of the draft tabled to the meeting, for which shareholder approval was required. The draft set of articles was approved by the directors for submission to the shareholders.

General Meeting
IT WAS RESOLVED THAT a general meeting of the Company be convened and held on [●] to consider and, if deemed fit, approve a special resolution to adopt new articles of association in the form attached to these minutes. It was further resolved that [**the company secretary or a director**] be authorised to sign and issue to the shareholders a notice convening the said meeting.

Close of Meeting
There being no further business the chairman declared the meeting closed.

CHAIRMAN

[●] LIMITED
("the Company")
Company Number: [●]

Notice of general meeting

NOTICE IS HEREBY GIVEN THAT a general meeting of the Company will be held at [●] on [●] at [●] to consider and, if deemed fit, approve the following resolution being proposed as a special resolution:

Special Resolution
THAT the regulations contained in the draft articles of association produced to this meeting be approved and adopted as the Company's articles of association in substitution for, and to the exclusion of, all existing articles of association.

Date: By order of the Board

Registered office:

—————————————
Company Secretary

Notes:

1. A member entitled to attend and vote at the meeting is entitled to appoint more than one proxy, to exercise all or any of their rights to attend, speak and vote in their place on a show of hands or on a poll provided that each proxy is appointed to a different share or shares, or to a different £10.00 or multiple of £10.00 of stock. Such proxy need not be a member of the Company.

2. To be valid, the completed and signed form of proxy must be returned to the Company's registered office not less than 48 hours (excluding weekends, Christmas Day, Good Friday or recognised public and bank holidays) before the time fixed for the meeting[1]. Lodging a form of proxy does not preclude a member from attending and voting at the meeting.

—————————————
[1] Articles must be checked to establish whether 1985 version of Table A applies, in which case 48 hours includes weekends, bank holidays etc.

[●] LIMITED
("the Company")
Company Number: [●]

Minutes of a general meeting of the Company
held at [●]
on [*date*] at [*time*]

Present:

In attendance:

Chairman
It was noted that [●] was chairman of the meeting.

Notice and Quorum
The chairman reported that notice of the meeting had been given to all persons entitled to receive the same and noted that the quorum necessary for a general meeting was present.

Adoption of Articles of Association
IT WAS RESOLVED THAT the regulations contained in the draft articles of association produced to this meeting be approved and adopted as the Company's articles of association in substitution for, and to the exclusion of, all existing articles of association.

Filing
[The company secretary or someone else] was instructed to file a copy of the special resolution at Companies House together with a copy of the new articles of association.

Close of Meeting
There being no further business the chairman declared the meeting closed.

_____

Chairman

Company Number: [●]

THE COMPANIES ACTS 1985

SPECIAL RESOLUTION

OF

[●] LIMITED

COMPANY LIMITED BY SHARES

At a general meeting of the above-named Company, duly convened and held at [●] on the [●] day of [*year*], the following **SPECIAL RESOLUTION** was duly passed:

IT WAS RESOLVED THAT the regulations contained in the draft articles of association produced to this meeting be approved and adopted as the Company's articles of association in substitution for, and to the exclusion of, all existing articles of association.

Director/ Secretary

6 Amend articles by written resolution

[●] LIMITED
("the Company")
Company Number: [●]

Resolutions in writing of the [sole] director[s] of the Company in accordance with [Article [●] of the Articles of Association of the Company] or [Regulation [●] of [*enter details of applicable version of Table A*] that forms part of the Articles of Association of the Company]

[*date*]

IT WAS RESOLVED THAT the [sole] member[s] be requested to approve a special resolution to alter the Company's articles of association in the following way:

a. by the deletion of articles [●] and the renumbering of articles [●] as articles [●].
b. by the insertion of the following new articles to be numbered [●].

[*set out numbering and full text of new articles here in inverted commas*]

[name]
Sole Director

[name of director]

[name of director]

Company Number: [●]

The Companies Acts 1985 and 2006

PRIVATE COMPANY LIMITED BY SHARES

WRITTEN RESOLUTION

LIMITED
("the Company")

We, the undersigned, being members of the Company eligible to attend and vote at general meetings of the Company, hereby pass the following resolution designated as a special resolution and agree that the said resolution shall be as valid and effective as if it had been passed at a general meeting the Company duly convened and held.

IT IS RESOLVED THAT the Company's articles of association be altered in the following way:

a. by the deletion of articles [●] and the renumbering of articles [●] as articles [●].
b. by the insertion of the following new articles to be numbered [●].

[*set out numbering and full text of new articles here in inverted commas*]

Signed:

…………………………………………… Date:………………..
[Name]

…………………………………………… Date:………………..
[Name]

Notes:

1. This written resolution has been proposed by the directors of the Company. The purpose of the resolution is to amend the articles to [*enter details of why the amendments are being proposed*].
2. The circulation date of the written resolution is [●].
3. Please signify your agreement to the resolution by signing against your name where indicated and entering the date on which you signed the document. Please then return the document to the Company.
4. If you do not date your signature we will assume you signed the document on the day immediately preceding the day on which the document was received by the Company.
5. If not passed by the requisite majority of the total voting rights of eligible members, these written resolutions shall lapse on [●].
6. As the resolution is a special resolution, the majority needed to pass the resolution is three-fourths of the total voting rights of eligible members.
7. Once the resolution has been signed and returned to the Company, your agreement to it may not be revoked.

7 Amend articles by board meeting and general meeting

[●] LIMITED
("the Company")
Company Number: [●]

Minutes of a Meeting of the Board of Directors of the Company
held at [●]
on [●] 200[●] at [●] am/pm

Present:

In attendance:

Chairman
It was noted that [●] was chairman of the meeting.

Notice and Quorum
The chairman reported that notice of the meeting had been given to all of the directors and noted that the quorum necessary for a meeting of the board of directors was present.

Alteration of Articles of Association:
The chairman reported the proposal to alter the Company's articles of association in the following way:

a.   by the deletion of articles [●] and the renumbering of articles [●] as articles [●].
b.   by the insertion of the following new articles to be numbered [●]:
[*set out numbering and full text of new articles here in inverted commas*]

General Meeting
The meeting considered the matter and **IT WAS RESOLVED THAT** a general meeting of the Company be convened and held on [●] to consider and, if deemed fit, approve a special resolution altering the Company's articles of association. It was further resolved that [**the company secretary or a director**] be authorised to sign and issue to the shareholders a notice convening the said meeting.

Close of Meeting
There being no further business the chairman declared the meeting closed.

_____
Chairman

[●] LIMITED
("the Company")
Company Number: [●]

Notice of general meeting

NOTICE IS HEREBY GIVEN THAT a general meeting of the Company will be held at [location] on [date] at [time] to consider and, if deemed fit, approve the following resolution being proposed as a special resolution:

Special Resolution

a.   by the deletion of articles [●] and the renumbering of articles [●] as articles [●].

b.   by the insertion of the following new articles to be numbered [●].

[set out numbering and full text of new articles here in inverted commas]

Date: **By order of the Board**

Registered office:

_____

Notes:

1.   A member entitled to attend and vote at the meeting is entitled to appoint more than one proxy, to exercise all or any of their rights to attend, speak and vote in their place on a show of hands or on a poll provided that each proxy is appointed to a different share or shares, or to a different £10.00 or multiple of £10.00 of stock. Such proxy need not be a member of the Company.

2.   To be valid, the completed and signed form of proxy must be returned to the Company's registered office not less than 48 hours[1] (excluding weekends, Christmas Day, Good Friday or recognised public and bank holidays) before the time fixed for the meeting. Lodging a form of proxy does not preclude a member from attending and voting at the meeting.

[1] Articles must be checked to establish whether the 1985 version of Table A applies, in which case 48 hours includes weekends, bank holidays etc.

[●] LIMITED
("the Company")
Company Number: [●]

Minutes of a General Meeting of the Company
held at [●]
on [●] 200[●] at [●] am/pm

Present:

Attending:

Chairman
It was noted that [●] was chairman of the meeting.

Notice and Quorum
The notice convening the meeting was taken as read.

Alteration of Articles of Association
IT WAS RESOLVED THAT the Company's articles of association be altered in the following way:

a. by the deletion of articles [●] and the renumbering of articles [●] as articles [●].
b. by the insertion of the following new articles to be numbered [●].

[set out numbering and full text of new articles here in inverted commas]

Filing
[The company secretary or someone else] was instructed to file a copy of the resolution at Companies House together with a revised copy of the articles of association as amended.

Close of Meeting
There being no further business the chairman declared the meeting closed.

_____

Chairman

Company Number: [●]

THE COMPANIES ACTS 1985 TO 2006

SPECIAL RESOLUTION

OF

[●] LIMITED

COMPANY LIMITED BY SHARES

At a general meeting of the above-named Company, duly convened and held at [*location*] on the [●] day of [*month*] [*year*], the following **SPECIAL RESOLUTION** was duly passed:

IT WAS RESOLVED THAT the Company's articles of association be altered in the following way:

a.   by the deletion of articles [●] and the renumbering of articles [●] as articles [●].

b.   by the insertion of the following new articles to be numbered [●].

[*set out numbering and full text of new articles here in inverted commas*]

_____

Director/ Secretary

Wording for conflicts of interest clause in articles

8

1.1 For the purposes of Section 175 of the 2006 Act, the Directors may authorise any matter proposed to them in accordance with these Articles which would, if not so authorised, constitute or give rise to an infringement of duty by a Director under that Section.

1.2 Authorisation of a matter under Article 1.1 shall be effective only if:
   (i) the matter in question shall have been proposed by any person for consideration at a meeting of the Directors, in accordance with the Directors' procedures, if any, for the time being relating to matters for consideration by the Directors or in such other manner as the Directors may approve;
   (ii) any requirement as to the quorum at the meeting of the Directors at which the matter is considered is met without counting the Director in question and any other interested Director (together the 'Interested Directors'); and
   (iii) the matter was agreed to without the Interested Directors voting or would have been agreed to if the votes of the Interested Directors had not been counted.

1.3 Any authorisation of a matter pursuant to Article 1.1 shall extend to any actual or potential conflict of interest which may reasonably be expected to arise out of the matter so authorised.

1.4 Any authorisation of a matter under Article 1.1 shall be subject to such conditions or limitations as the Directors may specify, whether at the time such authorisation is given or subsequently, and may be terminated or varied by the Directors at any time. A Director shall comply with any obligations imposed on him by the Directors pursuant to any such authorisation.

1.5 A Director shall not, by reason of his office or the fiduciary relationship thereby established, be accountable to the Company for any remuneration or other benefit which derives from any matter authorised by the Directors under Article 1.1 and any contract, transaction or arrangement relating thereto shall not be liable to be avoided on the grounds of any such remuneration or other benefit or on the ground of the Director having any interest as referred to in the said Section 175.

1.6 A Director shall be under no duty to the Company with respect to any information which he obtains or has obtained otherwise than as a director or officer or employee of the Company and in respect of which he owes a duty of confidentiality to another person. However, to the extent that his connection with that other person conflicts, or possibly may conflict, with the interests of the Company, this Article 1.6 applies only if the existence of that connection has been authorised by the Directors under Article 1.1. In particular, the Director shall not be in breach of the general duties he owes to the Company by virtue of Sections 171 to 177 of the 2006 Act because he fails –
    (i) to disclose any such information to the Directors or to any Director or other officer or employee of the Company; and/or
    (ii) to use any such information in performing his duties as a Director or officer or employee of the Company.

1.7 Where the existence of a Director's connection with another person has been authorised by the Directors under Article 1.1 and his connection with that person conflicts, or possibly may conflict, with the interests of the Company, the Director shall not be in breach of the general duties he owes to the Company by virtue of Sections 171 to 177 of the 2006 Act because he –
    (i) absents himself from meetings of the Directors or any committee thereof at which any matter relating to the conflict of interest or possible conflict of interest will or may be discussed or from the discussion of any such matter at a meeting or otherwise; and/or
    (ii) makes arrangements not to receive documents and information relating to any matter which gives rise to the conflict of interest or possible conflict of interest sent or supplied by the Company and/or for such documents and information to be received and read by a professional adviser, for so long as he reasonably believes such conflict of interest (or possible conflict of interest) subsists.

1.8 The provisions of Articles 1.6 and 1.7 are without prejudice to any equitable principle or rule of law which may excuse the Director from:
    (i) disclosing information, in circumstances where disclosure would otherwise be required under these Articles or otherwise; or
    (ii) attending meetings or discussions or receiving documents and information as referred to in Article 1.7, in circumstances where such attendance or receiving such documents and information would otherwise be required under these Articles.

1.9 For the purposes of this Article, a conflict of interest includes a conflict of Interest and duty and a conflict of duties.

Wording for electronic communication clause in articles

9

Electronic Communication

1.1 Notwithstanding anything in these articles to the contrary:

    1.1.1 Any document or information to be given, sent, supplied, delivered or provided to any person by the company, whether pursuant to these articles, the Companies Acts or otherwise, is also to be treated as given, sent, supplied, delivered or provided where it is made available on a website, or is sent in electronic form, in the manner provided by CA 2006 for the purposes of, inter alia, CA 2006 (subject to the provisions of these Articles).

    1.1.2 For the purposes of paragraph 10(2)(b) of Schedule 5 to the 2006 Act, the Company may give, send, supply, deliver or provide documents or information to members by making them available on a website.

    1.1.3 For the purposes of paragraph 6.1.8R(1) of the Disclosure and Transparency Rules, the Company may use electronic means (as defined therein) to convey information or documents to members.

    1.1.4 The directors may from time to time make such arrangements or regulations (if any) as they may from time to time in their absolute discretion think fit in relation to the giving of notices or other documents or information by electronic means by or to the company and otherwise for the purpose of implementing and/or supplementing the provisions of these articles and the Companies Acts in relation to electronic means; and such arrangements and regulations (as the case may be) shall have the same effect as if set out in this article.

10 Indemnity and insurance provisions

1. Indemnity

1.1 Subject to the Companies Acts but without prejudice to any indemnity to which a director may otherwise be entitled, every director or other officer of the Company shall be indemnified out of the assets of the Company against all losses or liabilities which he may sustain or incur in or about the lawful execution of the duties of his office or otherwise in relation thereto, including any liability incurred by him in defending any proceedings, whether civil or criminal, in which judgment is given in his favour or in which he is acquitted or in connection with any application in which relief is granted to him by the court, and no director or other officer shall be liable for any loss, damage or misfortune which may happen to or be incurred by the Company in the lawful execution of the duties of his office or in relation thereto.

1.2 The directors shall have power to purchase and maintain for any director, officer or auditor of the Company insurance against any such liability as is referred in section 232 of CA 2006 and, subject to the provisions of CA 2006, against any other liability which may attach to him or loss or expenditure which he may incur in relation to anything done or alleged to have been done or omitted to be done as a director, officer or auditor.

1.3 The directors may authorise the directors of companies within the same group of companies as the Company to purchase and maintain insurance at the expense of the Company for the benefit of any director, other officer or auditor of such Company in respect of such liability, loss or expenditure as is referred to in article 1.1.

Resolution for general authority to allot shares

11

That the directors of the Company be authorised generally and unconditionally pursuant to and in accordance with section 80 of the Companies Act 1985 ('the 1985 Act') to exercise all the powers of the Company to allot relevant securities (within the meaning of section 80(2) of the 1985 Act) up to an aggregate nominal amount of £[●] [(representing [●] per cent. of the Company's issued ordinary share capital on [●] 200[●], being [*specify applicable reference date*] provided that this authority shall expire on whichever is earlier of the date of the conclusion of the Company's next Annual General Meeting or 15 months from the date on which this resolution is passed save that the Company may, pursuant to this authority, make offers or agreements before the expiry of this authority which would or might require relevant securities to be allotted after such expiry and the directors may allot relevant securities in pursuance of such offers or agreements as if the authority conferred by this resolution had not expired.

PRECEDENT 12

Resolution to disapply statutory pre-emption rights on allotment

That, subject to the passing of resolution [•], the directors are hereby empowered pursuant to section 95(1) of the Companies Act 1985 (the '1985 Act') to allot equity securities (within the meaning of section 94(2) of the 1985 Act) for cash pursuant to the authority conferred by resolution [•] as if section 89(1) of the 1985 Act did not apply to such allotment, provided that this power shall be limited to the allotment of equity securities:

(i)   in connection with an offer of equity securities by way of rights to the holders of ordinary shares [and/or any other persons entitled to participate therein] [(other than the Company itself in respect of any shares held by it as treasury shares within the meaning of section 162A of the 1985 Act)] in proportion (as nearly as may be) to their respective holdings of ordinary shares [(or, as appropriate, the number of ordinary shares which such other persons are, for the purposes of such offer, deemed to hold)] on a record date fixed by the directors but subject to such exclusions or other arrangements as the directors may consider necessary or expedient to deal with [any legal or practical] problems under the laws of any territory or the requirements of any regulatory body or any stock exchange in any territory or in connection with fractional entitlements or otherwise howsoever; or

(ii) [pursuant to the terms of any share scheme for directors and employees of the Company and/or its subsidiaries approved by the shareholders of the Company in general meeting; or]

(iii) (other than pursuant to paragraph[s] (i) [or (ii)] above) having (in the case of relevant shares (as defined in section 94(5) of the 1985 Act)) a nominal amount or (in the case of any other equity securities) giving the right to subscribe for or convert into relevant shares having a nominal amount, not exceeding in aggregate £[•] [(the 'Relevant Amount')] [(representing [•] per cent. of the Company's issued ordinary share capital on [•] 200[•], being [specify applicable reference date];

Stock transfer form

STOCK TRANSFER FORM			
		(Above this line for Registrars only)	
	Consideration Money £[•]		Certificate lodged with the registrar
			(For completion by the Registrar/Stock Exchange)
	Full name of undertaking	**[•] LIMITED** **(Company No. [•])**	
	Full description of security	**Ordinary Shares of [£1.00] Each**	
	Number or amount of Shares, Stock or other security and, in figures column only, number and denomination of units, if any.	Words [•]	Figures [•] of £[•]
	Name(s) of registered holder(s) should be given in full; the address should be given where there is only one holder. If the transfer is not made by the registered holder(s) insert also name(s) and capacity (e.g. Executor(s)) of the person(s) making the transfer.	In the name(s) of	Account Designation (if any)

PLEASE SIGN HERE	I/We hereby transfer the above security out of the name(s) aforesaid to the person(s) named below (or to the several persons named in parts two of Brokers Transfer Forms relating to the above security): (Delete above words in brackets except for stock exchange transactions)	Stamp of selling broker(s) or for transactions which are not stock exchange transactions, of agent(s), if any, acting for the transferor(s).
	Signature(s) of transferor(s)	
	1.	
	2.	
	3.	
	4.	
	Bodies corporate should execute under their common seal	Date [•] 200[•]

Full name(s) and full postal address(es) (including County, if applicable, Postal District number) of the person(s) to whom the security is transferred. Please state title, if any, or whether Mr., Mrs., or Miss. Please complete in typewriting or in block capitals	

I/We request that such entries be made in the register as are necessary to give effect to this transfer.

Stamp of buying Broker(s) (if any)	Stamp or name and address of person lodging this form (if other than Buying Broker(s))

FORM OF CERTIFICATE WHERE THE CONSIDERATION IS £1,000 OR LESS

*Please
delete as
appropriate

I/We* certify that the transaction effected by this instrument does not form part of a larger transaction or series of transactions in respect of which the amount or value, or aggregate amount or value, of the consideration exceeds £1,000.

** Delete
second
sentence if
certificate is
given by
transferor

I/We* confirm that I/we* have been duly authorised by the transferor to sign this certificate and that the facts of the transaction are within my/our* knowledge.**

Signature(s)

Description ("Transferor", "Solicitor", etc

_____   _____

_____   _____

_____   _____

_____   _____

Date _____

Where the consideration for a particular transfer is £1,000 or less but the transfer forms part of a larger transaction or series of transactions in respect of which the amount or value, or aggregate value, of the consideration exceeds £1,000, the instrument will be chargeable with stamp duty and will need to be submitted to HMRC for stamping, together with the duty. Certification is not appropriate in these cases.

NOTES

(1) If the above certificate has been completed, this transfer does not need to be submitted to the Stamp Office but should be sent directly to the Company or its Registrars.

(2) If the above certificate is not completed, this transfer must be submitted to the Stamp Office and duly stamped.

Sample form of proxy for private and unlisted public companies

14

Adapted from proforma proxy form contained in ICSA guidance

Note: This sample form of proxy is intended for use by private and unlisted public companies and no account is taken of the CREST system. The form reflects the enhanced rights of proxies under CA 2006 and allows for the appointment of multiple proxies. For larger companies, both private and public, the format of the form of proxy is likely to be set by the Company's registrars.

Company Name Limited

Shareholder Name
Address line 1
Address line 2
Address line 3
Address line 4

Attendance Card
Please bring this card with you to the Meeting and present it on registration

The chairman of [Company Name] invites you to attend the Annual General Meeting of the Company to be held at [Address
]

On [date] at [time] a.m./ p.m.

Form of Proxy – Annual General Meeting to be held on [date]

Explanatory notes:

1. Every holder has the right to appoint some other person(s) of their choice, who need not be a shareholder, as their proxy to exercise all or any of their rights to attend, speak and vote on their behalf at the meeting. If you wish to appoint a person other than the chairman, please insert the name of your chosen proxy holder in the space provided (see reverse). If the proxy is being appointed in relation to less than your full voting entitlement, please enter in the box next to the proxy holder's name (see reverse) the number of shares in relation to which they are authorised to act as your proxy. If left blank your proxy will be deemed to be authorised in respect of your full voting entitlement.

2. To appoint more than one proxy you mat obtain additional proxy form(s) by contacting [ ] or you may photocopy this form. Please indicate in the box next to the proxy holder's name (see reverse) the number of shares in relation to which they are authorised to act as your proxy. Please also indicate by ticking the box provided if the proxy instruction is one of multiple instructions being given. All forms must be signed and should be returned together in the same envelope.

3. The 'Vote Withheld' option overleaf is provided to enable you to abstain on a resolution. Please note that a 'Vote Withheld' is not a vote in law and will not be counted in the proportion of the votes 'For' and 'Against' a resolution.

4. If the appointor is a corporation, this form must be under its common seal or under the hand of some officer or attorney duly authorised in that behalf.

5. In the case of joint holders, the signature of any one holder will be sufficient, but the names of all the joint holders should be stated.

6. If this form is returned without indication as to how the person appointed proxy shall vote, he will exercise his discretion as to how he votes or whether he abstains from voting.

7. To be valid, this form must be completed and deposited at [address] not less than 48 hours (excluding any day that is not a working day) before the time fixed for holding the meeting or adjourned meeting.

Form of Proxy

Please use a **black** pen. Mark with an **X** inside the box as shown in the example

I/ We hereby appoint the Chairman of the meeting OR the following person

Please leave this box blank if you have selected the chairman. Do not insert your own name.

as my/our proxy to exercise all or any of my/our rights to attend, speak and vote in respect of my/ our voting entitlement* on my/our behalf at the annual general meeting of [company name] to be held at [address] on [date] at [time] a.m/p.m. and at any adjourned meeting.

Please tick here if this proxy appointment is one of multiple appointments being made*

* For the appointment of more than one proxy please refer to note 2 (see front).

Ordinary resolutions	For	Against	Vote Withheld
1. To receive the report and accounts	☐	☐	☐
2. To declare a final dividend of [•] p per ordinary share	☐	☐	☐
3. To re-elect [•] as a director	☐	☐	☐
4. To re-elect [•] as a director	☐	☐	☐
5. To reappoint [•] as auditors and determine their remuneration	☐	☐	☐
6. To grant the directors authority to allot [•] shares up to [•]	☐	☐	☐
7. To authorise political donations exceeding £5,000	☐	☐	☐
Special resolutions			
8. To disapply pre-emption rights up to [•]	☐	☐	☐

Intention to attend

Please indicate if you wish to attend the AGM ☐

I/ We would like my/ our proxy to vote on the resolution proposed at the meeting as indicated on this form. Unless otherwise indicated the proxy may vote as he or she sees fit or abstain in relation to any business of the meeting.

Signature   **Date**

15

Alternative sample form of proxy

[Company Name]   **Company No. [ ]**

FORM OF PROXY

Please use a **black** pen. Mark with an **X** inside the box as shown in the example. | X |

I/ We hereby appoint the Chairman of the meeting OR the following person

| |

Please leave this box blank if you have selected the chairman. Do not insert your own name.

as my/ our proxy to exercise all or any of my/our rights to attend, speak and vote in respect of my/ our voting entitlement* on my/our behalf at the annual general meeting of [Company Name] to be held at [Address] on [Date] at [Time] a.m./p.m. and at any adjourned meeting.

Please tick here if this proxy appointment is one of multiple appointments being made*
* For the appointment of more than one proxy please refer to note 2 below.

Ordinary resolutions	For	Against	Vote Withheld
1. To receive the report and accounts	☐	☐	☐
2. To declare a final dividend of [ ]p per ordinary share	☐	☐	☐
3. To re-elect [ ] as a director	☐	☐	☐
4. To re-elect [ ] as a director	☐	☐	☐
5. To re-elect [ ] as a director	☐	☐	☐
6. To reappoint] as auditors and determine their remuneration	☐	☐	☐
7. To reappoint [ ] as auditors and determine their remuneration	☐	☐	☐
8. To reappoint [ ] as auditors and determine their remuneration	☐	☐	☐

Special Resolutions:

	For	Against	Vote Withheld
9. To reappoint [ ] as auditors and determine their remuneration	☐	☐	☐

I/ We would like my/ our proxy to vote on the resolution proposed at the meeting as indicated on this form. Unless otherwise indicated the proxy may vote as he or she sees fit or abstain in relation to any business of the meeting.

Signature   **Date**

Explanatory Notes:

1. You may appoint a proxy or proxies to exercise all or any of your rights to attend, speak and vote on your behalf at the meeting. If you wish to appoint a person other than the chairman, please insert the name of your chosen proxy holder in the space provided.
2. To appoint more than one proxy you may photocopy this form. Please indicate in the box next to the proxy holder's name the number of shares in relation to which they are authorised to act as your proxy. Please also indicate by ticking the box provided if the proxy instruction is one of multiple instructions being given. All forms must be signed and should be returned together in the same envelope.
3. The 'Vote Withheld' option is provided to enable you to abstain on a resolution. Please note that a 'Vote Withheld' is not a vote in law and will not be counted in the votes 'For' and 'Against' a resolution.
4. If the appointor is a corporation, this form must be under its common seal or under the hand of some officer or attorney duly authorised in that behalf.
5. In the case of joint holders, the signature of any one holder will be sufficient, but the names of all the joint holders should be stated.
6. If this form is returned without indication as to how the person appointed proxy shall vote, he will exercise his discretion as to how he votes or whether he abstains from voting.
7. To be valid, this form must be completed and deposited at the Company's registered office not less than 48 hours (excluding any day that is not a working day) before the time fixed for holding the meeting.

Appendices

1   1985 Table A

Commencement 22nd December 2000

COMPANIES (TABLES A TO F) REGULATIONS 1985 AS AMENDED BY SI 2000/3373

TABLE A
Regulations for management of a company limited by shares

Interpretation

1 In these regulations –

"the Act" means the Companies Act 1985 including any statutory modification or re-enactment thereof for the time being in force.
"the articles" means the articles of the company.
"clear days" in relation to the period of a notice means that period excluding the day when the notice is given or deemed to be given and the day for which it is given or on which it is to take effect.
"executed" includes any mode of execution.
"office" means the registered office of the company.
"the holder" in relation to shares means the member whose name is entered in the register of members as the holder of the shares.
"the seal" means the common seal of the company.
"secretary" means the secretary of the company or any other person appointed to perform the duties of the secretary of the company, including a joint, assistant or deputy secretary.
"the United Kingdom" means Great Britain and Northern Ireland.
"communication" means the same as in the Electronic Communications Act 2000.
"electronic communication" means the same as in the Electronic Communications Act 2000.

Unless the context otherwise requires, words or expressions contained in these regulations bear the same meaning as in the Act but excluding any statutory modification thereof not in force when these regulations become binding on the company.

Share capital

2 Subject to the provisions of the Act and without prejudice to any rights attached to any existing shares, any share may be issued with such rights or restrictions as the company may by ordinary resolution determine.

3 Subject to the provisions of the Act, shares may be issued which are to be redeemed or are to be liable to be redeemed at the option of the company or the holder on such terms and in such manner as may be provided by the articles.

4 The company may exercise the powers of paying commissions conferred by the Act. Subject to the provisions of the Act, any such commission may be satisfied by the payment of cash or by the allotment of fully or partly paid shares or partly in one way and partly in the other.

5 Except as required by law, no person shall be recognised by the company as holding any share upon any trust and (except as otherwise provided by the articles or by law) the company shall not be bound by or recognise any interest in any share except an absolute right to the entirety thereof in the holder.

Share certificates

6 Every member, upon becoming the holder of any shares, shall be entitled without payment to one certificate for all the shares of each class held by him (and, upon transferring a part of his holding of shares of any class, to a certificate for the balance of such holding) or several certificates each for one or more of his shares upon payment for every certificate after the first of such reasonable sum as the directors may determine. Every certificate shall be sealed with the seal and shall specify the number, class and distinguishing numbers (if any) of the shares to which it relates and the amount or respective amounts paid up thereon. The company shall not be bound to issue more than one certificate for shares held jointly by several persons and delivery of a certificate to one joint holder shall be a sufficient delivery to all of them.

7 If a share certificate is defaced, worn-out, lost or destroyed, it may be renewed on such terms (if any) as to evidence and indemnity and payment of the expenses reasonably incurred by the company in investigating evidence as the directors may determine but otherwise free of charge, and (in the case of defacement or wearing-out) on delivery up of the old certificate.

Lien

8 The company shall have a first and paramount lien on every share (not being a fully paid share) for all moneys (whether presently payable or not) payable at a fixed time or called in respect of that share. The directors may at any time declare any share to be wholly or in part exempt from the provisions of this regulation. The company's lien on a share shall extend to any amount payable in respect of it.

9 The company may sell in such manner as the directors determine any shares on which the company has a lien if a sum in respect of which the lien exists is presently payable and is not paid within fourteen clear days after notice has been given to the holder of the share or to the person entitled to it in consequence of the death or bankruptcy of the holder, demanding payment and stating that if the notice is not complied with the shares may be sold.

10 To give effect to a sale the directors may authorise some person to execute an instrument of transfer of the shares sold to, or in accordance with the directions of, the purchaser. The title of the transferee to the shares shall not be affected by any irregularity in or invalidity of the proceedings in reference to the sale.

11 The net proceeds of the sale, after payment of the costs, shall be applied in payment of so much of the sum for which the lien exists as is presently payable, and any residue shall (upon surrender to the company for cancellation of the certificate for the shares sold and subject to a like lien for any moneys not presently payable as existed upon the shares before the sale) be paid to the person entitled to the shares at the date of the sale.

Calls on shares and forfeiture

12 Subject to the terms of allotment, the directors may make calls upon the members in respect of any moneys unpaid on their shares (whether in respect of nominal value or premium) and each member shall (subject to receiving at least fourteen clear days' notice specifying when and where payment is to be

made) pay to the company as required by the notice the amount called on his shares. A call may be required to be paid by instalments. A call may, before receipt by the company of any sum due thereunder, be revoked in whole or part and payment of a call may be postponed in whole or part. A person upon whom a call is made shall remain liable for calls made upon him notwithstanding the subsequent transfer of the shares in respect whereof the call was made.

13 A call shall be deemed to have been made at the time when the resolution of the directors authorising the call was passed.

14 The joint holders of a share shall be jointly and severally liable to pay all calls in respect thereof.

15 If a call remains unpaid after it has become due and payable the person from whom it is due and payable shall pay interest on the amount unpaid from the day it became due and payable until it is paid at the rate fixed by the terms of allotment of the share or in the notice of the call or, if no rate is fixed, at the appropriate rate (as defined by the Act) but the directors may waive payment of the interest wholly or in part.

16 An amount payable in respect of a share on allotment or at any fixed date, whether in respect of nominal value or premium or as an instalment of a call, shall be deemed to be a call and if it is not paid the provisions of the articles shall apply as if that amount had become due and payable by virtue of a call.

17 Subject to the terms of allotment, the directors may make arrangements on the issue of shares for a difference between the holders in the amounts and times of payment of calls on their shares.

18 If a call remains unpaid after it has become due and payable the directors may give to the person from whom it is due not less than fourteen clear days' notice requiring payment of the amount unpaid together with any interest which may have accrued. The notice shall name the place where payment is to be made and shall state that if the notice is not complied with the shares in respect of which the call was made will be liable to be forfeited.

19 If the notice is not complied with any share in respect of which it was given may, before the payment required by the notice has been made, be forfeited by a resolution of the directors and the forfeiture shall include all dividends or other moneys payable in respect of the forfeited shares and not paid before the forfeiture.

20 Subject to the provisions of the Act, a forfeited share may be sold, re-allotted or otherwise disposed of on such terms and in such manner as the directors determine either to the person who was before the forfeiture the holder or to any other person and at any time before sale, re-allotment or other disposition, the forfeiture may be cancelled on such terms as the directors think fit. Where for the purposes of its disposal a forfeited share is to be transferred to any person the directors may authorise some person to execute an instrument of transfer of the share to that person.

21 A person any of whose shares have been forfeited shall cease to be a member in respect of them and shall surrender to the company for cancellation the certificate for the shares forfeited but shall remain liable to the company for all moneys which at the date of forfeiture were presently payable by him to the company in respect of those shares with interest at the rate at which interest was payable on those moneys before the forfeiture or, if no interest was so payable, at the appropriate rate (as defined in the Act) from the date of forfeiture until payment but the directors may waive payment wholly or in part or enforce payment without any allowance for the value of the shares at the time of forfeiture or for any consideration received on their disposal.

22 A statutory declaration by a director or the secretary that a share has been forfeited on a specified date shall be conclusive evidence of the facts stated in it as against all persons claiming to be entitled to the share and the declaration shall (subject to the execution of an instrument of transfer if necessary) constitute a good title to the share and the person to whom the share is disposed of shall not be bound to see to the application of the consideration, if any, nor shall his title to the share be affected by any irregularity in or invalidity of the proceedings in reference to the forfeiture or disposal of the share.

Transfer of shares

23 The instrument of transfer of a share may be in any usual form or in any other form which the directors may approve and shall be executed by or on behalf of the transferor and, unless the share is fully paid, by or on behalf of the transferee.

24 The directors may refuse to register the transfer of a share which is not fully paid to a person of whom they do not approve and they may refuse to register the transfer of a share on which the company has a lien. They may also refuse to register a transfer unless –

(a) it is lodged at the office or at such other place as the directors may appoint and is accompanied by the certificate for the shares to which it relates and such other evidence as the directors may reasonably require to show the right of the transferor to make the transfer;

(b) it is in respect of only one class of shares; and

(c) it is in favour of not more than four transferees.

25 If the directors refuse to register a transfer of a share, they shall within two months after the date on which the transfer was lodged with the company send to the transferee notice of the refusal.

26 The registration of transfers of shares or of transfers of any class of shares may be suspended at such times and for such periods (not exceeding thirty days in any year) as the directors may determine.

27 No fee shall be charged for the registration of any instrument of transfer or other document relating to or affecting the title to any share.

28 The company shall be entitled to retain any instrument of transfer which is registered, but any instrument of transfer which the directors refuse to register shall be returned to the person lodging it when notice of the refusal is given.

Transmission of shares

29 If a member dies the survivor or survivors where he was a joint holder, and his personal representatives where he was a sole holder or the only survivor of joint holders, shall be the only persons recognised by the company as having any title to his interest; but nothing herein contained shall release the estate of a deceased member from any liability in respect of any share which had been jointly held by him.

30 A person becoming entitled to a share in consequence of the death or bankruptcy of a member may, upon such evidence being produced as the directors may properly require, elect either to become the holder of the share or to have some person nominated by him registered as the transferee. If he elects to become the holder he shall give notice to the company to that effect. If he elects to have another person registered he shall execute an instrument of transfer of the share to that person. All the articles relating to the transfer of shares shall apply to the notice or instrument of transfer as if it were an instrument of transfer executed by the member and the death or bankruptcy of the member had not occurred.

31 A person becoming entitled to a share in consequence of the death or bankruptcy of a member shall have the rights to which he would be entitled if he were the holder of the share, except that he shall not, before being registered as the holder of the share, be entitled in respect of it to attend or vote at any meeting of the company or at any separate meeting of the holders of any class of shares in the company.

Alteration of share capital

32 The company may by ordinary resolution –
(a) increase its share capital by new shares of such amount as the resolution prescribes;
(b) consolidate and divide all or any of its share capital into shares of larger amount than its existing shares;
(c) subject to the provisions of the Act, sub-divide its shares, or any of them, into shares of smaller amount and the resolution may determine that, as between the shares resulting from the sub-division, any of them may have any preference or advantage as compared with the others; and
(d) cancel shares which, at the date of the passing of the resolution, have not been taken or agreed to be taken by any person and diminish the amount of its share capital by the amount of the shares so cancelled.

33 Whenever as a result of a consolidation of shares any members would become entitled to fractions of a share, the directors may, on behalf of those members, sell the shares representing the fractions for the best price reasonably obtainable to any person (including, subject to the provisions of the Act, the company) and distribute the net proceeds of sale in due proportion among those members, and the directors may authorise some person to execute an instrument of transfer of the shares to, or in accordance with the directions of, the purchaser. The transferee shall not be bound to see to the application of the purchase money nor shall his title to the shares be affected by any irregularity in or invalidity of the proceedings in reference to the sale.

34 Subject to the provisions of the Act, the company may by special resolution reduce its share capital, any capital redemption reserve and any share premium account in any way.

Purchase of own shares

35 Subject to the provisions of the Act, the company may purchase its own shares (including any redeemable shares) and, if it is a private company, make

a payment in respect of the redemption or purchase of its own shares otherwise than out of distributable profits of the company or the proceeds of a fresh issue of shares.

General meetings

36 All general meetings other than annual general meetings shall be called extraordinary general meetings.

37 The directors may call general meetings and, on the requisition of members pursuant to the provisions of the Act, shall forthwith proceed to convene an extraordinary general meeting for a date not later than eight weeks after receipt of the requisition. If there are not within the United Kingdom sufficient directors to call a general meeting, any director or any member of the company may call a general meeting.

Notice of general meetings

38 An annual general meeting and an extraordinary general meeting called for the passing of a special resolution or a resolution appointing a person as a director shall be called by at least twenty-one clear days' notice. All other extraordinary general meetings shall be called by at least fourteen clear days' notice but a general meeting may be called by shorter notice if it is so agreed –
(a) in the case of an annual general meeting, by all the members entitled to attend and vote thereat; and
(b) in the case of any other meeting by a majority in number of the members having a right to attend and vote being a majority together holding not less than ninety-five per cent. in nominal value of the shares giving that right.

The notice shall specify the time and place of the meeting and the general nature of the business to be transacted and, in the case of an annual general meeting, shall specify the meeting as such.

Subject to the provisions of the articles and to any restrictions imposed on any shares, the notice shall be given to all the members, to all persons entitled to a share in consequence of the death or bankruptcy of a member and to the directors and auditors.

39 The accidental omission to give notice of a meeting to, or the non-receipt of notice of a meeting by, any person entitled to receive notice shall not invalidate the proceedings at that meeting.

Proceedings at general meetings

40 No business shall be transacted at any meeting unless a quorum is present. Two persons entitled to vote upon the business to be transacted, each being a member or a proxy for a member or a duly authorised representative of a corporation, shall be a quorum.

41 If such a quorum is not present within half an hour from the time appointed for the meeting, or if during a meeting such a quorum ceases to be present, the meeting shall stand adjourned to the same day in the next week at the same time and place or to such time and place as the directors may determine.

42 The chairman, if any, of the board of directors or in his absence some other director nominated by the directors shall preside as chairman of the meeting, but if neither the chairman nor such other director (if any) be present within fifteen minutes after the time appointed for holding the meeting and willing to act, the directors present shall elect one of their number to be chairman and, if there is only one director present and willing to act, he shall be chairman.

43 If no director is willing to act as chairman, or if no director is present within fifteen minutes after the time appointed for holding the meeting, the members present and entitled to vote shall choose one of their number to be chairman.

44 A director shall, notwithstanding that he is not a member, be entitled to attend and speak at any general meeting and at any separate meeting of the holders of any class of shares in the company.

45 The chairman may, with the consent of a meeting at which a quorum is present (and shall if so directed by the meeting), adjourn the meeting from time to time and from place to place, but no business shall be transacted at an adjourned meeting other than business which might properly have been transacted at the meeting had the adjournment not taken place. When a meeting is adjourned for fourteen days or more, at least seven clear days' notice shall be given specifying the time and place of the adjourned meeting and the general nature of the business to be transacted. Otherwise it shall not be necessary to give any such notice.

46 A resolution put to the vote of a meeting shall be decided on a show of hands unless before, or on the declaration of the result of, the show of hands a poll is duly demanded. Subject to the provisions of the Act, a poll may be demanded –

(a) by the chairman; or

(b) by at least two members having the right to vote at the meeting; or

(c) by a member or members representing not less than one-tenth of the total voting rights of all the members having the right to vote at the meeting; or

(d) by a member or members holding shares conferring a right to vote at the meeting being shares on which an aggregate sum has been paid up equal to not less than one-tenth of the total sum paid up on all the shares conferring that right;

and a demand by a person as proxy for a member shall be the same as a demand by the member.

47 Unless a poll is duly demanded a declaration by the chairman that a resolution has been carried or carried unanimously, or by a particular majority, or lost, or not carried by a particular majority and an entry to that effect in the minutes of the meeting shall be conclusive evidence of the fact without proof of the number or proportion of the votes recorded in favour of or against the resolution.

48 The demand for a poll may, before the poll is taken, be withdrawn but only with the consent of the chairman and a demand so withdrawn shall not be taken to have invalidated the result of a show of hands declared before the demand was made.

49 A poll shall be taken as the chairman directs and he may appoint scrutineers (who need not be members) and fix a time and place for declaring the result of the poll. The result of the poll shall be deemed to be the resolution of the meeting at which the poll was demanded.

50 In the case of an equality of votes, whether on a show of hands or on a poll, the chairman shall be entitled to a casting vote in addition to any other vote he may have.

51 A poll demanded on the election of a chairman or on a question of adjournment shall be taken forthwith. A poll demanded on any other question shall be taken either forthwith or at such time and place as the chairman directs not being more than thirty days after the poll is demanded. The demand for a poll shall not prevent the continuance of a meeting for the transaction of any business other than the question on which the poll was demanded. If a poll is demanded before the declaration of the result of a show

of hands and the demand is duly withdrawn, the meeting shall continue as if the demand had not been made.

52 No notice need be given of a poll not taken forthwith if the time and place at which it is to be taken are announced at the meeting at which it is demanded. In any other case at least seven clear days' notice shall be given specifying the time and place at which the poll is to be taken.

53 A resolution in writing executed by or on behalf of each member who would have been entitled to vote upon it if it had been proposed at a general meeting at which he was present shall be as effectual as if it had been passed at a general meeting duly convened and held and may consist of several instruments in the like form each executed by or on behalf of one or more members.

Votes of members

54 Subject to any rights or restrictions attached to any shares, on a show of hands every member who (being an individual) is present in person or (being a corporation) is present by a duly authorised representative, not being himself a member entitled to vote, shall have one vote and on a poll every member shall have one vote for every share of which he is the holder.

55 In the case of joint holders the vote of the senior who tenders a vote, whether in person or by proxy, shall be accepted to the exclusion of the votes of the other joint holders; and seniority shall be determined by the order in which the names of the holders stand in the register of members.

56 A member in respect of whom an order has been made by any court having jurisdiction (whether in the United Kingdom or elsewhere) in matters concerning mental disorder may vote, whether on a show of hands or on a poll, by his receiver, curator bonis or other person authorised in that behalf appointed by that court, and any such receiver, curator bonis or other person may, on a poll, vote by proxy. Evidence to the satisfaction of the directors of the authority of the person claiming to exercise the right to vote shall be deposited at the office, or at such other place as is specified in accordance with the articles for the deposit of instruments of proxy, not less than 48 hours before the time appointed for holding the meeting or adjourned meeting at which the right to vote is to be exercised and in default the right to vote shall not be exercisable.

57 No member shall vote at any general meeting or at any separate meeting of

the holders of any class of shares in the company, either in person or by proxy, in respect of any share held by him unless all moneys presently payable by him in respect of that share have been paid.

58 No objection shall be raised to the qualification of any voter except at the meeting or adjourned meeting at which the vote objected to is tendered, and every vote not disallowed at the meeting shall be valid. Any objection made in due time shall be referred to the chairman whose decision shall be final and conclusive.

59 On a poll votes may be given either personally or by proxy. A member may appoint more than one proxy to attend on the same occasion.

60 The appointment of a proxy shall be executed by or on behalf of the appointor and shall be in the following form (or in a form as near thereto as circumstances allow or in any other form which is usual or which the directors may approve) –

"_____PLC/Limited

I/We,   of
being a member/members of the above-named company, hereby appoint
                                                         of
or failing him,   of
as my/our proxy to vote in my/our name[s] and on my/our behalf at the annual/ extraordinary general meeting of the company to be held on 19
    , and at any adjournment thereof.

Signed on   19 ."

61 Where it is desired to afford members an opportunity of instructing the proxy how he shall act the appointment of a proxy shall be in the following form (or in a form as near thereto as circumstances allow or in any other form which is usual or which the directors may approve)

"_____PLC/Limited

I/We,   of
being a member/members of the above-named company, hereby appoint
                                                         of
or failing him,   of
as my/our proxy to vote in my/our name[s] and on my/our behalf at the

annual/ extraordinary general meeting of the company to be held on 19
, and at any adjournment thereof.

This form is to be used in respect of the resolutions mentioned below as
follows:

Resolution No.1 *for *against
Resolution No.2 *for *against.

*Strike out whichever is not desired.

Unless otherwise instructed, the proxy may vote as he thinks fit or abstain
from voting.
Signed this   day of   19   ."

62 The appointment of a proxy and any authority under which it is
executed or a copy of such authority certified notarially or in some other
way approved by the directors may –
(a) in the case of an instrument in writing be deposited at the office or at
    such other place within the United Kingdom as is specified in the notice
    convening the meeting or in any instrument of proxy sent out by the
    company in relation to the meeting not less than 48 hours before the time
    for holding the meeting or adjourned meeting at which the person named
    in the instrument proposes to vote; or (aa) in the case of an appointment
    contained in an electronic communication, where an address has been
    specified for the purpose of receiving electronic communications –
    (i)   in the notice convening the meeting, or
    (ii) in any instrument of proxy sent out by the company in relation to the
          meeting, or
    (iii) in any invitation contained in an electronic communication to appoint
          a proxy issued by the company in relation to the meeting, be received
          at such address not less than 48hours before the time for holding
          the meeting or adjourned meeting at which the person named in the
          appointment proposes to vote;
(b) in the case of a poll taken more than 48 hours after it is demanded, be
    deposited or received as aforesaid after the poll has been demanded and
    not less than 24 hours before the time appointed for the taking of the poll;
    or
(c) where the poll is not taken forthwith but is taken not more than 48 hours
    after it was demanded, be delivered at the meeting at which the poll was
    demanded to the chairman or to the secretary or to any director; and an

appointment of proxy which is not deposited, delivered or received in a manner so permitted shall be invalid.

In this regulation and the next, "address", in relation to electronic communications, includes any number or address used for the purposes of such communications.

63 A vote given or poll demanded by proxy or by the duly authorised representative of a corporation shall be valid notwithstanding the previous determination of the authority of the person voting or demanding a poll unless notice of the determination was received by the company at the office or at such other place at which the instrument of proxy was duly deposited or, where the appointment of the proxy was contained in an electronic communication, at the address at which such appointment was duly received before the commencement of the meeting or adjourned meeting at which the vote is given or the poll demanded or (in the case of a poll taken otherwise than on the same day as the meeting or adjourned meeting) the time appointed for taking the poll.

Number of directors

64 Unless otherwise determined by ordinary resolution, the number of directors (other than alternate directors) shall not be subject to any maximum but shall be not less than two.

Alternate directors

65 Any director (other than an alternate director) may appoint any other director, or any other person approved by resolution of the directors and willing to act, to be an alternate director and may remove from office an alternate director so appointed by him.

66 An alternate director shall be entitled to receive notice of all meetings of directors and of all meetings of committees of directors of which his appointor is a member, to attend and vote at any such meeting at which the director appointing him is not personally present, and generally to perform all the functions of his appointor as a director in his absence but shall not be entitled to receive any remuneration from the company for his services as an alternate director. But it shall not be necessary to give notice of such a meeting to an alternate director who is absent from the United Kingdom.

67 An alternate director shall cease to be an alternate director if his appointor ceases to be a director; but, if a director retires by rotation or otherwise but is reappointed or deemed to have been reappointed at the meeting at which he retires, any appointment of an alternate director made by him which was in force immediately prior to his retirement shall continue after his reappointment.

68 Any appointment or removal of an alternate director shall be by notice to the company signed by the director making or revoking the appointment or in any other manner approved by the directors.

69 Save as otherwise provided in the articles, an alternate director shall be deemed for all purposes to be a director and shall alone be responsible for his own acts and defaults and he shall not be deemed to be the agent of the director appointing him.

Powers of directors

70 Subject to the provisions of the Act, the memorandum and the articles and to any directions given by special resolution, the business of the company shall be managed by the directors who may exercise all the powers of the company. No alteration of the memorandum or articles and no such direction shall invalidate any prior act of the directors which would have been valid if that alteration had not been made or that direction had not been given. The powers given by this regulation shall not be limited by any special power given to the directors by the articles and a meeting of directors at which a quorum is present may exercise all powers exercisable by the directors.

71 The directors may, by power of attorney or otherwise, appoint any person to be the agent of the company for such purposes and on such conditions as they determine, including authority for the agent to delegate all or any of his powers.

Delegation of directors' powers

72 The directors may delegate any of their powers to any committee consisting of one or more directors. They may also delegate to any managing director or any director holding any other executive office such of their powers as they consider desirable to be exercised by him. Any such delegation may be made subject to any conditions the directors may impose, and either collaterally with or to the exclusion of their own powers and may be revoked or altered. Subject to any such conditions, the proceedings of a committee with two or more members shall be governed by the articles regulating the proceedings of directors so far as they are capable of applying.

Appointment and retirement of directors

73 At the first annual general meeting all the directors shall retire from office, and at every subsequent annual general meeting one-third of the directors who are subject to retirement by rotation or, if their number is not three or a multiple of three, the number nearest to one-third shall retire from office; but, if there is only one director who is subject to retirement by rotation, he shall retire.

74 Subject to the provisions of the Act, the directors to retire by rotation shall be those who have been longest in office since their last appointment or reappointment, but as between persons who became or were last reappointed directors on the same day those to retire shall (unless they otherwise agree among themselves) be determined by lot.

75 If the company, at the meeting at which a director retires by rotation, does not fill the vacancy the retiring director shall, if willing to act, be deemed to have been reappointed unless at the meeting it is resolved not to fill the vacancy or unless a resolution for the reappointment of the director is put to the meeting and lost.

76 No person other than a director retiring by rotation shall be appointed or reappointed a director at any general meeting unless –
(a) he is recommended by the directors; or
(b) not less than fourteen nor more than thirty-five clear days before the date appointed for the meeting, notice executed by a member qualified to vote at the meeting has been given to the company of the intention to propose that person for appointment or reappointment stating the particulars which would, if he were so appointed or reappointed, be required to be included in the company's register of directors together with notice executed by that person of his willingness to be appointed or reappointed.

77 Not less than seven nor more than twenty-eight clear days before the date appointed for holding a general meeting notice shall be given to all who are entitled to receive notice of the meeting of any person (other than a director retiring by rotation at the meeting) who is recommended by the directors for appointment or reappointment as a director at the meeting or in respect of

whom notice has been duly given to the company of the intention to propose him at the meeting for appointment or reappointment as a director. The notice shall give the particulars of that person which would, if he were so appointed or reappointed, be required to be included in the company's register of directors.

78 Subject as aforesaid, the company may by ordinary resolution appoint a person who is willing to act to be a director either to fill a vacancy or as an additional director and may also determine the rotation in which any additional directors are to retire.

79 The directors may appoint a person who is willing to act to be a director, either to fill a vacancy or as an additional director, provided that the appointment does not cause the number of directors to exceed any number fixed by or in accordance with the articles as the maximum number of directors. A director so appointed shall hold office only until the next following annual general meeting and shall not be taken into account in determining the directors who are to retire by rotation at the meeting. If not reappointed at such annual general meeting, he shall vacate office at the conclusion thereof.

80 Subject as aforesaid, a director who retires at an annual general meeting may, if willing to act, be reappointed. If he is not reappointed, he shall retain office until the meeting appoints someone in his place, or if it does not do so, until the end of the meeting.

Disqualification and removal of directors

81 The office of a director shall be vacated if –
(a) he ceases to be a director by virtue of any provision of the Act or he becomes prohibited by law from being a director; or
(b) he becomes bankrupt or makes any arrangement or composition with his creditors generally; or
(c) he is, or may be, suffering from mental disorder and either-
   (i) he is admitted to hospital in pursuance of an application for admission for treatment under the Mental Health Act 1983 or, in Scotland, an application for admission under the Mental Health (Scotland) Act 1960, or
   (ii) an order is made by a court having jurisdiction (whether in the United Kingdom or elsewhere) in matters concerning mental disorder for his detention or for the appointment of a receiver, curator bonis or other person to exercise powers with respect to his property or affairs; or

(d) he resigns his office by notice to the company; or

(e) he shall for more than six consecutive months have been absent without permission of the directors from meetings of directors held during that period and the directors resolve that his office be vacated.

Remuneration of directors

82 The directors shall be entitled to such remuneration as the company may by ordinary resolution determine and, unless the resolution provides otherwise, the remuneration shall be deemed to accrue from day to day.

Directors' expenses

83 The directors may be paid all travelling, hotel, and other expenses properly incurred by them in connection with their attendance at meetings of directors or committees of directors or general meetings or separate meetings of the holders of any class of shares or of debentures of the company or otherwise in connection with the discharge of their duties.

Directors' appointments and interest

84 Subject to the provisions of the Act, the directors may appoint one or more of their number to the office of managing director or to any other executive office under the company and may enter into an agreement or arrangement with any director for his employment by the company or for the provision by him of any services outside the scope of the ordinary duties of a director. Any such appointment, agreement or arrangement may be made upon such terms as the directors determine and they may remunerate any such director for his services as they think fit. Any appointment of a director to an executive office shall terminate if he ceases to be a director but without prejudice to any claim to damages for breach of the contract of service between the director and the company. A managing director and a director holding any other executive office shall not be subject to retirement by rotation.

85 Subject to the provisions of the Act, and provided that he has disclosed to the directors the nature and extent of any material interest of his, a director notwithstanding his office –

(a) may be a party to, or otherwise interested in, any transaction or arrangement with the company or in which the company is otherwise interested;

(b) may be a director or other officer of, or employed by, or a party to any transaction or arrangement with, or otherwise interested in, any body corporate promoted by the company or in which the company is otherwise interested; and

(c) shall not, by reason of his office, be accountable to the company for any benefit which he derives from any such office or employment or from any such transaction or arrangement or from any interest in any such body corporate and no such transaction or arrangement shall be liable to be avoided on the ground of any such interest or benefit.

86 For the purposes of regulation 85 –

(a) a general notice given to the directors that a director is to be regarded as having an interest of the nature and extent specified in the notice in any transaction or arrangement in which a specified person or class of persons is interested shall be deemed to be a disclosure that the director has an interest in any such transaction of the nature and extent so specified; and

(b) an interest of which a director has no knowledge and of which it is unreasonable to expect him to have knowledge shall not be treated as an interest of his.

Directors' gratuities and pensions

87 The directors may provide benefits, whether by the payment of gratuities or pensions or by insurance or otherwise, for any director who has held but no longer holds any executive office or employment with the company or with any body corporate which is or has been a subsidiary of the company or a predecessor in business of the company or of any such subsidiary , and for any member of his family (including a spouse and a former spouse) or any person who is or was dependent on him, and may (as well before as after he ceases to hold such office or employment) contribute to any fund and pay premiums for the purchase or provision of any such benefit.

Proceedings of directors

88 Subject to the provisions of the articles, the directors may regulate their proceedings as they think fit. A director may, and the secretary at the request of a director shall, call a meeting of the directors. It shall not be necessary to give notice of a meeting to a director who is absent from the United Kingdom. Questions arising at a meeting shall be decided by a majority of votes. In the case of an equality of votes, the chairman shall have a second or casting vote.

A director who is also an alternate director shall be entitled in the absence of his appointor to a separate vote on behalf of his appointor in addition to his own vote.

89 The quorum for the transaction of the business of the directors may be fixed by the directors and unless so fixed at any other number shall be two. A person who holds office only as an alternate director shall, if his appointor is not present, be counted in the quorum.

90 The continuing directors or a sole continuing director may act notwithstanding any vacancies in their number, but, if the number of directors is less than the number fixed as the quorum, the continuing directors or director may act only for the purpose of filling vacancies or of calling a general meeting.

91 The directors may appoint one of their number to be the chairman of the board of directors and may at any time remove him from that office. Unless he is unwilling to do so, the director so appointed shall preside at every meeting of directors at which he is present. But if there is no director holding that office, or if the director holding it is unwilling to preside or is not present within five minutes after the time appointed for the meeting, the directors present may appoint one of their number to be chairman of the meeting.

92 All acts done by a meeting of directors, or of a committee of directors, or by a person acting as a director shall, notwithstanding that it be afterwards discovered that there was a defect in the appointment of any director or that any of them were disqualified from holding office, or had vacated office, or were not entitled to vote, be as valid as if every such person had been duly appointed and was qualified and had continued to be a director and had been entitled to vote.

93 A resolution in writing signed by all the directors entitled to receive notice of a meeting of directors or of a committee of directors shall be as valid and effectual as if it had been passed at a meeting of directors or (as the case may be) a committee of directors duly convened and held and may consist of several documents in the like form each signed by one or more directors; but a resolution signed by an alternate director need not also be signed by his appointor and, if it is signed by a director who has appointed an alternate director, it need not be signed by the alternate director in that capacity.

94 Save as otherwise provided by the articles, a director shall not vote at a meeting of directors or of a committee of directors on any resolution concerning a matter in which he has, directly or indirectly, an interest or duty which is material and which conflicts or may conflict with the interests of the company unless his interest or duty arises only because the case falls within one or more of the following paragraphs –

(a) the resolution relates to the giving to him of a guarantee, security, or indemnity in respect of money lent to, or an obligation incurred by him for the benefit of, the company or any of its subsidiaries;

(b) the resolution relates to the giving to a third party of a guarantee, security, or indemnity in respect of an obligation of the company or any of its subsidiaries for which the director has assumed responsibility in whole or part and whether alone or jointly with others under a guarantee or indemnity or by the giving of security;

(c) his interest arises by virtue of his subscribing or agreeing to subscribe for any shares, debentures or other securities of the company or any of its subsidiaries, or by virtue of his being, or intending to become, a participant in the underwriting or sub-underwriting of an offer of any such shares, debentures, or other securities by the company or any of its subsidiaries for subscription, purchase or exchange;

(d) the resolution relates in any way to a retirement benefits scheme which has been approved, or is conditional upon approval, by the Board of Inland Revenue for taxation purposes.

For the purposes of this regulation, an interest of a person who is, for any purpose of the Act (excluding any statutory modification thereof not in force when this regulation becomes binding on the company), connected with a director shall be treated as an interest of the director and, in relation to an alternate director, an interest of his appointor shall be treated as an interest of the alternate director without prejudice to any interest which the alternate director has otherwise.

95 A director shall not be counted in the quorum present at a meeting in relation to a resolution on which he is not entitled to vote.

96 The company may by ordinary resolution suspend or relax to any extent, either generally or in respect of any particular matter, any provision of the articles prohibiting a director from voting at a meeting of directors or of a committee of directors.

97 Where proposals are under consideration concerning the appointment of two or more directors to offices or employments with the company or any body corporate in which the company is interested the proposals may be divided and considered in relation to each director separately and (provided he is not for another reason precluded from voting) each of the directors concerned shall be entitled to vote and be counted in the quorum in respect of each resolution except that concerning his own appointment.

98 If a question arises at a meeting of directors or of a committee of directors as to the right of a director to vote, the question may, before the conclusion of the meeting, be referred to the chairman of the meeting and his ruling in relation to any director other than himself shall be final and conclusive.

Secretary

99 Subject to the provisions of the Act, the secretary shall be appointed by the directors for such term, at such remuneration and upon such conditions as they may think fit; and any secretary so appointed may be removed by them.

Minutes

100 The directors shall cause minutes to be made in books kept for the purpose –
(a) of all appointments of officers made by the directors; and
(b) of all proceedings at meetings of the company, of the holders of any class of shares in the company, and of the directors, and of committees of directors, including the names of the directors present at each such meeting.

The seal

101 The seal shall only be used by the authority of the directors or of a committee of directors authorised by the directors. The directors may determine who shall sign any instrument to which the seal is affixed and unless otherwise so determined it shall be signed by a director and by the secretary or by a second director.

Dividends

102 Subject to the provisions of the Act, the company may by ordinary resolution declare dividends in accordance with the respective rights of the members, but no dividend shall exceed the amount recommended by the directors.

103 Subject to the provisions of the Act, the directors may pay interim dividends if it appears to them that they are justified by the profits of the company available for distribution. If the share capital is divided into different classes, the directors may pay interim dividends on shares which confer deferred or non-preferred rights with regard to dividend as well as on shares which confer

preferential rights with regard to dividend, but no interim dividend shall be paid on shares carrying deferred or non-preferred rights if, at the time of payment, any preferential dividend is in arrear. The directors may also pay at intervals settled by them any dividend payable at a fixed rate if it appears to them that the profits available for distribution justify the payment. Provided the directors act in good faith they shall not incur any liability to the holders of shares conferring preferred rights for any loss they may suffer by the lawful payment of an interim dividend on any shares having deferred or non-preferred rights.

104 Except as otherwise provided by the rights attached to shares, all dividends shall be declared and paid according to the amounts paid up on the shares on which the dividend is paid. All dividends shall be apportioned and paid proportionately to the amounts paid up on the shares during any portion or portions of the period in respect of which the dividend is paid; but, if any share is issued on terms providing that it shall rank for dividend as from a particular date, that share shall rank for dividend accordingly.

105 A general meeting declaring a dividend may, upon the recommendation of the directors, direct that it shall be satisfied wholly or partly by the distribution of assets and, where any difficulty arises in regard to the distribution, the directors may settle the same and in particular may issue fractional certificates and fix the value for distribution of any assets and may determine that cash shall be paid to any member upon the footing of the value so fixed in order to adjust the rights of members and may vest any assets in trustees.

106 Any dividend or other moneys payable in respect of a share may be paid by cheque sent by post to the registered address of the person entitled or, if two or more persons are the holders of the share or are jointly entitled to it by reason of the death or bankruptcy of the holder, to the registered address of that one of those persons who is first named in the register of members or to such person and to such address as the person or persons entitled may in writing direct. Every cheque shall be made payable to the order of the person or persons entitled or to such other person as the person or persons entitled may in writing direct and payment of the cheque shall be a good discharge to the company. Any joint holder or other person jointly entitled to a share as aforesaid may give receipts for any dividend or other moneys payable in respect of the share.

107 No dividend or other moneys payable in respect of a share shall bear interest against the company unless otherwise provided by the rights attached to the share.

108 Any dividend which has remained unclaimed for twelve years from the date when it became due for payment shall, if the directors so resolve, be forfeited and cease to remain owing by the company.

Accounts

109 No member shall (as such) have any right of inspecting any accounting records or other book or document of the company except as conferred by statute or authorised by the directors or by ordinary resolution of the company.

Capitalisation of profits

110 The directors may with the authority of an ordinary resolution of the company –

(a) subject as hereinafter provided, resolve to capitalise any undivided profits of the company not required for paying any preferential dividend (whether or not they are available for distribution) or any sum standing to the credit of the company's share premium account or capital redemption reserve;

(b) appropriate the sum resolved to be capitalised to the members who would have been entitled to it if it were distributed by way of dividend and in the same proportions and apply such sum on their behalf either in or towards paying up the amounts, if any, for the time being unpaid on any shares held by them respectively, or in paying up in full unissued shares or debentures of the company of a nominal amount equal to that sum, and allot the shares or debentures credited as fully paid to those members, or as they may direct, in those proportions, or partly in one way and partly in the other: but the share premium account, the capital redemption reserve, and any profits which are not available for distribution may, for the purposes of this regulation, only be applied in paying up unissued shares to be allotted to members credited as fully paid;

(c) make such provision by the issue of fractional certificates or by payment in cash or otherwise as they determine in the case of shares or debentures becoming distributable under this regulation in fractions; and

(d) authorise any person to enter on behalf of all the members concerned into an agreement with the company providing for the allotment to them respectively, credited as fully paid, of any shares or debentures to which they are entitled upon such capitalisation, any agreement made under such authority being binding on all such members.

Notices

111 Any notice to be given to or by any person pursuant to the articles (other than a notice calling the meeting of the directors) shall be in writing or shall be given using electronic communications to an address for the time being notified for that purpose to the person giving the notice. In this regulation, "address", in relation to electronic communications, includes any number or address used for the purpose of such communications.

112 The company may give any notice to a member either personally or by sending it by post in a prepaid envelope addressed to the member at his registered address or by leaving it at that address or by giving it using electronic communications to an address for the time being notified to the company by the member. In the case of joint holders of a share, all notices shall be given to the joint holder whose name stands first in the register of members in respect of the joint holding and notice so given shall be sufficient notice to all the joint holders. A member whose registered address is not within the United Kingdom and who gives to the company an address within the United Kingdom at which notices may be given to him or an address to which notices may be sent using electronic communications, shall be entitled to have notices given to him at that address, but otherwise no such member shall be entitled to receive any notice from the company. In this regulation and the next, "address" in relation to electronic communications, includes any number or address used for the purpose of such communications.

113 A member present, either in person or by proxy, at any meeting of the company or of the holders of any class of shares in the company shall be deemed to have received notice of the meeting and, where requisite, of the purposes for which it was called.

114 Every person who becomes entitled to a share shall be bound by any notice in respect of that share which, before his name is entered in the register of members, has been duly given to a person from whom he derives his title.

115 Proof that an envelope containing a notice was properly addressed, prepaid and posted shall be conclusive evidence that the notice was given. Proof that a notice contained in an electronic communication was sent in accordance with guidance issued by the Institute of Chartered Secretaries and Administrators shall be conclusive evidence that the notice was given. A notice shall be deemed to be given at the expiration of 48 hours after the envelope containing it was posted or, in the case of a notice contained in an electronic communication, at the expiration of 48 hours after the time it was sent.

116 A notice may be given by the company to the persons entitled to a share in consequence of the death or bankruptcy of a member by sending or delivering it, in any manner authorised by the articles for the giving of notice to a member, addressed to them by name, or by the title of representatives of the deceased, or trustee of the bankrupt or by any like description at the address, if any, within the United Kingdom supplied for that purpose by the persons claiming to be so entitled. Until such an address has been supplied, a notice may be given in any manner in which it might have been given if the death or bankruptcy had not occurred.

Winding up

117 If the company is wound up, the liquidator may, with the sanction of an extraordinary resolution of the company and any other sanction required by the Act, divide among the members in specie the whole or any part of the assets of the company and may, for that purpose, value any assets and determine how the division shall be carried out as between the members or different classes of members. The liquidator may, with the like sanction, vest the whole or any part of the assets in trustees upon such trusts for the benefit of the members as he with the like sanction determines, but no member shall be compelled to accept any assets upon which there is a liability.

Indemnity

118 Subject to the provisions of the Act but without prejudice to any indemnity to which a director may otherwise be entitled, every director or other officer or auditor of the company shall be indemnified out of the assets of the company against any liability incurred by him in defending any proceedings, whether civil or criminal, in which judgment is given in his favour or in which he is acquitted or in connection with any application in which relief is granted to him by the court from liability for negligence, default, breach of duty or breach of trust in relation to the affairs of the company.

Companies Act 2006 Model Articles for private companies – destinations

1

Under the Companies Act 2006 Table A is being replaced by Model Articles of association for:

1 private companies limited by shares;
2 private companies limited by guarantee;
3 public companies.

These Model Articles will automatically be the articles of association for companies formed under CA 2006 from 1 October 2009 which do not register their own articles of association, or which register their own articles but do not exclude the Model Articles in whole or in part as was the case with Table A.

The table below compares the 1985 version of Table A (not the transitional version) with the Model Articles for a private company. It shows on a clause-by-clause basis which regulations of Table A have no equivalent in the Model Articles and where a regulation is re-enacted it shows the corresponding article number in the Model Articles.

Regulation of 1985 Table A	Destination in Model Articles
1 Interpretation	Article1 (changed)
2 Power to issue different classes of share	Article 22(1) (changed)
3 Allowing issue of redeemable shares	Article 22(2) (changed)
4 Company may pay commission when issuing shares	–
5 Company not bound by less than absolute interests	Article 23
6 Right to share certificate	Article 24(1)
7 Replacement share certificates	Article 25(1)
8 Company to have lien on partly paid shares	–
9 Company may sell shares on which it has a lien	–
10 Directors may authorise someone to execute an instrument of transfer for shares being sold pursuant to exercise of lien	–
11 Proceeds of sale arising from exercise of lien	–

continued

Regulation of 1985 Table A		Destination in Model Articles
12	Directors may make calls on partly paid shares	–
13	Call made when directors resolve it should be made	–
14	Joint holders jointly and severally liable to pay calls	–
15	Interest payable on moneys due under unpaid calls	–
16	Moneys payable on shares are deemed to be moneys due to the company as if a call had been made.	–
17	Directors may make different call arrangements on the issue of shares	–
18	Notice of calls remaining unpaid	–
19	Directors may resolve unpaid shares forfeit	–
20	Company permitted to deal with forfeited shares	–
21	On forfeiture shareholder ceases to be a member in respect of the forfeited shares	–
22	Declaration by director or secretary of forfeiture is conclusive evidence against anyone claiming to be entitled to the shares	–
23	Form of instrument of transfer	Article 26(1)
24	Directors right to refuse to register transfer of a partly paid share	Article 26(5) (changed)
25	Directors to notify refusal to register transfer within 2 months	Article 26(5) (changed)
26	Registration of transfers may be suspended by the directors for up to 30 days a year	–
27	No fee to be charged for transfer	Article 26(2)
28	Right to retain instrument of transfer/ instrument of transfer to be returned when transfer refused	Articles 26(3) and (5) (changed)
29	Transmission on death of a member	–
30	Transmittee may elect to hold shares or transfer to third party	Article 27(2)
31	Transmittee can attend and vote once registered as holder	Article 27(3)
32	Alteration of share capital by ordinary resolution	–
33	Dealing with fractional entitlement following a consolidation	–
34	Reduction of capital, reserves or share premium by special resolution	–
35	Company can purchase its own shares	–
36	Extraordinary general meetings	–
37	Calling general meetings	–
38	Notice requirements for AGMs and EGMs	–
39	Accidental omission to give notice	–
40	Quorum for general meetings	–
41	Arrangements where quorum not present within half an hour	Article 42(1) (changed)
42	Company chairman or other director to chair meeting	Article 40(1) (changed)
43	Members to elect chairman if no director willing to act	Article 40(2) (changed)
44	Director entitled to attend and speak at general meeting even though not a member	Article 41(1)
45	Chairman may adjourn meeting	Article 42(2) (changed)
46	Voting arrangements	Article 43 (changed)

continued

Regulation of 1985 Table A	Destination in Model Articles
47 Chairman to declare voting result; entry in minutes conclusive evidence of result	–
48 Demand for poll may be withdrawn	Article 45(3) (changed)
49 Chairman's discretion over poll arrangements	Article 45(4) (changed)
50 Chairman to have casting vote	–
51 Timing of polls	Article 45(4) (changed)
52 Notice of polls	–
53 Written resolutions of members	–
54 Every member to have one vote on a show of hands and on a poll one vote per share	–
55 First named in a joint holding is the one who should vote	–
56 Votes of members with mental disorders	–
57 Member cannot vote on a partly paid share where moneys payable	–
58 Objections about the qualification of a voter	Article 44
59 Poll voting	Article 45
60 Form of proxy	Article 46 (changed)
61 Form of proxy (plc)	–
62 Deposit/ delivery of forms of proxy	Article 47 (changed)
63 Demanding a poll	Article 45(2) (changed)
64 Number of directors	–
65 Directors may appoint alternates	–
66 Alternate entitled to receive notice & to attend & vote when appointor not present	–
67 Cessation of alternate's appointment	–
68 Form of appointment or removal of an alternate	–
69 Alternate deemed for all purposes to be a director	–
70 Directors general authority	Articles 3 and 4
71 Appointment of agents	–
72 Delegation of directors' power to committees	Article 5(1)
73 Directors to retire by rotation	–
74 Determining who to retire by rotation	–
75 Deemed reappointment of director retiring by rotation	–
76 Notice to appoint someone other than a retiring director at a general meeting	–
77 Notice to be given to members of appointment of directors other than those retiring by rotation.	–
78 Directors may be appointed by ordinary resolution	Article 17(1)(a)
79 Board may appoint directors	Article 17(1)(b)
80 Retiring director is eligible for re–appointment	–
81 Termination of director's appointment	Article 18 (changed)
82 Directors' remuneration	Article 19 (changed)
83 Directors' expenses	Article 20
84 Executives not to retire by rotation	–

continued

Regulation of 1985 Table A	Destination in Model Articles
85 Director may be interested in a transaction provided he has disclosed his interest	Article 14 (changed)
86 General disclosure of interest by directors	–
87 Directors gratuities and pensions	Article 19(3)(b) (changed)
88 Directors discretion to regulate their proceedings	Articles 9, 13 and 16 (changed)
89 Quorum for directors' meetings	Article 11
90 Directors may act when number falls below minimum/ only to appoint another director if quorum cannot be met	Article 11(3)
91 Directors may appoint chairman	Article 12 (changed)
92 Acts of director valid notwithstanding any defect in appointment	–
93 Directors' written resolutions	Article 7(3)
94 Director cannot vote on a matter of personal interest	Article 14 (changed)
95 Director cannot be counted in the quorum for a resolution on which he is not entitled to vote	Article 14 (changed)
96 Members may suspend provision of articles precluding a director from voting	Article 14 (changed)
97 Appointment of directors should be made individually	–
98 Chairman to decide whether a director may vote	Article 14(6)
99 Directors may appoint secretary	–
100 Minutes of meetings to be kept	Article 15 (changed)
101 Company seals	Article 50 (changed)
102 Declaration of dividends	Article 30 (1) & (2)
103 Payment of interim dividends	Article 30
104 Payment of dividends on pro–rata basis	Article 30
105 Approval of dividend in specie	Article 35
106 Dividends to be sent to first–named joint holder	Article 31(2)(b)
107 No interest payable on dividends	Article 33
108 Unclaimed distributions	Article 34
109 No right to inspect accounts and other records	Article 51
110 Capitalisation of profits	Article 37 (changed)
111 Notice to be in writing or electronic form, save for notice of Board meetings	Articles 9 and 49 (changed)
112 Manner of giving notice to members	Article 49 (changed)
113 Any member present at a general meeting is deemed to have received notice	–
114 Transferee bound by notice given to former holder	Article 29
115 Deeming provisions for notices	–
116 Notice to person taking shares by transmission	–
117 Distribution of surplus assets in a liquidation can be made in kind when resolution passed	–
118 Indemnity	Article 53 (changed)

Companies Act 2006 Model Articles for private companies – derivations

Under the Companies Act 2006 Table A is being replaced by Model Articles of association for:

1 private companies limited by shares;
2 private companies limited by guarantee;
3 public companies.

These Model Articles will automatically be the articles of association for companies formed under CA 2006 from 1 October 2009 which do not register their own articles of association, or which register their own articles but do not exclude the Model Articles in whole or in part as was the case with Table A.

The table below compares the Model Articles for a private company with the 1985 version of Table A. It shows on a clause-by-clause basis the provisions of the Model Articles and, where applicable, the equivalent regulation of Table A.

Provision of Model Articles	Origin in 1985 Table A
1 Defined terms	Regulation 1
2 Liability of members	Regulation 8
3 Directors' general authority	Regulation 70
4 Shareholders' reserve power	Regulation 70
5 Directors may delegate	Regulations 71 and 72
6 Committees	Regulation 72
7 Directors to take decisions collectively	Regulation 88
8 Unanimous decisions	Regulation 93
9 Calling a directors' meeting	Regulation 88
10 Participation in directors' meetings	–
11 Quorum for directors' meetings	Regulation 89
12 Chairing of directors' meetings	Regulation 91
13 Casting vote	Regulation 88
14 Conflicts of interest	Regulations 85, 86 and 94

continued

Provision of Model Articles	Origin in 1985 Table A
15 Records of decisions to be kept	Regulation 100(b)
16 Directors' discretion to make further rules	Regulation 88
17 Methods of appointing directors	Regulations 78 and 79
18 Termination of director's appointment	Regulation 81
19 Directors' remuneration	Regulations 82, 84 and 87
20 Directors' expenses	Regulation 83
21 All shares to be fully paid up	-
22 Powers to issue different classes of share	Regulations 2 and 3
23 Company not bound by less than absolute interests	Regulation 5
24 Share certificates	Regulation 6
25 Replacement share certificates	Regulation 7
26 Share transfers	Regulations 23, 25, 26, 27 and 28
27 Transmission of shares	Regulations 29 to 31
28 Exercise of transmittees' rights	Regulations 29 to 31
29 Transmittees bound by prior notices	Regulations 29 to 31
30 Procedure for declaring dividends	Regulations 102 to 104
31 Payment of dividends and other distributions	Regulation 106
32 No interest on distributions	Regulation 107
33 Unclaimed distributions	Regulation 108
34 Non-cash distributions	Regulation 105
35 Waiver of distributions	–
36 Authority to capitalise and appropriation of capitalised sums	Regulation 110
37 Attendance and speaking at general meetings	–
38 Quorum for general meetings	Regulation 40
39 Chairing general meetings	Regulation 42 and 43
40 Attendance and speaking by directors and non-shareholders	Regulation 44
41 Adjournment	Regulations 41 and 45
42 Voting: general	Regulation 46
43 Errors and disputes	Regulation 58
44 Poll votes	Regulations 46 to 52
45 Content of proxy notices	Regulations 60 and 61
46 Delivery of proxy notices	Regulation 63
47 Amendments to resolutions	–
48 Means of communication to be used	Regulations 111 to 116
49 Company seals	Regulation 101
50 No right to inspect accounts and other records	Regulation 109
51 Provision for employees on cessation of business	–
52 Indemnity	Regulation 118
53 Insurance	Regulation 87

Companies Act 2006 Model Articles for private companies limited by shares

The following Model Articles for private companies limited by shares are the first of three sets of Model Articles contained in the Companies (Model Articles) Regulations 2008 which were made on 16 December 2008 to come into force on 1 October 2009.

For private limited companies formed under CA 2006 on or after 1 October 2009 these Model Articles will automatically be the company's articles unless the company chooses to adopt its own tailor-made articles in place of some or all of the Model Articles.

MODEL ARTICLES FOR PRIVATE COMPANIES LIMITED BY SHARES

INDEX TO THE ARTICLES

11. Quorum for directors' meetings
12. Chairing of directors' meetings
13. Casting vote
14. Conflicts of interest
15. Records of decisions to be kept
16. Directors' discretion to make further rules

APPOINTMENT OF DIRECTORS

17. Methods of appointing directors
18. Termination of director's appointment
19. Directors' remuneration
20. Directors' expenses

PART 3
SHARES AND DISTRIBUTIONS

SHARES

21. All shares to be fully paid up
22. Powers to issue different classes of share
23. Company not bound by less than absolute interests
24. Share certificates
25. Replacement share certificates
26. Share transfers
27. Transmission of shares
28. Exercise of transmittees' rights
29. Transmittees bound by prior notices

DIVIDENDS AND OTHER DISTRIBUTIONS

30. Procedure for declaring dividends
31. Payment of dividends and other distributions
32. No interest on distributions
33. Unclaimed distributions
34. Non-cash distributions
35. Waiver of distributions

CAPITALISATION OF PROFITS

36. Authority to capitalise and appropriation of capitalised sums

PART 4
DECISION-MAKING BY SHAREHOLDERS

ORGANISATION OF GENERAL MEETINGS

37. Attendance and speaking at general meetings

38. Quorum for general meetings
39. Chairing general meetings
40. Attendance and speaking by directors and non-shareholders
41. Adjournment

VOTING AT GENERAL MEETINGS

42. Voting: general
43. Errors and disputes
44. Poll votes
45. Content of proxy notices
46. Delivery of proxy notices
47. Amendments to resolutions

PART 5
ADMINISTRATIVE ARRANGEMENTS

48. Means of communication to be used
49. Company seals
50. No right to inspect accounts and other records
51. Provisions for employees on cessation of business

DIRECTORS' INDEMNITY AND INSURANCE

52. Indemnity
53. Insurance

PART 1
INTERPRETATION AND LIMITATION OF LIABILITY

Defined terms

1. In the articles, unless the context requires otherwise—

"articles" means the company's articles of association;

"bankruptcy" includes individual insolvency proceedings in a jurisdiction other than England and Wales or Northern Ireland which have an effect similar to that of bankruptcy;

"chairman" has the meaning given in article 12;

"chairman of the meeting" has the meaning given in article 39;
"Companies Acts" means the Companies Acts (as defined in section 2 of the Companies Act 2006), in so far as they apply to the company;

"director" means a director of the company, and includes any person occupying the position of director, by whatever name called;

"distribution recipient" has the meaning given in article 31;

"document" includes, unless otherwise specified, any document sent or supplied in electronic form;

"electronic form" has the meaning given in section 1168 of the Companies Act 2006;

"fully paid" in relation to a share, means that the nominal value and any premium to be paid to the company in respect of that share have been paid to the company;

"hard copy form" has the meaning given in section 1168 of the Companies Act 2006;

"holder" in relation to shares means the person whose name is entered in the register of members as the holder of the shares;

"instrument" means a document in hard copy form;

"ordinary resolution" has the meaning given in section 282 of the Companies Act 2006;

"paid" means paid or credited as paid;

"participate", in relation to a directors' meeting, has the meaning given in article 10;

"proxy notice" has the meaning given in article 45;

"shareholder" means a person who is the holder of a share;

"shares" means shares in the company;

"special resolution" has the meaning given in section 283 of the Companies Act 2006;

"subsidiary" has the meaning given in section 1159 of the Companies Act 2006;

"transmittee" means a person entitled to a share by reason of the death or bankruptcy of a shareholder or otherwise by operation of law; and

"writing" means the representation or reproduction of words, symbols or other information in a visible form by any method or combination of methods, whether sent or supplied in electronic form or otherwise.

Unless the context otherwise requires, other words or expressions contained in these articles bear the same meaning as in the Companies Act 2006 as in force on the date when these articles become binding on the company.

Liability of members

2. The liability of the members is limited to the amount, if any, unpaid on the shares held by them.

PART 2
DIRECTORS

DIRECTORS' POWERS AND RESPONSIBILITIES

Directors' general authority

3. Subject to the articles, the directors are responsible for the management of the company's business, for which purpose they may exercise all the powers of the company.

Shareholders' reserve power

4.—(1) The shareholders may, by special resolution, direct the directors to take, or refrain from taking, specified action.

(2) No such special resolution invalidates anything which the directors have done before the passing of the resolution.

Directors may delegate

5.—(1) Subject to the articles, the directors may delegate any of the powers which are conferred on them under the articles—

(a) to such person or committee;
(b) by such means (including by power of attorney);
(c) to such an extent;
(d) in relation to such matters or territories; and
(e) on such terms and conditions;

as they think fit.

(2) If the directors so specify, any such delegation may authorise further delegation of the directors' powers by any person to whom they are delegated.

(3) The directors may revoke any delegation in whole or part, or alter its terms and conditions.

Committees

6.—(1) Committees to which the directors delegate any of their powers must follow procedures which are based as far as they are applicable on those provisions of the articles which govern the taking of decisions by directors.

(2) The directors may make rules of procedure for all or any committees, which prevail over rules derived from the articles if they are not consistent with them.

DECISION-MAKING BY DIRECTORS

Directors to take decisions collectively

7.—(1) The general rule about decision-making by directors is that any decision of the directors must be either a majority decision at a meeting or a decision taken in accordance with article 8.

(2) If—

(a) the company only has one director, and
(b) no provision of the articles requires it to have more than one director,

the general rule does not apply, and the director may take decisions without regard to any of the provisions of the articles relating to directors' decision-making.

Unanimous decisions

8.—(1) A decision of the directors is taken in accordance with this article when all eligible directors indicate to each other by any means that they share a common view on a matter.

(2) Such a decision may take the form of a resolution in writing, copies of which have been signed by each eligible director or to which each eligible director has otherwise indicated agreement in writing.

(3) References in this article to eligible directors are to directors who would have been entitled to vote on the matter had it been proposed as a resolution at a directors' meeting.

(4) A decision may not be taken in accordance with this article if the eligible directors would not have formed a quorum at such a meeting.

Calling a directors' meeting

9.—(1) Any director may call a directors' meeting by giving notice of the meeting to the directors or by authorising the company secretary (if any) to give such notice.

(2) Notice of any directors' meeting must indicate—

(a) its proposed date and time;
(b) where it is to take place; and
(c) if it is anticipated that directors participating in the meeting will not be in the same place, how it is proposed that they should communicate with each other during the meeting.

(3) Notice of a directors' meeting must be given to each director, but need not be in writing.

(4) Notice of a directors' meeting need not be given to directors who waive their entitlement to notice of that meeting, by giving notice to that effect to the company not more than 7 days after the date on which the meeting is held. Where such notice is given after the meeting has been held, that does not affect the validity of the meeting, or of any business conducted at it.

Participation in directors' meetings

10.—(1) Subject to the articles, directors participate in a directors' meeting, or part of a directors' meeting, when—

(a) the meeting has been called and takes place in accordance with the articles, and
(b) they can each communicate to the others any information or opinions they have on any particular item of the business of the meeting.

(2) In determining whether directors are participating in a directors' meeting, it is irrelevant where any director is or how they communicate with each other.

(3) If all the directors participating in a meeting are not in the same place, they may decide that the meeting is to be treated as taking place wherever any of them is.

Quorum for directors' meetings

11.—(1) At a directors' meeting, unless a quorum is participating, no proposal is to be voted on, except a proposal to call another meeting.

(2) The quorum for directors' meetings may be fixed from time to time by a decision of the directors, but it must never be less than two, and unless otherwise fixed it is two.

(3) If the total number of directors for the time being is less than the quorum required, the directors must not take any decision other than a decision—

(a) to appoint further directors, or
(b) to call a general meeting so as to enable the shareholders to appoint further directors.

Chairing of directors' meetings

12.—(1) The directors may appoint a director to chair their meetings.

(2) The person so appointed for the time being is known as the chairman.

(3) The directors may terminate the chairman's appointment at any time.

(4) If the chairman is not participating in a directors' meeting within ten minutes of the time at which it was to start, the participating directors must appoint one of themselves to chair it.

Casting vote

13.—(1) If the numbers of votes for and against a proposal are equal, the chairman or other director chairing the meeting has a casting vote.

(2) But this does not apply if, in accordance with the articles, the chairman or other director is not to be counted as participating in the decision-making process for quorum or voting purposes.

Conflicts of interest

14.—(1) If a proposed decision of the directors is concerned with an actual or proposed transaction or arrangement with the company in which a director is interested, that director is not to be counted as participating in the decision-making process for quorum or voting purposes.

(2) But if paragraph (3) applies, a director who is interested in an actual or proposed transaction or arrangement with the company is to be counted as participating in the decision-making process for quorum and voting purposes.

(3) This paragraph applies when—

(a) the company by ordinary resolution disapplies the provision of the articles which would otherwise prevent a director from being counted as participating in the decision-making process;
(b) the director's interest cannot reasonably be regarded as likely to give rise to a conflict of interest; or
(c) the director's conflict of interest arises from a permitted cause.

(4) For the purposes of this article, the following are permitted causes—

(a) a guarantee given, or to be given, by or to a director in respect of an obligation incurred by or on behalf of the company or any of its subsidiaries;
(b) subscription, or an agreement to subscribe, for shares or other securities of the company or any of its subsidiaries, or to underwrite, sub-underwrite, or guarantee subscription for any such shares or securities; and
(c) arrangements pursuant to which benefits are made available to employees and directors or former employees and directors of the company or any

of its subsidiaries which do not provide special benefits for directors or former directors.

(5) For the purposes of this article, references to proposed decisions and decision-making processes include any directors' meeting or part of a directors' meeting.

(6) Subject to paragraph (7), if a question arises at a meeting of directors or of a committee of directors as to the right of a director to participate in the meeting (or part of the meeting) for voting or quorum purposes, the question may, before the conclusion of the meeting, be referred to the chairman whose ruling in relation to any director other than the chairman is to be final and conclusive.

(7) If any question as to the right to participate in the meeting (or part of the meeting) should arise in respect of the chairman, the question is to be decided by a decision of the directors at that meeting, for which purpose the chairman is not to be counted as participating in the meeting (or that part of the meeting) for voting or quorum purposes.

Records of decisions to be kept

15. The directors must ensure that the company keeps a record, in writing, for at least 10 years from the date of the decision recorded, of every unanimous or majority decision taken by the directors.

Directors' discretion to make further rules

16. Subject to the articles, the directors may make any rule which they think fit about how they take decisions, and about how such rules are to be recorded or communicated to directors.

APPOINTMENT OF DIRECTORS

Methods of appointing directors

17.—(1) Any person who is willing to act as a director, and is permitted by law to do so, may be appointed to be a director—

(a) by ordinary resolution, or
(b) by a decision of the directors.

(2) In any case where, as a result of death, the company has no shareholders and no directors, the personal representatives of the last shareholder to have died have the right, by notice in writing, to appoint a person to be a director.

(3) For the purposes of paragraph (2), where 2 or more shareholders die in circumstances rendering it uncertain who was the last to die, a younger shareholder is deemed to have survived an older shareholder.

Termination of director's appointment

18. A person ceases to be a director as soon as—

(a) that person ceases to be a director by virtue of any provision of the Companies Act 2006 or is prohibited from being a director by law;

(b) a bankruptcy order is made against that person;

(c) a composition is made with that person's creditors generally in satisfaction of that person's debts;

(d) a registered medical practitioner who is treating that person gives a written opinion to the company stating that that person has become physically or mentally incapable of acting as a director and may remain so for more than three months;

(e) by reason of that person's mental health, a court makes an order which wholly or partly prevents that person from personally exercising any powers or rights which that person would otherwise have;

(f) notification is received by the company from the director that the director is resigning from office, and such resignation has taken effect in accordance with its terms.

Directors' remuneration

19.—(1) Directors may undertake any services for the company that the directors decide.

(2) Directors are entitled to such remuneration as the directors determine—

(a) for their services to the company as directors, and

(b) for any other service which they undertake for the company.

(3) Subject to the articles, a director's remuneration may—

(a) take any form, and

(b) include any arrangements in connection with the payment of a pension, allowance or gratuity, or any death, sickness or disability benefits, to or in respect of that director.

(4) Unless the directors decide otherwise, directors' remuneration accrues from day to day.

(5) Unless the directors decide otherwise, directors are not accountable to the company for any remuneration which they receive as directors or other officers

or employees of the company's subsidiaries or of any other body corporate in which the company is interested.

Directors' expenses

20. The company may pay any reasonable expenses which the directors properly incur in connection with their attendance at—

(a) meetings of directors or committees of directors,
(b) general meetings, or
(c) separate meetings of the holders of any class of shares or of debentures of the company,

or otherwise in connection with the exercise of their powers and the discharge of their responsibilities in relation to the company.

PART 3
SHARES AND DISTRIBUTIONS

SHARES

All shares to be fully paid up

21.—(1) No share is to be issued for less than the aggregate of its nominal value and any premium to be paid to the company in consideration for its issue.

(2) This does not apply to shares taken on the formation of the company by the subscribers to the company's memorandum.

Powers to issue different classes of share

22.—(1) Subject to the articles, but without prejudice to the rights attached to any existing share, the company may issue shares with such rights or restrictions as may be determined by ordinary resolution.

(2) The company may issue shares which are to be redeemed, or are liable to be redeemed at the option of the company or the holder, and the directors may determine the terms, conditions and manner of redemption of any such shares.

Company not bound by less than absolute interests

23. Except as required by law, no person is to be recognised by the company as holding any share upon any trust, and except as otherwise required by law or the articles, the company is not in any way to be bound by or recognise any interest in a share other than the holder's absolute ownership of it and all the rights attaching to it.

Share certificates

24.—(1) The company must issue each shareholder, free of charge, with one or more certificates in respect of the shares which that shareholder holds.

(2) Every certificate must specify—

(a) in respect of how many shares, of what class, it is issued;
(b) the nominal value of those shares;
(c) that the shares are fully paid; and
(d) any distinguishing numbers assigned to them.

(3) No certificate may be issued in respect of shares of more than one class.

(4) If more than one person holds a share, only one certificate may be issued in respect of it.

(5) Certificates must—

(a) have affixed to them the company's common seal, or
(b) be otherwise executed in accordance with the Companies Acts.

Replacement share certificates

25.—(1) If a certificate issued in respect of a shareholder's shares is—

(a) damaged or defaced, or
(b) said to be lost, stolen or destroyed,

that shareholder is entitled to be issued with a replacement certificate in respect of the same shares.

(2) A shareholder exercising the right to be issued with such a replacement certificate—

(a) may at the same time exercise the right to be issued with a single certificate or separate certificates;
(b) must return the certificate which is to be replaced to the company if it is damaged or defaced; and
(c) must comply with such conditions as to evidence, indemnity and the payment of a reasonable fee as the directors decide.

Share transfers

26.—(1) Shares may be transferred by means of an instrument of transfer in any usual form or any other form approved by the directors, which is executed by or on behalf of the transferor.

(2) No fee may be charged for registering any instrument of transfer or other document relating to or affecting the title to any share.

(3) The company may retain any instrument of transfer which is registered.

(4) The transferor remains the holder of a share until the transferee's name is entered in the register of members as holder of it.

(5) The directors may refuse to register the transfer of a share, and if they do so, the instrument of transfer must be returned to the transferee with the notice of refusal unless they suspect that the proposed transfer may be fraudulent.

Transmission of shares

27.—(1) If title to a share passes to a transmittee, the company may only recognise the transmittee as having any title to that share.

(2) A transmittee who produces such evidence of entitlement to shares as the directors may properly require—

(a) may, subject to the articles, choose either to become the holder of those shares or to have them transferred to another person, and
(b) subject to the articles, and pending any transfer of the shares to another person, has the same rights as the holder had.

(3) But transmittees do not have the right to attend or vote at a general meeting, or agree to a proposed written resolution, in respect of shares to which they are entitled, by reason of the holder's death or bankruptcy or otherwise, unless they become the holders of those shares.

Exercise of transmittees' rights

28.—(1) Transmittees who wish to become the holders of shares to which they have become entitled must notify the company in writing of that wish.

(2) If the transmittee wishes to have a share transferred to another person, the transmittee must execute an instrument of transfer in respect of it.

(3) Any transfer made or executed under this article is to be treated as if it were made or executed by the person from whom the transmittee has derived rights in respect of the share, and as if the event which gave rise to the transmission had not occurred.

Transmittees bound by prior notices

29. If a notice is given to a shareholder in respect of shares and a transmittee is entitled to those shares, the transmittee is bound by the notice if it was given to the shareholder before the transmittee's name has been entered in the register of members.

DIVIDENDS AND OTHER DISTRIBUTIONS

Procedure for declaring dividends

30.—(1) The company may by ordinary resolution declare dividends, and the directors may decide to pay interim dividends.

(2) A dividend must not be declared unless the directors have made a recommendation as to its amount. Such a dividend must not exceed the amount recommended by the directors.

(3) No dividend may be declared or paid unless it is in accordance with shareholders' respective rights.

(4) Unless the shareholders' resolution to declare or directors' decision to pay a dividend, or the terms on which shares are issued, specify otherwise, it must be paid by reference to each shareholder's holding of shares on the date of the resolution or decision to declare or pay it.

(5) If the company's share capital is divided into different classes, no interim dividend may be paid on shares carrying deferred or non-preferred rights if, at the time of payment, any preferential dividend is in arrear.

(6) The directors may pay at intervals any dividend payable at a fixed rate if it appears to them that the profits available for distribution justify the payment.

(7) If the directors act in good faith, they do not incur any liability to the holders of shares conferring preferred rights for any loss they may suffer by the lawful payment of an interim dividend on shares with deferred or non-preferred rights.

Payment of dividends and other distributions

31.—(1) Where a dividend or other sum which is a distribution is payable in respect of a share, it must be paid by one or more of the following means—

(a) transfer to a bank or building society account specified by the distribution recipient either in writing or as the directors may otherwise decide;

(b) sending a cheque made payable to the distribution recipient by post to the distribution recipient at the distribution recipient's registered address (if the distribution recipient is a holder of the share), or (in any other case) to an address specified by the distribution recipient either in writing or as the directors may otherwise decide;

(c) sending a cheque made payable to such person by post to such person at such address as the distribution recipient has specified either in writing or as the directors may otherwise decide; or

(d) any other means of payment as the directors agree with the distribution recipient either in writing or by such other means as the directors decide.

(2) In the articles, "the distribution recipient" means, in respect of a share in respect of which a dividend or other sum is payable—

(a) the holder of the share; or

(b) if the share has two or more joint holders, whichever of them is named first in the register of members; or

(c) if the holder is no longer entitled to the share by reason of death or bankruptcy, or otherwise by operation of law, the transmittee.

No interest on distributions

32. The company may not pay interest on any dividend or other sum payable in respect of a share unless otherwise provided by—

(a) the terms on which the share was issued, or

(b) the provisions of another agreement between the holder of that share and the company.

Unclaimed distributions

33.—(1) All dividends or other sums which are—

(a) payable in respect of shares, and

(b) unclaimed after having been declared or become payable,

may be invested or otherwise made use of by the directors for the benefit of the company until claimed.

(2) The payment of any such dividend or other sum into a separate account does not make the company a trustee in respect of it.

(3) If—

(a) twelve years have passed from the date on which a dividend or other sum became due for payment, and

(b) the distribution recipient has not claimed it,

the distribution recipient is no longer entitled to that dividend or other sum and it ceases to remain owing by the company.

Non-cash distributions

34.—(1) Subject to the terms of issue of the share in question, the company may, by ordinary resolution on the recommendation of the directors, decide to pay all or part of a dividend or other distribution payable in respect of a share by transferring non-cash assets of equivalent value (including, without limitation, shares or other securities in any company).

(2) For the purposes of paying a non-cash distribution, the directors may make whatever arrangements they think fit, including, where any difficulty arises regarding the distribution—

(a) fixing the value of any assets;
(b) paying cash to any distribution recipient on the basis of that value in order to adjust the rights of recipients; and
(c) vesting any assets in trustees.

Waiver of distributions

35. Distribution recipients may waive their entitlement to a dividend or other distribution payable in respect of a share by giving the company notice in writing to that effect, but if—

(a) the share has more than one holder, or
(b) more than one person is entitled to the share, whether by reason of the death or bankruptcy of one or more joint holders, or otherwise,

the notice is not effective unless it is expressed to be given, and signed, by all the holders or persons otherwise entitled to the share.

CAPITALISATION OF PROFITS

Authority to capitalise and appropriation of capitalised sums

36.—(1) Subject to the articles, the directors may, if they are so authorised by an ordinary resolution—

(a) decide to capitalise any profits of the company (whether or not they are available for distribution) which are not required for paying a preferential dividend, or any sum standing to the credit of the company's share premium account or capital redemption reserve; and
(b) appropriate any sum which they so decide to capitalise (a "capitalised sum") to the persons who would have been entitled to it if it were distributed by way of dividend (the "persons entitled") and in the same proportions.

(2) Capitalised sums must be applied—

(a) on behalf of the persons entitled, and

174

(b) in the same proportions as a dividend would have been distributed to them.

(3) Any capitalised sum may be applied in paying up new shares of a nominal amount equal to the capitalised sum which are then allotted credited as fully paid to the persons entitled or as they may direct.

(4) A capitalised sum which was appropriated from profits available for distribution may be applied in paying up new debentures of the company which are then allotted credited as fully paid to the persons entitled or as they may direct.

(5) Subject to the articles the directors may—

(a) apply capitalised sums in accordance with paragraphs (3) and (4) partly in one way and partly in another;
(b) make such arrangements as they think fit to deal with shares or debentures becoming distributable in fractions under this article (including the issuing of fractional certificates or the making of cash payments); and
(c) authorise any person to enter into an agreement with the company on behalf of all the persons entitled which is binding on them in respect of the allotment of shares and debentures to them under this article.

PART 4
DECISION-MAKING BY SHAREHOLDERS

ORGANISATION OF GENERAL MEETINGS

Attendance and speaking at general meetings

37.—(1) A person is able to exercise the right to speak at a general meeting when that person is in a position to communicate to all those attending the meeting, during the meeting, any information or opinions which that person has on the business of the meeting.

(2) A person is able to exercise the right to vote at a general meeting when—

(a) that person is able to vote, during the meeting, on resolutions put to the vote at the meeting, and
(b) that person's vote can be taken into account in determining whether or not such resolutions are passed at the same time as the votes of all the other persons attending the meeting.

(3) The directors may make whatever arrangements they consider appropriate to enable those attending a general meeting to exercise their rights to speak or vote at it.

(4) In determining attendance at a general meeting, it is immaterial whether any two or more members attending it are in the same place as each other.

(5) Two or more persons who are not in the same place as each other attend a general meeting if their circumstances are such that if they have (or were to have) rights to speak and vote at that meeting, they are (or would be) able to exercise them.

Quorum for general meetings

38. No business other than the appointment of the chairman of the meeting is to be transacted at a general meeting if the persons attending it do not constitute a quorum.

Chairing general meetings

39.—(1) If the directors have appointed a chairman, the chairman shall chair general meetings if present and willing to do so.

(2) If the directors have not appointed a chairman, or if the chairman is unwilling to chair the meeting or is not present within ten minutes of the time at which a meeting was due to start—

(a) the directors present, or
(b) (if no directors are present), the meeting,

must appoint a director or shareholder to chair the meeting, and the appointment of the chairman of the meeting must be the first business of the meeting.

(3) The person chairing a meeting in accordance with this article is referred to as "the chairman of the meeting".

Attendance and speaking by directors and non-shareholders

40.—(1) Directors may attend and speak at general meetings, whether or not they are shareholders.

(2) The chairman of the meeting may permit other persons who are not—

(a) shareholders of the company, or
(b) otherwise entitled to exercise the rights of shareholders in relation to general meetings,

to attend and speak at a general meeting.

Adjournment

41.—(1) If the persons attending a general meeting within half an hour of the time at which the meeting was due to start do not constitute a quorum, or if during a meeting a quorum ceases to be present, the chairman of the meeting must adjourn it.

(2) The chairman of the meeting may adjourn a general meeting at which a quorum is present if—

(a) the meeting consents to an adjournment, or
(b) it appears to the chairman of the meeting that an adjournment is necessary to protect the safety of any person attending the meeting or ensure that the business of the meeting is conducted in an orderly manner.

(3) The chairman of the meeting must adjourn a general meeting if directed to do so by the meeting.

(4) When adjourning a general meeting, the chairman of the meeting must—

(a) either specify the time and place to which it is adjourned or state that it is to continue at a time and place to be fixed by the directors, and
(b) have regard to any directions as to the time and place of any adjournment which have been given by the meeting.

(5) If the continuation of an adjourned meeting is to take place more than 14 days after it was adjourned, the company must give at least 7 clear days' notice of it (that is, excluding the day of the adjourned meeting and the day on which the notice is given)—

(a) to the same persons to whom notice of the company's general meetings is required to be given, and
(b) containing the same information which such notice is required to contain.

(6) No business may be transacted at an adjourned general meeting which could not properly have been transacted at the meeting if the adjournment had not taken place.

VOTING AT GENERAL MEETINGS

Voting: general

42. A resolution put to the vote of a general meeting must be decided on a show of hands unless a poll is duly demanded in accordance with the articles. Errors and disputes

43.—(1) No objection may be raised to the qualification of any person voting at a general meeting except at the meeting or adjourned meeting at which the vote objected to is tendered, and every vote not disallowed at the meeting is valid.

(2) Any such objection must be referred to the chairman of the meeting, whose decision is final.

Poll votes

44.—(1) A poll on a resolution may be demanded—

(a) in advance of the general meeting where it is to be put to the vote, or
(b) at a general meeting, either before a show of hands on that resolution or immediately after the result of a show of hands on that resolution is declared.

(2) A poll may be demanded by—

(a) the chairman of the meeting;
(b) the directors;
(c) two or more persons having the right to vote on the resolution; or
(d) a person or persons representing not less than one tenth of the total voting rights of all the shareholders having the right to vote on the resolution.

(3) A demand for a poll may be withdrawn if—

(a) the poll has not yet been taken, and
(b) the chairman of the meeting consents to the withdrawal.

(4) Polls must be taken immediately and in such manner as the chairman of the meeting directs.

Content of proxy notices

45.—(1) Proxies may only validly be appointed by a notice in writing (a "proxy notice") which—

(a) states the name and address of the shareholder appointing the proxy;
(b) identifies the person appointed to be that shareholder's proxy and the general meeting in relation to which that person is appointed;
(c) is signed by or on behalf of the shareholder appointing the proxy, or is authenticated in such manner as the directors may determine; and
(d) is delivered to the company in accordance with the articles and any instructions contained in the notice of the general meeting to which they relate.

(2) The company may require proxy notices to be delivered in a particular form, and may specify different forms for different purposes.

(3) Proxy notices may specify how the proxy appointed under them is to vote (or that the proxy is to abstain from voting) on one or more resolutions.

(4) Unless a proxy notice indicates otherwise, it must be treated as—
(a) allowing the person appointed under it as a proxy discretion as to how to vote on any ancillary or procedural resolutions put to the meeting, and
(b) appointing that person as a proxy in relation to any adjournment of the general meeting to which it relates as well as the meeting itself.

Delivery of proxy notices

46.—(1) A person who is entitled to attend, speak or vote (either on a show of hands or on a poll) at a general meeting remains so entitled in respect of that meeting or any adjournment of it, even though a valid proxy notice has been delivered to the company by or on behalf of that person.

(2) An appointment under a proxy notice may be revoked by delivering to the company a notice in writing given by or on behalf of the person by whom or on whose behalf the proxy notice was given.

(3) A notice revoking a proxy appointment only takes effect if it is delivered before the start of the meeting or adjourned meeting to which it relates.

(4) If a proxy notice is not executed by the person appointing the proxy, it must be accompanied by written evidence of the authority of the person who executed it to execute it on the appointor's behalf.

Amendments to resolutions

47.—(1) An ordinary resolution to be proposed at a general meeting may be amended by ordinary resolution if—

(a) notice of the proposed amendment is given to the company in writing by a person entitled to vote at the general meeting at which it is to be proposed not less than 48 hours before the meeting is to take place (or such later time as the chairman of the meeting may determine), and
(b) the proposed amendment does not, in the reasonable opinion of the chairman of the meeting, materially alter the scope of the resolution.

(2) A special resolution to be proposed at a general meeting may be amended by ordinary resolution, if—

(a) the chairman of the meeting proposes the amendment at the general meeting at which the resolution is to be proposed, and
(b) the amendment does not go beyond what is necessary to correct a grammatical or other non-substantive error in the resolution.

(3) If the chairman of the meeting, acting in good faith, wrongly decides that an amendment to a resolution is out of order, the chairman's error does not invalidate the vote on that resolution.

PART 5
ADMINISTRATIVE ARRANGEMENTS

Means of communication to be used

48.—(1) Subject to the articles, anything sent or supplied by or to the company under the articles may be sent or supplied in any way in which the Companies Act 2006 provides for documents or information which are authorised or required by any provision of that Act to be sent or supplied by or to the company.

(2) Subject to the articles, any notice or document to be sent or supplied to a director in connection with the taking of decisions by directors may also be sent or supplied by the means by which that director has asked to be sent or supplied with such notices or documents for the time being.

(3) A director may agree with the company that notices or documents sent to that director in a particular way are to be deemed to have been received within a specified time of their being sent, and for the specified time to be less than 48 hours.

Company seals

49.—(1) Any common seal may only be used by the authority of the directors.

(2) The directors may decide by what means and in what form any common seal is to be used.

(3) Unless otherwise decided by the directors, if the company has a common seal and it is affixed to a document, the document must also be signed by at least one authorised person in the presence of a witness who attests the signature.

(4) For the purposes of this article, an authorised person is—

(a) any director of the company;
(b) the company secretary (if any); or
(c) any person authorised by the directors for the purpose of signing documents to which the common seal is applied.

No right to inspect accounts and other records

50. Except as provided by law or authorised by the directors or an ordinary resolution of the company, no person is entitled to inspect any of the company's accounting or other records or documents merely by virtue of being a shareholder.

Provision for employees on cessation of business

51. The directors may decide to make provision for the benefit of persons employed or formerly employed by the company or any of its subsidiaries (other than a director or former director or shadow director) in connection with the cessation or transfer to any person of the whole or part of the undertaking of the company or that subsidiary.

DIRECTORS' INDEMNITY AND INSURANCE

Indemnity

52.—(1) Subject to paragraph (2), a relevant director of the company or an associated company may be indemnified out of the company's assets against—

(a) any liability incurred by that director in connection with any negligence, default, breach of duty or breach of trust in relation to the company or an associated company,

(b) any liability incurred by that director in connection with the activities of the company or an associated company in its capacity as a trustee of an occupational pension scheme (as defined in section 235(6) of the Companies Act 2006),

(c) any other liability incurred by that director as an officer of the company or an associated company.

(2) This article does not authorise any indemnity which would be prohibited or rendered void by any provision of the Companies Acts or by any other provision of law.

(3) In this article—

(a) companies are associated if one is a subsidiary of the other or both are subsidiaries of the same body corporate, and

(b) a "relevant director" means any director or former director of the company or an associated company.

Insurance

53.—(1) The directors may decide to purchase and maintain insurance, at the expense of the company, for the benefit of any relevant director in respect of any relevant loss.

(2) In this article—

(a) a "relevant director" means any director or former director of the company or an associated company,

(b) a "relevant loss" means any loss or liability which has been or may be incurred by a relevant director in connection with that director's duties or powers in relation to the company, any associated company or any pension fund or employees' share scheme of the company or associated company, and

(c) companies are associated if one is a subsidiary of the other or both are subsidiaries of the same body corporate.

Companies Act 2006 Model Articles for private companies limited by guarantee

The following Model Articles for private companies limited by guarantee are contained in Schedule 2 to the Companies (Model Articles) Regulations 2008 which were made on 16 December 2008 to come into force on 1 October 2009.

For private companies limited by guarantee formed under CA 2006 on or after 1 October 2009 these Model Articles will automatically be the company's articles unless the company chooses to adopt its own tailor-made articles in place of some or all of the Model Articles.

MODEL ARTICLES FOR PRIVATE COMPANIES LIMITED BY GUARANTEE

INDEX TO THE ARTICLES

PART 1
INTERPRETATION AND LIMITATION OF LIABILITY

PART 2
DIRECTORS

DIRECTORS' POWERS AND RESPONSIBILITIES

DECISION-MAKING BY DIRECTORS

36. No right to inspect accounts and other records
37. Provision for employees on cessation of business

DIRECTORS' INDEMNITY AND INSURANCE

38. Indemnity
39. Insurance

PART 1
INTERPRETATION AND LIMITATION OF LIABILITY

Defined terms

1. In the articles, unless the context requires otherwise—

"articles" means the company's articles of association;

"bankruptcy" includes individual insolvency proceedings in a jurisdiction other than England and Wales or Northern Ireland which have an effect similar to that of bankruptcy;

"chairman" has the meaning given in article 12;

"chairman of the meeting" has the meaning given in article 25;

"Companies Acts" means the Companies Acts (as defined in section 2 of the Companies Act 2006), in so far as they apply to the company;

"director" means a director of the company, and includes any person occupying the position of director, by whatever name called;

"document" includes, unless otherwise specified, any document sent or supplied in electronic form;

"electronic form" has the meaning given in section 1168 of the Companies Act 2006;

"member" has the meaning given in section 112 of the Companies Act 2006;

"ordinary resolution" has the meaning given in section 282 of the Companies Act 2006;

"participate", in relation to a directors' meeting, has the meaning given in article 10;

"proxy notice" has the meaning given in article 31;

"special resolution" has the meaning given in section 283 of the Companies Act 2006;

"subsidiary" has the meaning given in section 1159 of the Companies Act 2006; and "writing" means the representation or reproduction of words, symbols or other information in a visible form by any method or combination of methods, whether sent or supplied in electronic form or otherwise.

Unless the context otherwise requires, other words or expressions contained in these articles bear the same meaning as in the Companies Act 2006 as in force on the date when these articles become binding on the company.

Liability of members

2. The liability of each member is limited to £1, being the amount that each member undertakes to contribute to the assets of the company in the event of its being wound up while he is a member or within one year after he ceases to be a member, for—

(a) payment of the company's debts and liabilities contracted before he ceases to be a member,
(b) payment of the costs, charges and expenses of winding up, and
(c) adjustment of the rights of the contributories among themselves.

PART 2
DIRECTORS

DIRECTORS' POWERS AND RESPONSIBILITIES

Directors' general authority

3. Subject to the articles, the directors are responsible for the management of the company's business, for which purpose they may exercise all the powers of the company.

Members' reserve power

4.—(1) The members may, by special resolution, direct the directors to take, or refrain from taking, specified action.

(2) No such special resolution invalidates anything which the directors have done before the passing of the resolution.
Directors may delegate

5.—(1) Subject to the articles, the directors may delegate any of the powers which are conferred on them under the articles—

(a) to such person or committee;
(b) by such means (including by power of attorney);

(c) to such an extent;
(d) in relation to such matters or territories; and
(e) on such terms and conditions;

as they think fit.

(2) If the directors so specify, any such delegation may authorise further delegation of the directors' powers by any person to whom they are delegated.

(3) The directors may revoke any delegation in whole or part, or alter its terms and conditions.

Committees

6.—(1) Committees to which the directors delegate any of their powers must follow procedures which are based as far as they are applicable on those provisions of the articles which govern the taking of decisions by directors.

(2) The directors may make rules of procedure for all or any committees, which prevail over rules derived from the articles if they are not consistent with them.

DECISION-MAKING BY DIRECTORS

Directors to take decisions collectively

7.—(1) The general rule about decision-making by directors is that any decision of the directors must be either a majority decision at a meeting or a decision taken in accordance with article 8.

(2) If—

(a) the company only has one director, and
(b) no provision of the articles requires it to have more than one director,

the general rule does not apply, and the director may take decisions without regard to any of the provisions of the articles relating to directors' decision-making.

Unanimous decisions

8.—(1) A decision of the directors is taken in accordance with this article when all eligible directors indicate to each other by any means that they share a common view on a matter.

(2) Such a decision may take the form of a resolution in writing, copies of which have been signed by each eligible director or to which each eligible director has otherwise indicated agreement in writing.

187

(3) References in this article to eligible directors are to directors who would have been entitled to vote on the matter had it been proposed as a resolution at a directors' meeting.

(4) A decision may not be taken in accordance with this article if the eligible directors would not have formed a quorum at such a meeting.

Calling a directors' meeting

9.—(1) Any director may call a directors' meeting by giving notice of the meeting to the directors or by authorising the company secretary (if any) to give such notice.

(2) Notice of any directors' meeting must indicate—

(a) its proposed date and time;
(b) where it is to take place; and
(c) if it is anticipated that directors participating in the meeting will not be in the same place, how it is proposed that they should communicate with each other during the meeting.

(3) Notice of a directors' meeting must be given to each director, but need not be in writing.

(4) Notice of a directors' meeting need not be given to directors who waive their entitlement to notice of that meeting, by giving notice to that effect to the company not more than 7 days after the date on which the meeting is held. Where such notice is given after the meeting has been held, that does not affect the validity of the meeting, or of any business conducted at it.

Participation in directors' meetings

10.—(1) Subject to the articles, directors participate in a directors' meeting, or part of a directors' meeting, when—

(a) the meeting has been called and takes place in accordance with the articles, and
(b) they can each communicate to the others any information or opinions they have on any particular item of the business of the meeting.

(2) In determining whether directors are participating in a directors' meeting, it is irrelevant where any director is or how they communicate with each other.

(3) If all the directors participating in a meeting are not in the same place, they may decide that the meeting is to be treated as taking place wherever any of them is.

Quorum for directors' meetings

11.—(1) At a directors' meeting, unless a quorum is participating, no proposal is to be voted on, except a proposal to call another meeting.

(2) The quorum for directors' meetings may be fixed from time to time by a decision of the directors, but it must never be less than two, and unless otherwise fixed it is two.

(3) If the total number of directors for the time being is less than the quorum required, the directors must not take any decision other than a decision—

(a) to appoint further directors, or
(b) to call a general meeting so as to enable the members to appoint further directors.

Chairing of directors' meetings

12.—(1) The directors may appoint a director to chair their meetings.

(2) The person so appointed for the time being is known as the chairman.

(3) The directors may terminate the chairman's appointment at any time.

(4) If the chairman is not participating in a directors' meeting within ten minutes of the time at which it was to start, the participating directors must appoint one of themselves to chair it.

Casting vote

13.—(1) If the numbers of votes for and against a proposal are equal, the chairman or other director chairing the meeting has a casting vote.

(2) But this does not apply if, in accordance with the articles, the chairman or other director is not to be counted as participating in the decision-making process for quorum or voting purposes.

Conflicts of interest

14.—(1) If a proposed decision of the directors is concerned with an actual or proposed transaction or arrangement with the company in which a director is interested, that director is not to be counted as participating in the decision-making process for quorum or voting purposes.

(2) But if paragraph (3) applies, a director who is interested in an actual or proposed transaction or arrangement with the company is to be counted as participating in the decision-making process for quorum and voting purposes.

(3) This paragraph applies when—

(a) the company by ordinary resolution disapplies the provision of the articles which would otherwise prevent a director from being counted as participating in the decision-making process;

(b) the director's interest cannot reasonably be regarded as likely to give rise to a conflict of interest; or

(c) the director's conflict of interest arises from a permitted cause.

(4) For the purposes of this article, the following are permitted causes—

(a) a guarantee given, or to be given, by or to a director in respect of an obligation incurred by or on behalf of the company or any of its subsidiaries;

(b) subscription, or an agreement to subscribe, for securities of the company or any of its subsidiaries, or to underwrite, sub-underwrite, or guarantee subscription for any such securities; and

(c) arrangements pursuant to which benefits are made available to employees and directors or former employees and directors of the company or any of its subsidiaries which do not provide special benefits for directors or former directors.

(5) For the purposes of this article, references to proposed decisions and decision-making processes include any directors' meeting or part of a directors' meeting.

(6) Subject to paragraph (7), if a question arises at a meeting of directors or of a committee of directors as to the right of a director to participate in the meeting (or part of the meeting) for voting or quorum purposes, the question may, before the conclusion of the meeting, be referred to the chairman whose ruling in relation to any director other than the chairman is to be final and conclusive.

(7) If any question as to the right to participate in the meeting (or part of the meeting) should arise in respect of the chairman, the question is to be decided by a decision of the directors at that meeting, for which purpose the chairman is not to be counted as participating in the meeting (or that part of the meeting) for voting or quorum purposes.

Records of decisions to be kept

15. The directors must ensure that the company keeps a record, in writing, for at least 10 years from the date of the decision recorded, of every unanimous or majority decision taken by the directors.

Directors' discretion to make further rules

16. Subject to the articles, the directors may make any rule which they think fit about how they take decisions, and about how such rules are to be recorded or communicated to directors.

APPOINTMENT OF DIRECTORS

Methods of appointing directors

17.—(1) Any person who is willing to act as a director, and is permitted by law to do so, may be appointed to be a director—

(a) by ordinary resolution, or
(b) by a decision of the directors.

(2) In any case where, as a result of death, the company has no members and no directors, the personal representatives of the last member to have died have the right, by notice in writing, to appoint a person to be a director.

(3) For the purposes of paragraph (2), where 2 or more members die in circumstances rendering it uncertain who was the last to die, a younger member is deemed to have survived an older member.

Termination of director's appointment

18. A person ceases to be a director as soon as—

(a) that person ceases to be a director by virtue of any provision of the Companies Act 2006 or is prohibited from being a director by law;
(b) a bankruptcy order is made against that person;
(c) a composition is made with that person's creditors generally in satisfaction of that person's debts;
(d) a registered medical practitioner who is treating that person gives a written opinion to the company stating that that person has become physically or mentally incapable of acting as a director and may remain so for more than three months;
(e) by reason of that person's mental health, a court makes an order which wholly or partly prevents that person from personally exercising any powers or rights which that person would otherwise have;
(f) notification is received by the company from the director that the director is resigning from office, and such resignation has taken effect in accordance with its terms.

Directors' remuneration

19.—(1) Directors may undertake any services for the company that the directors decide.

(2) Directors are entitled to such remuneration as the directors determine—

(a) for their services to the company as directors, and

(b) for any other service which they undertake for the company.

(3) Subject to the articles, a director's remuneration may—

(a) take any form, and

(b) include any arrangements in connection with the payment of a pension, allowance or gratuity, or any death, sickness or disability benefits, to or in respect of that director.

(4) Unless the directors decide otherwise, directors' remuneration accrues from day to day.

(5) Unless the directors decide otherwise, directors are not accountable to the company for any remuneration which they receive as directors or other officers or employees of the company's subsidiaries or of any other body corporate in which the company is interested.

Directors' expenses

20. The company may pay any reasonable expenses which the directors properly incur in connection with their attendance at—

(a) meetings of directors or committees of directors,

(b) general meetings, or

(c) separate meetings of the holders of debentures of the company,

or otherwise in connection with the exercise of their powers and the discharge of their responsibilities in relation to the company.

PART 3
MEMBERS

BECOMING AND CEASING TO BE A MEMBER

Applications for membership

21. No person shall become a member of the company unless—

(a) that person has completed an application for membership in a form approved by the directors, and

(b) the directors have approved the application.

Termination of membership

22.—(1) A member may withdraw from membership of the company by giving 7 days' notice to the company in writing.

(2) Membership is not transferable.

(3) A person's membership terminates when that person dies or ceases to exist.

ORGANISATION OF GENERAL MEETINGS

Attendance and speaking at general meetings

23.—(1) A person is able to exercise the right to speak at a general meeting when that person is in a position to communicate to all those attending the meeting, during the meeting, any information or opinions which that person has on the business of the meeting.

(2) A person is able to exercise the right to vote at a general meeting when—

(a) that person is able to vote, during the meeting, on resolutions put to the vote at the meeting, and
(b) that person's vote can be taken into account in determining whether or not such resolutions are passed at the same time as the votes of all the other persons attending the meeting.

(3) The directors may make whatever arrangements they consider appropriate to enable those attending a general meeting to exercise their rights to speak or vote at it.

(4) In determining attendance at a general meeting, it is immaterial whether any two or more members attending it are in the same place as each other.

(5) Two or more persons who are not in the same place as each other attend a general meeting if their circumstances are such that if they have (or were to have) rights to speak and vote at that meeting, they are (or would be) able to exercise them.

Quorum for general meetings

24. No business other than the appointment of the chairman of the meeting is to be transacted at a general meeting if the persons attending it do not constitute a quorum.

Chairing general meetings

25.—(1) If the directors have appointed a chairman, the chairman shall chair general meetings if present and willing to do so.

(2) If the directors have not appointed a chairman, or if the chairman is unwilling to chair the meeting or is not present within ten minutes of the time at which a meeting was due to start—

(a) the directors present, or
(b) (if no directors are present), the meeting,

must appoint a director or member to chair the meeting, and the appointment of the chairman of the meeting must be the first business of the meeting.

(3) The person chairing a meeting in accordance with this article is referred to as "the chairman of the meeting".

Attendance and speaking by directors and non-members

26.—(1) Directors may attend and speak at general meetings, whether or not they are members.

(2) The chairman of the meeting may permit other persons who are not members of the company to attend and speak at a general meeting.

Adjournment

27.—(1) If the persons attending a general meeting within half an hour of the time at which the meeting was due to start do not constitute a quorum, or if during a meeting a quorum ceases to be present, the chairman of the meeting must adjourn it.

(2) The chairman of the meeting may adjourn a general meeting at which a quorum is present if—

(a) the meeting consents to an adjournment, or
(b) it appears to the chairman of the meeting that an adjournment is necessary to protect the safety of any person attending the meeting or ensure that the business of the meeting is conducted in an orderly manner.

(3) The chairman of the meeting must adjourn a general meeting if directed to do so by the meeting.

(4) When adjourning a general meeting, the chairman of the meeting must—

(a) either specify the time and place to which it is adjourned or state that it is to continue at a time and place to be fixed by the directors, and
(b) have regard to any directions as to the time and place of any adjournment which have been given by the meeting.

(5) If the continuation of an adjourned meeting is to take place more than

14 days after it was adjourned, the company must give at least 7 clear days' notice of it (that is, excluding the day of the adjourned meeting and the day on which the notice is given)—

(a) to the same persons to whom notice of the company's general meetings is required to be given, and
(b) containing the same information which such notice is required to contain.

(6) No business may be transacted at an adjourned general meeting which could not properly have been transacted at the meeting if the adjournment had not taken place.

VOTING AT GENERAL MEETINGS

Voting: general

28. A resolution put to the vote of a general meeting must be decided on a show of hands unless a poll is duly demanded in accordance with the articles.

Errors and disputes

29.—(1) No objection may be raised to the qualification of any person voting at a general meeting except at the meeting or adjourned meeting at which the vote objected to is tendered, and every vote not disallowed at the meeting is valid.

(2) Any such objection must be referred to the chairman of the meeting whose decision is final.

Poll votes

30.—(1) A poll on a resolution may be demanded—

(a) in advance of the general meeting where it is to be put to the vote, or
(b) at a general meeting, either before a show of hands on that resolution or immediately after the result of a show of hands on that resolution is declared.

(2) A poll may be demanded by—

(a) the chairman of the meeting;
(b) the directors;
(c) two or more persons having the right to vote on the resolution; or
(d) a person or persons representing not less than one tenth of the total voting rights of all the members having the right to vote on the resolution.

(3) A demand for a poll may be withdrawn if—

(a) the poll has not yet been taken, and
(b) the chairman of the meeting consents to the withdrawal.

(4) Polls must be taken immediately and in such manner as the chairman of the meeting directs.

Content of proxy notices

31.—(1) Proxies may only validly be appointed by a notice in writing (a "proxy notice") which—

(a) states the name and address of the member appointing the proxy;
(b) identifies the person appointed to be that member's proxy and the general meeting in relation to which that person is appointed;
(c) is signed by or on behalf of the member appointing the proxy, or is authenticated in such manner as the directors may determine; and
(d) is delivered to the company in accordance with the articles and any instructions contained in the notice of the general meeting to which they relate.

(2) The company may require proxy notices to be delivered in a particular form, and may specify different forms for different purposes.

(3) Proxy notices may specify how the proxy appointed under them is to vote (or that the proxy is to abstain from voting) on one or more resolutions.

(4) Unless a proxy notice indicates otherwise, it must be treated as—

(a) allowing the person appointed under it as a proxy discretion as to how to vote on any ancillary or procedural resolutions put to the meeting, and
(b) appointing that person as a proxy in relation to any adjournment of the general meeting to which it relates as well as the meeting itself.

Delivery of proxy notices

32.—(1) A person who is entitled to attend, speak or vote (either on a show of hands or on a poll) at a general meeting remains so entitled in respect of that meeting or any adjournment of it, even though a valid proxy notice has been delivered to the company by or on behalf of that person.

(2) An appointment under a proxy notice may be revoked by delivering to the company a notice in writing given by or on behalf of the person by whom or on whose behalf the proxy notice was given.

(3) A notice revoking a proxy appointment only takes effect if it is delivered before the start of the meeting or adjourned meeting to which it relates.

(4) If a proxy notice is not executed by the person appointing the proxy, it must be accompanied by written evidence of the authority of the person who executed it to execute it on the appointor's behalf.

Amendments to resolutions

33.—(1) An ordinary resolution to be proposed at a general meeting may be amended by ordinary resolution if—

(a) notice of the proposed amendment is given to the company in writing by a person entitled to vote at the general meeting at which it is to be proposed not less than 48 hours before the meeting is to take place (or such later time as the chairman of the meeting may determine), and

(b) the proposed amendment does not, in the reasonable opinion of the chairman of the meeting, materially alter the scope of the resolution.

(2) A special resolution to be proposed at a general meeting may be amended by ordinary resolution, if—

(a) the chairman of the meeting proposes the amendment at the general meeting at which the resolution is to be proposed, and

(b) the amendment does not go beyond what is necessary to correct a grammatical or other non-substantive error in the resolution.

(3) If the chairman of the meeting, acting in good faith, wrongly decides that an amendment to a resolution is out of order, the chairman's error does not invalidate the vote on that resolution.

PART 4
ADMINISTRATIVE ARRANGEMENTS

Means of communication to be used

34.—(1) Subject to the articles, anything sent or supplied by or to the company under the articles may be sent or supplied in any way in which the Companies Act 2006 provides for documents or information which are authorised or required by any provision of that Act to be sent or supplied by or to the company.

(2) Subject to the articles, any notice or document to be sent or supplied to a director in connection with the taking of decisions by directors may also be sent or supplied by the means by which that director has asked to be sent or supplied with such notices or documents for the time being.

(3) A director may agree with the company that notices or documents sent to that director in a particular way are to be deemed to have been received within

a specified time of their being sent, and for the specified time to be less than 48 hours.

Company seals

35.—(1) Any common seal may only be used by the authority of the directors.

(2) The directors may decide by what means and in what form any common seal is to be used.

(3) Unless otherwise decided by the directors, if the company has a common seal and it is affixed to a document, the document must also be signed by at least one authorised person in the presence of a witness who attests the signature.

(4) For the purposes of this article, an authorised person is—

(a) any director of the company;
(b) the company secretary (if any); or
(c) any person authorised by the directors for the purpose of signing documents to which the common seal is applied.

No right to inspect accounts and other records

36. Except as provided by law or authorised by the directors or an ordinary resolution of the company, no person is entitled to inspect any of the company's accounting or other records or documents merely by virtue of being a member.

Provision for employees on cessation of business

37. The directors may decide to make provision for the benefit of persons employed or formerly employed by the company or any of its subsidiaries (other than a director or former director or shadow director) in connection with the cessation or transfer to any person of the whole or part of the undertaking of the company or that subsidiary.

DIRECTORS' INDEMNITY AND INSURANCE

Indemnity

38.—(1) Subject to paragraph (2), a relevant director of the company or an associated company may be indemnified out of the company's assets against—

(a) any liability incurred by that director in connection with any negligence, default, breach of duty or breach of trust in relation to the company or an associated company,

(b) any liability incurred by that director in connection with the activities of the company or an associated company in its capacity as a trustee of an occupational pension scheme (as defined in section 235(6) of the Companies Act 2006),

(c) any other liability incurred by that director as an officer of the company or an associated company.

(2) This article does not authorise any indemnity which would be prohibited or rendered void by any provision of the Companies Acts or by any other provision of law.

(3) In this article—

(a) companies are associated if one is a subsidiary of the other or both are subsidiaries of the same body corporate, and

(b) a "relevant director" means any director or former director of the company or an associated company.

Insurance

39.—(1) The directors may decide to purchase and maintain insurance, at the expense of the company, for the benefit of any relevant director in respect of any relevant loss.

(2) In this article—

(a) a "relevant director" means any director or former director of the company or an associated company,

(b) a "relevant loss" means any loss or liability which has been or may be incurred by a relevant director in connection with that director's duties or powers in relation to the company, any associated company or any pension fund or employees' share scheme of the company or associated company, and

(c) companies are associated if one is a subsidiary of the other or both are subsidiaries of the same body corporate.

Companies Act 2006 Model articles for public companies

The following Model Articles for public companies are contained in Schedule 3 to the Companies (Model Articles) Regulations 2008 which were made on 16 December 2008 to come into force on 1 October 2009.

For public companies formed under CA 2006 on or after 1 October 2009 these Model Articles will automatically be the company's articles unless the company chooses to adopt its own tailor-made articles in place of some or all of the Model Articles.

MODEL ARTICLES FOR PUBLIC COMPANIES

INDEX TO THE ARTICLES

TRANSFER AND TRANSMISSION OF SHARES

CONSOLIDATION OF SHARES

DISTRIBUTIONS

CAPITALISATION OF PROFITS

PART 5
MISCELLANEOUS PROVISIONS

COMMUNICATIONS

ADMINISTRATIVE ARRANGEMENTS

DIRECTORS' INDEMNITY AND INSURANCE

PART 1
INTERPRETATION AND LIMITATION OF LIABILITY

Defined terms

1. In the articles, unless the context requires otherwise—

"alternate" or "alternate director" has the meaning given in article 25;

"appointor" has the meaning given in article 25;

"articles" means the company's articles of association;

"bankruptcy" includes individual insolvency proceedings in a jurisdiction other than England and Wales or Northern Ireland which have an effect similar to that of bankruptcy;

"call" has the meaning given in article 54;

"call notice" has the meaning given in article 54;

"certificate" means a paper certificate (other than a share warrant) evidencing a person's title to specified shares or other securities;

"certificated" in relation to a share, means that it is not an uncertificated share or a share in respect of which a share warrant has been issued and is current;

"chairman" has the meaning given in article 12;

"chairman of the meeting" has the meaning given in article 31;

"Companies Acts" means the Companies Acts (as defined in section 2 of the Companies Act 2006), in so far as they apply to the company;

"company's lien" has the meaning given in article 52;

"director" means a director of the company, and includes any person occupying the position of director, by whatever name called;

"distribution recipient" has the meaning given in article 72;

"document" includes, unless otherwise specified, any document sent or supplied in electronic form;

"electronic form" has the meaning given in section 1168 of the Companies Act 2006;

"fully paid" in relation to a share, means that the nominal value and any premium to be paid to the company in respect of that share have been paid to the company;

"hard copy form" has the meaning given in section 1168 of the Companies Act 2006;

"holder" in relation to shares means the person whose name is entered in the register of members as the holder of the shares, or, in the case of a share in respect of which a share warrant has been issued (and not cancelled), the person in possession of that warrant;

"instrument" means a document in hard copy form;

"lien enforcement notice" has the meaning given in article 53;

"member" has the meaning given in section 112 of the Companies Act 2006;

"ordinary resolution" has the meaning given in section 282 of the Companies Act 2006;

"paid" means paid or credited as paid;

"participate", in relation to a directors' meeting, has the meaning given in article 9;

"partly paid" in relation to a share means that part of that share's nominal value or any premium at which it was issued has not been paid to the company;

"proxy notice" has the meaning given in article 38;

"securities seal" has the meaning given in article 47;

"shares" means shares in the company;

"special resolution" has the meaning given in section 283 of the Companies Act 2006;

"subsidiary" has the meaning given in section 1159 of the Companies Act 2006;

"transmittee" means a person entitled to a share by reason of the death or bankruptcy of a shareholder or otherwise by operation of law;

"uncertificated" in relation to a share means that, by virtue of legislation (other than section 778 of the Companies Act 2006) permitting title to shares to be evidenced and transferred without a certificate, title to that share is evidenced and may be transferred without a certificate; and

"writing" means the representation or reproduction of words, symbols or other information in a visible form by any method or combination of methods, whether sent or supplied in electronic form or otherwise.

Unless the context otherwise requires, other words or expressions contained in these articles bear the same meaning as in the Companies Act 2006 as in force on the date when these articles become binding on the company.

Liability of members

2. The liability of the members is limited to the amount, if any, unpaid on the shares held by them.

PART 2
DIRECTORS

DIRECTORS' POWERS AND RESPONSIBILITIES

Directors' general authority

3. Subject to the articles, the directors are responsible for the management of the company's business, for which purpose they may exercise all the powers of the company.

Members' reserve power

4.—(1) The members may, by special resolution, direct the directors to take, or refrain from taking, specified action.

(2) No such special resolution invalidates anything which the directors have done before the passing of the resolution.

Directors may delegate

5.—(1) Subject to the articles, the directors may delegate any of the powers which are conferred on them under the articles—

(a) to such person or committee;
(b) by such means (including by power of attorney);
(c) to such an extent;
(d) in relation to such matters or territories; and
(e) on such terms and conditions;

as they think fit.

(2) If the directors so specify, any such delegation may authorise further delegation of the directors' powers by any person to whom they are delegated.

(3) The directors may revoke any delegation in whole or part, or alter its terms and conditions.

Committees

6.—(1) Committees to which the directors delegate any of their powers must follow procedures which are based as far as they are applicable on those provisions of the articles which govern the taking of decisions by directors.

(2) The directors may make rules of procedure for all or any committees, which prevail over rules derived from the articles if they are not consistent with them.

DECISION-MAKING BY DIRECTORS

Directors to take decisions collectively

7. Decisions of the directors may be taken—

(a) at a directors' meeting, or
(b) in the form of a directors' written resolution.

Calling a directors' meeting

8.—(1) Any director may call a directors' meeting.

(2) The company secretary must call a directors' meeting if a director so requests.

(3) A directors' meeting is called by giving notice of the meeting to the directors.

(4) Notice of any directors' meeting must indicate—

(a) its proposed date and time;
(b) where it is to take place; and
(c) if it is anticipated that directors participating in the meeting will not be in the same place, how it is proposed that they should communicate with each other during the meeting.

(5) Notice of a directors' meeting must be given to each director, but need not be in writing.

(6) Notice of a directors' meeting need not be given to directors who waive their entitlement to notice of that meeting, by giving notice to that effect to the company not more than 7 days after the date on which the meeting is held. Where such notice is given after the meeting has been held, that does not affect the validity of the meeting, or of any business conducted at it.

Participation in directors' meetings

9.—(1) Subject to the articles, directors participate in a directors' meeting, or part of a directors' meeting, when—

(a) the meeting has been called and takes place in accordance with the articles, and
(b) they can each communicate to the others any information or opinions they have on any particular item of the business of the meeting.

(2) In determining whether directors are participating in a directors' meeting, it is irrelevant where any director is or how they communicate with each other.

(3) If all the directors participating in a meeting are not in the same place, they may decide that the meeting is to be treated as taking place wherever any of them is.

Quorum for directors' meetings

10.—(1) At a directors' meeting, unless a quorum is participating, no proposal is to be voted on, except a proposal to call another meeting.

(2) The quorum for directors' meetings may be fixed from time to time by a decision of the directors, but it must never be less than two, and unless otherwise fixed it is two.

Meetings where total number of directors less than quorum

11.—(1) This article applies where the total number of directors for the time being is less than the quorum for directors' meetings.

(2) If there is only one director, that director may appoint sufficient directors to make up a quorum or call a general meeting to do so.

(3) If there is more than one director—

(a) a directors' meeting may take place, if it is called in accordance with the articles and at least two directors participate in it, with a view to appointing sufficient directors to make up a quorum or calling a general meeting to do so, and
(b) if a directors' meeting is called but only one director attends at the appointed date and time to participate in it, that director may appoint sufficient directors to make up a quorum or call a general meeting to do so.

Chairing directors' meetings

12.—(1) The directors may appoint a director to chair their meetings.

(2) The person so appointed for the time being is known as the chairman.

(3) The directors may appoint other directors as deputy or assistant chairmen to chair directors' meetings in the chairman's absence.

(4) The directors may terminate the appointment of the chairman, deputy or assistant chairman at any time.

(5) If neither the chairman nor any director appointed generally to chair directors' meetings in the chairman's absence is participating in a meeting

within ten minutes of the time at which it was to start, the participating directors must appoint one of themselves to chair it.

Voting at directors' meetings: general rules

13.—(1) Subject to the articles, a decision is taken at a directors' meeting by a majority of the votes of the participating directors.

(2) Subject to the articles, each director participating in a directors' meeting has one vote.

(3) Subject to the articles, if a director has an interest in an actual or proposed transaction or arrangement with the company—

(a) that director and that director's alternate may not vote on any proposal relating to it, but
(b) this does not preclude the alternate from voting in relation to that transaction or arrangement on behalf of another appointor who does not have such an interest.

Chairman's casting vote at directors' meetings

14.—(1) If the numbers of votes for and against a proposal are equal, the chairman or other director chairing the meeting has a casting vote.

(2) But this does not apply if, in accordance with the articles, the chairman or other director is not to be counted as participating in the decision-making process for quorum or voting purposes.

Alternates voting at directors' meetings

15. A director who is also an alternate director has an additional vote on behalf of each appointor who is—

(a) not participating in a directors' meeting, and
(b) would have been entitled to vote if they were participating in it.

Conflicts of interest

16.—(1) If a directors' meeting, or part of a directors' meeting, is concerned with an actual or proposed transaction or arrangement with the company in which a director is interested, that director is not to be counted as participating in that meeting, or part of a meeting, for quorum or voting purposes.

(2) But if paragraph (3) applies, a director who is interested in an actual or proposed transaction or arrangement with the company is to be counted

as participating in a decision at a directors' meeting, or part of a directors' meeting, relating to it for quorum and voting purposes.

(3) This paragraph applies when—

(a) the company by ordinary resolution disapplies the provision of the articles which would otherwise prevent a director from being counted as participating in, or voting at, a directors' meeting;

(b) the director's interest cannot reasonably be regarded as likely to give rise to a conflict of interest; or

(c) the director's conflict of interest arises from a permitted cause.

(4) For the purposes of this article, the following are permitted causes—

(a) a guarantee given, or to be given, by or to a director in respect of an obligation incurred by or on behalf of the company or any of its subsidiaries;

(b) subscription, or an agreement to subscribe, for shares or other securities of the company or any of its subsidiaries, or to underwrite, sub-underwrite, or guarantee subscription for any such shares or securities; and

(c) arrangements pursuant to which benefits are made available to employees and directors or former employees and directors of the company or any of its subsidiaries which do not provide special benefits for directors or former directors.

(5) Subject to paragraph (6), if a question arises at a meeting of directors or of a committee of directors as to the right of a director to participate in the meeting (or part of the meeting) for voting or quorum purposes, the question may, before the conclusion of the meeting, be referred to the chairman whose ruling in relation to any director other than the chairman is to be final and conclusive.

(6) If any question as to the right to participate in the meeting (or part of the meeting) should arise in respect of the chairman, the question is to be decided by a decision of the directors at that meeting, for which purpose the chairman is not to be counted as participating in the meeting (or that part of the meeting) for voting or quorum purposes.

Proposing directors' written resolutions

17.—(1) Any director may propose a directors' written resolution.

(2) The company secretary must propose a directors' written resolution if a director so requests.

(3) A directors' written resolution is proposed by giving notice of the proposed resolution to the directors.

(4) Notice of a proposed directors' written resolution must indicate—

(a) the proposed resolution, and
(b) the time by which it is proposed that the directors should adopt it.

(5) Notice of a proposed directors' written resolution must be given in writing to each director.

(6) Any decision which a person giving notice of a proposed directors' written resolution takes regarding the process of adopting that resolution must be taken reasonably in good faith.

Adoption of directors' written resolutions

18.—(1) A proposed directors' written resolution is adopted when all the directors who would have been entitled to vote on the resolution at a directors' meeting have signed one or more copies of it, provided that those directors would have formed a quorum at such a meeting.

(2) It is immaterial whether any director signs the resolution before or after the time by which the notice proposed that it should be adopted.

(3) Once a directors' written resolution has been adopted, it must be treated as if it had been a decision taken at a directors' meeting in accordance with the articles.

(4) The company secretary must ensure that the company keeps a record, in writing, of all directors' written resolutions for at least ten years from the date of their adoption.

Directors' discretion to make further rules

19. Subject to the articles, the directors may make any rule which they think fit about how they take decisions, and about how such rules are to be recorded or communicated to directors.

APPOINTMENT OF DIRECTORS

Methods of appointing directors

20. Any person who is willing to act as a director, and is permitted by law to do so, may be appointed to be a director—

(a) by ordinary resolution, or
(b) by a decision of the directors.

Retirement of directors by rotation

21.—(1) At the first annual general meeting all the directors must retire from office.

(2) At every subsequent annual general meeting any directors—

(a) who have been appointed by the directors since the last annual general meeting, or
(b) who were not appointed or reappointed at one of the preceding two annual general meetings,

must retire from office and may offer themselves for reappointment by the members.

Termination of director's appointment

22. A person ceases to be a director as soon as—

(a) that person ceases to be a director by virtue of any provision of the Companies Act 2006 or is prohibited from being a director by law;
(b) a bankruptcy order is made against that person;
(c) a composition is made with that person's creditors generally in satisfaction of that person's debts;
(d) a registered medical practitioner who is treating that person gives a written opinion to the company stating that that person has become physically or mentally incapable of acting as a director and may remain so for more than three months;
(e) by reason of that person's mental health, a court makes an order which wholly or partly prevents that person from personally exercising any powers or rights which that person would otherwise have;
(f) notification is received by the company from the director that the director is resigning from office as director, and such resignation has taken effect in accordance with its terms.

Directors' remuneration

23.—(1) Directors may undertake any services for the company that the directors decide.

(2) Directors are entitled to such remuneration as the directors determine—

(a) for their services to the company as directors, and
(b) for any other service which they undertake for the company.

(3) Subject to the articles, a director's remuneration may—

(a) take any form, and
(b) include any arrangements in connection with the payment of a pension,

allowance or gratuity, or any death, sickness or disability benefits, to or in respect of that director.

(4) Unless the directors decide otherwise, directors' remuneration accrues from day to day.

(5) Unless the directors decide otherwise, directors are not accountable to the company for any remuneration which they receive as directors or other officers or employees of the company's subsidiaries or of any other body corporate in which the company is interested.

Directors' expenses

24. The company may pay any reasonable expenses which the directors properly incur in connection with their attendance at—

(a) meetings of directors or committees of directors,
(b) general meetings, or
(c) separate meetings of the holders of any class of shares or of debentures of the company,

or otherwise in connection with the exercise of their powers and the discharge of their responsibilities in relation to the company.

ALTERNATE DIRECTORS

Appointment and removal of alternates

25.—(1) Any director (the "appointor") may appoint as an alternate any other director, or any other person approved by resolution of the directors, to—

(a) exercise that director's powers, and
(b) carry out that director's responsibilities,

in relation to the taking of decisions by the directors in the absence of the alternate's appointor.

(2) Any appointment or removal of an alternate must be effected by notice in writing to the company signed by the appointor, or in any other manner approved by the directors.

(3) The notice must—

(a) identify the proposed alternate, and
(b) in the case of a notice of appointment, contain a statement signed by the proposed alternate that the proposed alternate is willing to act as the alternate of the director giving the notice.

Rights and responsibilities of alternate directors

26.—(1) An alternate director has the same rights, in relation to any directors' meeting or directors' written resolution, as the alternate's appointor.

(2) Except as the articles specify otherwise, alternate directors—

(a) are deemed for all purposes to be directors;
(b) are liable for their own acts and omissions;
(c) are subject to the same restrictions as their appointors; and
(d) are not deemed to be agents of or for their appointors.

(3) A person who is an alternate director but not a director—

(a) may be counted as participating for the purposes of determining whether a quorum is participating (but only if that person's appointor is not participating), and
(b) may sign a written resolution (but only if it is not signed or to be signed by that person's appointor).

No alternate may be counted as more than one director for such purposes.

(4) An alternate director is not entitled to receive any remuneration from the company for serving as an alternate director except such part of the alternate's appointor's remuneration as the appointor may direct by notice in writing made to the company.

Termination of alternate directorship

27. An alternate director's appointment as an alternate terminates—

(a) when the alternate's appointor revokes the appointment by notice to the company in writing specifying when it is to terminate;
(b) on the occurrence in relation to the alternate of any event which, if it occurred in relation to the alternate's appointor, would result in the termination of the appointor's appointment as a director;
(c) on the death of the alternate's appointor; or
(d) when the alternate's appointor's appointment as a director terminates, except that an alternate's appointment as an alternate does not terminate when the appointor retires by rotation at a general meeting and is then re-appointed as a director at the same general meeting.

PART 3
DECISION-MAKING BY MEMBERS

ORGANISATION OF GENERAL MEETINGS

Members can call general meeting if not enough directors

28. If—

(a) the company has fewer than two directors, and
(b) the director (if any) is unable or unwilling to appoint sufficient directors to make up a quorum or to call a general meeting to do so,

then two or more members may call a general meeting (or instruct the company secretary to do so) for the purpose of appointing one or more directors.

Attendance and speaking at general meetings

29.—(1) A person is able to exercise the right to speak at a general meeting when that person is in a position to communicate to all those attending the meeting, during the meeting, any information or opinions which that person has on the business of the meeting.

(2) A person is able to exercise the right to vote at a general meeting when—

(a) that person is able to vote, during the meeting, on resolutions put to the vote at the meeting, and
(b) that person's vote can be taken into account in determining whether or not such resolutions are passed at the same time as the votes of all the other persons attending the meeting.

(3) The directors may make whatever arrangements they consider appropriate to enable those attending a general meeting to exercise their rights to speak or vote at it.

(4) In determining attendance at a general meeting, it is immaterial whether any two or more members attending it are in the same place as each other.

(5) Two or more persons who are not in the same place as each other attend a general meeting if their circumstances are such that if they have (or were to have) rights to speak and vote at that meeting, they are (or would be) able to exercise them.

Quorum for general meetings

30. No business other than the appointment of the chairman of the meeting is to be transacted at a general meeting if the persons attending it do not constitute a quorum.

Chairing general meetings

31.—(1) If the directors have appointed a chairman, the chairman shall chair general meetings if present and willing to do so.

(2) If the directors have not appointed a chairman, or if the chairman is unwilling to chair the meeting or is not present within ten minutes of the time at which a meeting was due to start—

(a) the directors present, or
(b) (if no directors are present), the meeting,

must appoint a director or member to chair the meeting, and the appointment of the chairman of the meeting must be the first business of the meeting.

(3) The person chairing a meeting in accordance with this article is referred to as "the chairman of the meeting".

Attendance and speaking by directors and non-members

32.—(1) Directors may attend and speak at general meetings, whether or not they are members.

(2) The chairman of the meeting may permit other persons who are not—

(a) members of the company, or
(b) otherwise entitled to exercise the rights of members in relation to general meetings,

to attend and speak at a general meeting.

Adjournment

33.—(1) If the persons attending a general meeting within half an hour of the time at which the meeting was due to start do not constitute a quorum, or if during a meeting a quorum ceases to be present, the chairman of the meeting must adjourn it.

(2) The chairman of the meeting may adjourn a general meeting at which a quorum is present if—

(a) the meeting consents to an adjournment, or
(b) it appears to the chairman of the meeting that an adjournment is necessary to protect the safety of any person attending the meeting or ensure that the business of the meeting is conducted in an orderly manner.

(3) The chairman of the meeting must adjourn a general meeting if directed to do so by the meeting.

(4) When adjourning a general meeting, the chairman of the meeting must—

(a) either specify the time and place to which it is adjourned or state that it is to continue at a time and place to be fixed by the directors, and

(b) have regard to any directions as to the time and place of any adjournment which have been given by the meeting.

(5) If the continuation of an adjourned meeting is to take place more than 14 days after it was adjourned, the company must give at least 7 clear days' notice of it (that is, excluding the day of the adjourned meeting and the day on which the notice is given)—

(a) to the same persons to whom notice of the company's general meetings is required to be given, and

(b) containing the same information which such notice is required to contain.

(6) No business may be transacted at an adjourned general meeting which could not properly have been transacted at the meeting if the adjournment had not taken place.

VOTING AT GENERAL MEETINGS

Voting: general

34. A resolution put to the vote of a general meeting must be decided on a show of hands unless a poll is duly demanded in accordance with the articles.

Errors and disputes

35.—(1) No objection may be raised to the qualification of any person voting at a general meeting except at the meeting or adjourned meeting at which the vote objected to is tendered, and every vote not disallowed at the meeting is valid.

(2) Any such objection must be referred to the chairman of the meeting whose decision is final.

Demanding a poll

36.—(1) A poll on a resolution may be demanded—

(a) in advance of the general meeting where it is to be put to the vote, or

(b) at a general meeting, either before a show of hands on that resolution or immediately after the result of a show of hands on that resolution is declared.

(2) A poll may be demanded by—

(a) the chairman of the meeting;

(b) the directors;

(c) two or more persons having the right to vote on the resolution; or

(d) a person or persons representing not less than one tenth of the total voting rights of all the members having the right to vote on the resolution.

(3) A demand for a poll may be withdrawn if—

(a) the poll has not yet been taken, and

(b) the chairman of the meeting consents to the withdrawal.

Procedure on a poll

37.—(1) Subject to the articles, polls at general meetings must be taken when, where and in such manner as the chairman of the meeting directs.

(2) The chairman of the meeting may appoint scrutineers (who need not be members) and decide how and when the result of the poll is to be declared.

(3) The result of a poll shall be the decision of the meeting in respect of the resolution on which the poll was demanded.

(4) A poll on—

(a) the election of the chairman of the meeting, or

(b) a question of adjournment,

must be taken immediately.

(5) Other polls must be taken within 30 days of their being demanded.

(6) A demand for a poll does not prevent a general meeting from continuing, except as regards the question on which the poll was demanded.

(7) No notice need be given of a poll not taken immediately if the time and place at which it is to be taken are announced at the meeting at which it is demanded.

(8) In any other case, at least 7 days' notice must be given specifying the time and place at which the poll is to be taken.

Content of proxy notices

38.—(1) Proxies may only validly be appointed by a notice in writing (a "proxy notice") which—

(a) states the name and address of the member appointing the proxy;

(b) identifies the person appointed to be that member's proxy and the general meeting in relation to which that person is appointed;

(c) is signed by or on behalf of the member appointing the proxy, or is authenticated in such manner as the directors may determine; and

(d) is delivered to the company in accordance with the articles and any instructions contained in the notice of the general meeting to which they relate.

(2) The company may require proxy notices to be delivered in a particular form, and may specify different forms for different purposes.

(3) Proxy notices may specify how the proxy appointed under them is to vote (or that the proxy is to abstain from voting) on one or more resolutions.

(4) Unless a proxy notice indicates otherwise, it must be treated as—

(a) allowing the person appointed under it as a proxy discretion as to how to vote on any ancillary or procedural resolutions put to the meeting, and

(b) appointing that person as a proxy in relation to any adjournment of the general meeting to which it relates as well as the meeting itself.

Delivery of proxy notices

39.—(1) Any notice of a general meeting must specify the address or addresses ("proxy notification address") at which the company or its agents will receive proxy notices relating to that meeting, or any adjournment of it, delivered in hard copy or electronic form.

(2) A person who is entitled to attend, speak or vote (either on a show of hands or on a poll) at a general meeting remains so entitled in respect of that meeting or any adjournment of it, even though a valid proxy notice has been delivered to the company by or on behalf of that person.

(3) Subject to paragraphs (4) and (5), a proxy notice must be delivered to a proxy notification address not less than 48 hours before the general meeting or adjourned meeting to which it relates.

(4) In the case of a poll taken more than 48 hours after it is demanded, the notice must be delivered to a proxy notification address not less than 24 hours before the time appointed for the taking of the poll.

(5) In the case of a poll not taken during the meeting but taken not more than 48 hours after it was demanded, the proxy notice must be delivered—

(a) in accordance with paragraph (3), or

(b) at the meeting at which the poll was demanded to the chairman, secretary or any director.

(6) An appointment under a proxy notice may be revoked by delivering a notice in writing given by or on behalf of the person by whom or on whose behalf the proxy notice was given to a proxy notification address.

(7) A notice revoking a proxy appointment only takes effect if it is delivered before—

(a) the start of the meeting or adjourned meeting to which it relates, or
(b) (in the case of a poll not taken on the same day as the meeting or adjourned meeting) the time appointed for taking the poll to which it relates.

(8) If a proxy notice is not signed by the person appointing the proxy, it must be accompanied by written evidence of the authority of the person who executed it to execute it on the appointor's behalf.

Amendments to resolutions

40.—(1) An ordinary resolution to be proposed at a general meeting may be amended by ordinary resolution if—

(a) notice of the proposed amendment is given to the company secretary in writing by a person entitled to vote at the general meeting at which it is to be proposed not less than 48 hours before the meeting is to take place (or such later time as the chairman of the meeting may determine), and
(b) the proposed amendment does not, in the reasonable opinion of the chairman of the meeting, materially alter the scope of the resolution.

(2) A special resolution to be proposed at a general meeting may be amended by ordinary resolution, if—

(a) the chairman of the meeting proposes the amendment at the general meeting at which the resolution is to be proposed, and
(b) the amendment does not go beyond what is necessary to correct a grammatical or other non-substantive error in the resolution.

(3) If the chairman of the meeting, acting in good faith, wrongly decides that an amendment to a resolution is out of order, the chairman's error does not invalidate the vote on that resolution.

RESTRICTIONS ON MEMBERS' RIGHTS

No voting of shares on which money owed to company

41. No voting rights attached to a share may be exercised at any general meeting, at any adjournment of it, or on any poll called at or in relation to it, unless all amounts payable to the company in respect of that share have been paid.

APPLICATION OF RULES TO CLASS MEETINGS

Class meetings

42. The provisions of the articles relating to general meetings apply, with any necessary modifications, to meetings of the holders of any class of shares.

PART 4
SHARES AND DISTRIBUTIONS

ISSUE OF SHARES

Powers to issue different classes of share

43.—(1) Subject to the articles, but without prejudice to the rights attached to any existing share, the company may issue shares with such rights or restrictions as may be determined by ordinary resolution.

(2) The company may issue shares which are to be redeemed, or are liable to be redeemed at the option of the company or the holder, and the directors may determine the terms, conditions and manner of redemption of any such shares.

Payment of commissions on subscription for shares

44.—(1) The company may pay any person a commission in consideration for that person—

(a) subscribing, or agreeing to subscribe, for shares, or
(b) procuring, or agreeing to procure, subscriptions for shares.

(2) Any such commission may be paid—

(a) in cash, or in fully paid or partly paid shares or other securities, or partly in one way and partly in the other, and
(b) in respect of a conditional or an absolute subscription.

INTERESTS IN SHARES

Company not bound by less than absolute interests

45. Except as required by law, no person is to be recognised by the company as holding any share upon any trust, and except as otherwise required by law or the articles, the company is not in any way to be bound by or recognise any interest in a share other than the holder's absolute ownership of it and all the rights attaching to it.

SHARE CERTIFICATES

Certificates to be issued except in certain cases

46.—(1) The company must issue each member with one or more certificates in respect of the shares which that member holds.

(2) This article does not apply to—

(a) uncertificated shares;
(b) shares in respect of which a share warrant has been issued; or
(c) shares in respect of which the Companies Acts permit the company not to issue a certificate.

(3) Except as otherwise specified in the articles, all certificates must be issued free of charge.

(4) No certificate may be issued in respect of shares of more than one class.

(5) If more than one person holds a share, only one certificate may be issued in respect of it.

Contents and execution of share certificates

47.—(1) Every certificate must specify—

(a) in respect of how many shares, of what class, it is issued;
(b) the nominal value of those shares;
(c) the amount paid up on them; and
(d) any distinguishing numbers assigned to them.

(2) Certificates must—

(a) have affixed to them the company's common seal or an official seal which is a facsimile of the company's common seal with the addition on its face of the word "Securities" (a "securities seal"), or
(b) be otherwise executed in accordance with the Companies Acts.

Consolidated share certificates

48.—(1) When a member's holding of shares of a particular class increases, the company may issue that member with—

(a) a single, consolidated certificate in respect of all the shares of a particular class which that member holds, or
(b) a separate certificate in respect of only those shares by which that member's holding has increased.

(2) When a member's holding of shares of a particular class is reduced, the company must ensure that the member is issued with one or more certificates in respect of the number of shares held by the member after that reduction. But the company need not (in the absence of a request from the member) issue any new certificate if—

(a) all the shares which the member no longer holds as a result of the reduction, and
(b) none of the shares which the member retains following the reduction, were, immediately before the reduction, represented by the same certificate.

(3) A member may request the company, in writing, to replace—

(a) the member's separate certificates with a consolidated certificate, or
(b) the member's consolidated certificate with two or more separate certificates representing such proportion of the shares as the member may specify.

(4) When the company complies with such a request it may charge such reasonable fee as the directors may decide for doing so.

(5) A consolidated certificate must not be issued unless any certificates which it is to replace have first been returned to the company for cancellation.

Replacement share certificates

49.—(1) If a certificate issued in respect of a member's shares is—

(a) damaged or defaced, or
(b) said to be lost, stolen or destroyed,

that member is entitled to be issued with a replacement certificate in respect of the same shares.

(2) A member exercising the right to be issued with such a replacement certificate—

(a) may at the same time exercise the right to be issued with a single certificate or separate certificates;
(b) must return the certificate which is to be replaced to the company if it is damaged or defaced; and
(c) must comply with such conditions as to evidence, indemnity and the payment of a reasonable fee as the directors decide.

SHARES NOT HELD IN CERTIFICATED FORM

Uncertificated shares

50.—(1) In this article, "the relevant rules" means—

(a) any applicable provision of the Companies Acts about the holding, evidencing of title to, or transfer of shares other than in certificated form, and

(b) any applicable legislation, rules or other arrangements made under or by virtue of such provision.

(2) The provisions of this article have effect subject to the relevant rules.

(3) Any provision of the articles which is inconsistent with the relevant rules must be disregarded, to the extent that it is inconsistent, whenever the relevant rules apply.

(4) Any share or class of shares of the company may be issued or held on such terms, or in such a way, that—

(a) title to it or them is not, or must not be, evidenced by a certificate, or

(b) it or they may or must be transferred wholly or partly without a certificate.

(5) The directors have power to take such steps as they think fit in relation to—

(a) the evidencing of and transfer of title to uncertificated shares (including in connection with the issue of such shares);

(b) any records relating to the holding of uncertificated shares;

(c) the conversion of certificated shares into uncertificated shares; or

(d) the conversion of uncertificated shares into certificated shares.

(6) The company may by notice to the holder of a share require that share—

(a) if it is uncertificated, to be converted into certificated form, and

(b) if it is certificated, to be converted into uncertificated form,

to enable it to be dealt with in accordance with the articles.

(7) If—

(a) the articles give the directors power to take action, or require other persons to take action, in order to sell, transfer or otherwise dispose of shares, and

(b) uncertificated shares are subject to that power, but the power is expressed in terms which assume the use of a certificate or other written instrument,

the directors may take such action as is necessary or expedient to achieve the same results when exercising that power in relation to uncertificated shares.

(8) In particular, the directors may take such action as they consider appropriate to achieve the sale, transfer, disposal, forfeiture, re-allotment or surrender of an uncertificated share or otherwise to enforce a lien in respect of it.

(9) Unless the directors otherwise determine, shares which a member holds in uncertificated form must be treated as separate holdings from any shares which that member holds in certificated form.

(10) A class of shares must not be treated as two classes simply because some shares of that class are held in certificated form and others are held in uncertificated form.

Share warrants

51.—(1) The directors may issue a share warrant in respect of any fully paid share.

(2) Share warrants must be—

(a) issued in such form, and
(b) executed in such manner,

as the directors decide.

(3) A share represented by a share warrant may be transferred by delivery of the warrant representing it.

(4) The directors may make provision for the payment of dividends in respect of any share represented by a share warrant.

(5) Subject to the articles, the directors may decide the conditions on which any share warrant is issued. In particular, they may—

(a) decide the conditions on which new warrants are to be issued in place of warrants which are damaged or defaced, or said to have been lost, stolen or destroyed;
(b) decide the conditions on which bearers of warrants are entitled to attend and vote at general meetings;
(c) decide the conditions subject to which bearers of warrants may surrender their warrant so as to hold their shares in certificated or uncertificated form instead; and
(d) vary the conditions of issue of any warrant from time to time,

and the bearer of a warrant is subject to the conditions and procedures in force in relation to it, whether or not they were decided or specified before the warrant was issued.

(6) Subject to the conditions on which the warrants are issued from time to time, bearers of share warrants have the same rights and privileges as they would if their names had been included in the register as holders of the shares represented by their warrants.

(7) The company must not in any way be bound by or recognise any interest in a share represented by a share warrant other than the absolute right of the bearer of that warrant to that warrant.

PARTLY PAID SHARES

Company's lien over partly paid shares

52.—(1) The company has a lien ("the company's lien") over every share which is partly paid for any part of—

(a) that share's nominal value, and
(b) any premium at which it was issued,

which has not been paid to the company, and which is payable immediately or at some time in the future, whether or not a call notice has been sent in respect of it.

(2) The company's lien over a share—

(a) takes priority over any third party's interest in that share, and
(b) extends to any dividend or other money payable by the company in respect of that share and (if the lien is enforced and the share is sold by the company) the proceeds of sale of that share.

(3) The directors may at any time decide that a share which is or would otherwise be subject to the company's lien shall not be subject to it, either wholly or in part.

Enforcement of the company's lien

53.—(1) Subject to the provisions of this article, if—

(a) a lien enforcement notice has been given in respect of a share, and
(b) the person to whom the notice was given has failed to comply with it,

the company may sell that share in such manner as the directors decide.

(2) A lien enforcement notice—

(a) may only be given in respect of a share which is subject to the company's lien, in respect of which a sum is payable and the due date for payment of that sum has passed;
(b) must specify the share concerned;
(c) must require payment of the sum payable within 14 days of the notice;
(d) must be addressed either to the holder of the share or to a person entitled to it by reason of the holder's death, bankruptcy or otherwise; and
(e) must state the company's intention to sell the share if the notice is not complied with.

(3) Where shares are sold under this article—

(a) the directors may authorise any person to execute an instrument of transfer of the shares to the purchaser or a person nominated by the purchaser, and

(b) the transferee is not bound to see to the application of the consideration, and the transferee's title is not affected by any irregularity in or invalidity of the process leading to the sale.

(4) The net proceeds of any such sale (after payment of the costs of sale and any other costs of enforcing the lien) must be applied—

(a) first, in payment of so much of the sum for which the lien exists as was payable at the date of the lien enforcement notice,

(b) second, to the person entitled to the shares at the date of the sale, but only after the certificate for the shares sold has been surrendered to the company for cancellation or a suitable indemnity has been given for any lost certificates, and subject to a lien equivalent to the company's lien over the shares before the sale for any money payable in respect of the shares after the date of the lien enforcement notice.

(5) A statutory declaration by a director or the company secretary that the declarant is a director or the company secretary and that a share has been sold to satisfy the company's lien on a specified date—

(a) is conclusive evidence of the facts stated in it as against all persons claiming to be entitled to the share, and

(b) subject to compliance with any other formalities of transfer required by the articles or by law, constitutes a good title to the share.

Call notices

54.—(1) Subject to the articles and the terms on which shares are allotted, the directors may send a notice (a "call notice") to a member requiring the member to pay the company a specified sum of money (a "call") which is payable in respect of shares which that member holds at the date when the directors decide to send the call notice.

(2) A call notice—

(a) may not require a member to pay a call which exceeds the total sum unpaid on that member's shares (whether as to the share's nominal value or any amount payable to the company by way of premium);

(b) must state when and how any call to which it relates it is to be paid; and

(c) may permit or require the call to be paid by instalments.

(3) A member must comply with the requirements of a call notice, but no member is obliged to pay any call before 14 days have passed since the notice was sent.

(4) Before the company has received any call due under a call notice the directors may—

(a) revoke it wholly or in part, or
(b) specify a later time for payment than is specified in the notice,

by a further notice in writing to the member in respect of whose shares the call is made.

Liability to pay calls

55.—(1) Liability to pay a call is not extinguished or transferred by transferring the shares in respect of which it is required to be paid.

(2) Joint holders of a share are jointly and severally liable to pay all calls in respect of that share.

(3) Subject to the terms on which shares are allotted, the directors may, when issuing shares, provide that call notices sent to the holders of those shares may require them—

(a) to pay calls which are not the same, or
(b) to pay calls at different times.

When call notice need not be issued

56.—(1) A call notice need not be issued in respect of sums which are specified, in the terms on which a share is issued, as being payable to the company in respect of that share (whether in respect of nominal value or premium)—

(a) on allotment;
(b) on the occurrence of a particular event; or
(c) on a date fixed by or in accordance with the terms of issue.

(2) But if the due date for payment of such a sum has passed and it has not been paid, the holder of the share concerned is treated in all respects as having failed to comply with a call notice in respect of that sum, and is liable to the same consequences as regards the payment of interest and forfeiture.

Failure to comply with call notice: automatic consequences

57.—(1) If a person is liable to pay a call and fails to do so by the call payment date—

(a) the directors may issue a notice of intended forfeiture to that person, and
(b) until the call is paid, that person must pay the company interest on the call from the call payment date at the relevant rate.

(2) For the purposes of this article—

(a) the "call payment date" is the time when the call notice states that a call is payable, unless the directors give a notice specifying a later date, in which case the "call payment date" is that later date;

(b) the "relevant rate" is—

    (i) the rate fixed by the terms on which the share in respect of which the call is due was allotted;

    (ii) such other rate as was fixed in the call notice which required payment of the call, or has otherwise been determined by the directors; or

    (iii) if no rate is fixed in either of these ways, 5 per cent per annum.

(3) The relevant rate must not exceed by more than 5 percentage points the base lending rate most recently set by the Monetary Policy Committee of the Bank of England in connection with its responsibilities under Part 2 of the Bank of England Act 1998(2).

(4) The directors may waive any obligation to pay interest on a call wholly or in part.

Notice of intended forfeiture

58. A notice of intended forfeiture—

(a) may be sent in respect of any share in respect of which a call has not been paid as required by a call notice;

(b) must be sent to the holder of that share or to a person entitled to it by reason of the holder's death, bankruptcy or otherwise;

(c) must require payment of the call and any accrued interest by a date which is not less than 14 days after the date of the notice;

(d) must state how the payment is to be made; and

(e) must state that if the notice is not complied with, the shares in respect of which the call is payable will be liable to be forfeited.

Directors' power to forfeit shares

59. If a notice of intended forfeiture is not complied with before the date by which payment of the call is required in the notice of intended forfeiture, the directors may decide that any share in respect of which it was given is forfeited, and the forfeiture is to include all dividends or other moneys payable in respect of the forfeited shares and not paid before the forfeiture.

Effect of forfeiture

60.—(1) Subject to the articles, the forfeiture of a share extinguishes—

(a) all interests in that share, and all claims and demands against the company in respect of it, and

(b) all other rights and liabilities incidental to the share as between the person whose share it was prior to the forfeiture and the company.

(2) Any share which is forfeited in accordance with the articles—

(a) is deemed to have been forfeited when the directors decide that it is forfeited;
(b) is deemed to be the property of the company; and
(c) may be sold, re-allotted or otherwise disposed of as the directors think fit.

(3) If a person's shares have been forfeited—

(a) the company must send that person notice that forfeiture has occurred and record it in the register of members;
(b) that person ceases to be a member in respect of those shares;
(c) that person must surrender the certificate for the shares forfeited to the company for cancellation;
(d) that person remains liable to the company for all sums payable by that person under the articles at the date of forfeiture in respect of those shares, including any interest (whether accrued before or after the date of forfeiture); and
(e) the directors may waive payment of such sums wholly or in part or enforce payment without any allowance for the value of the shares at the time of forfeiture or for any consideration received on their disposal.

(4) At any time before the company disposes of a forfeited share, the directors may decide to cancel the forfeiture on payment of all calls and interest due in respect of it and on such other terms as they think fit.

Procedure following forfeiture

61.—(1) If a forfeited share is to be disposed of by being transferred, the company may receive the consideration for the transfer and the directors may authorise any person to execute the instrument of transfer.

(2) A statutory declaration by a director or the company secretary that the declarant is a director or the company secretary and that a share has been forfeited on a specified date—

(a) is conclusive evidence of the facts stated in it as against all persons claiming to be entitled to the share, and
(b) subject to compliance with any other formalities of transfer required by the articles or by law, constitutes a good title to the share.

(3) A person to whom a forfeited share is transferred is not bound to see to the application of the consideration (if any) nor is that person's title to the share affected by any irregularity in or invalidity of the process leading to the forfeiture or transfer of the share.

(4) If the company sells a forfeited share, the person who held it prior to its forfeiture is entitled to receive from the company the proceeds of such sale, net of any commission, and excluding any amount which—

(a) was, or would have become, payable, and
(b) had not, when that share was forfeited, been paid by that person in respect of that share,

but no interest is payable to such a person in respect of such proceeds and the company is not required to account for any money earned on them.

Surrender of shares

62.—(1) A member may surrender any share—

(a) in respect of which the directors may issue a notice of intended forfeiture;
(b) which the directors may forfeit; or
(c) which has been forfeited.

(2) The directors may accept the surrender of any such share.

(3) The effect of surrender on a share is the same as the effect of forfeiture on that share.

(4) A share which has been surrendered may be dealt with in the same way as a share which has been forfeited.

TRANSFER AND TRANSMISSION OF SHARES

Transfers of certificated shares

63.—(1) Certificated shares may be transferred by means of an instrument of transfer in any usual form or any other form approved by the directors, which is executed by or on behalf of—

(a) the transferor, and
(b) (if any of the shares is partly paid) the transferee.

(2) No fee may be charged for registering any instrument of transfer or other document relating to or affecting the title to any share.

(3) The company may retain any instrument of transfer which is registered.

(4) The transferor remains the holder of a certificated share until the transferee's name is entered in the register of members as holder of it.

(5) The directors may refuse to register the transfer of a certificated share if—

(a) the share is not fully paid;

(b) the transfer is not lodged at the company's registered office or such other place as the directors have appointed;

(c) the transfer is not accompanied by the certificate for the shares to which it relates, or such other evidence as the directors may reasonably require to show the transferor's right to make the transfer, or evidence of the right of someone other than the transferor to make the transfer on the transferor's behalf;

(d) the transfer is in respect of more than one class of share; or

(e) the transfer is in favour of more than four transferees.

(6) If the directors refuse to register the transfer of a share, the instrument of transfer must be returned to the transferee with the notice of refusal unless they suspect that the proposed transfer may be fraudulent.

Transfer of uncertificated shares

64. A transfer of an uncertificated share must not be registered if it is in favour of more than four transferees.

Transmission of shares

65.—(1) If title to a share passes to a transmittee, the company may only recognise the transmittee as having any title to that share.

(2) Nothing in these articles releases the estate of a deceased member from any liability in respect of a share solely or jointly held by that member.

Transmittees' rights

66.—(1) A transmittee who produces such evidence of entitlement to shares as the directors may properly require—

(a) may, subject to the articles, choose either to become the holder of those shares or to have them transferred to another person, and

(b) subject to the articles, and pending any transfer of the shares to another person, has the same rights as the holder had.

(2) But transmittees do not have the right to attend or vote at a general meeting in respect of shares to which they are entitled, by reason of the holder's death or bankruptcy or otherwise, unless they become the holders of those shares

Exercise of transmittees' rights

67.—(1) Transmittees who wish to become the holders of shares to which they have become entitled must notify the company in writing of that wish.

(2) If the share is a certificated share and a transmittee wishes to have it transferred to another person, the transmittee must execute an instrument of transfer in respect of it.

(3) If the share is an uncertificated share and the transmittee wishes to have it transferred to another person, the transmittee must—

(a) procure that all appropriate instructions are given to effect the transfer, or
(b) procure that the uncertificated share is changed into certificated form and then execute an instrument of transfer in respect of it.

(4) Any transfer made or executed under this article is to be treated as if it were made or executed by the person from whom the transmittee has derived rights in respect of the share, and as if the event which gave rise to the transmission had not occurred.

Transmittees bound by prior notices

68. If a notice is given to a member in respect of shares and a transmittee is entitled to those shares, the transmittee is bound by the notice if it was given to the member before the transmittee's name has been entered in the register of members.

CONSOLIDATION OF SHARES

Procedure for disposing of fractions of shares

69.—(1) This article applies where—

(a) there has been a consolidation or division of shares, and
(b) as a result, members are entitled to fractions of shares.

(2) The directors may—

(a) sell the shares representing the fractions to any person including the company for the best price reasonably obtainable;
(b) in the case of a certificated share, authorise any person to execute an instrument of transfer of the shares to the purchaser or a person nominated by the purchaser; and
(c) distribute the net proceeds of sale in due proportion among the holders of the shares.

(3) Where any holder's entitlement to a portion of the proceeds of sale amounts to less than a minimum figure determined by the directors, that member's portion may be distributed to an organisation which is a charity for the purposes of the law of England and Wales, Scotland or Northern Ireland.

(4) The person to whom the shares are transferred is not obliged to ensure that any purchase money is received by the person entitled to the relevant fractions.

(5) The transferee's title to the shares is not affected by any irregularity in or invalidity of the process leading to their sale.

DISTRIBUTIONS

Procedure for declaring dividends

70.—(1) The company may by ordinary resolution declare dividends, and the directors may decide to pay interim dividends.

(2) A dividend must not be declared unless the directors have made a recommendation as to its amount. Such a dividend must not exceed the amount recommended by the directors.

(3) No dividend may be declared or paid unless it is in accordance with members' respective rights.

(4) Unless the members' resolution to declare or directors' decision to pay a dividend, or the terms on which shares are issued, specify otherwise, it must be paid by reference to each member's holding of shares on the date of the resolution or decision to declare or pay it.

(5) If the company's share capital is divided into different classes, no interim dividend may be paid on shares carrying deferred or non-preferred rights if, at the time of payment, any preferential dividend is in arrear.

(6) The directors may pay at intervals any dividend payable at a fixed rate if it appears to them that the profits available for distribution justify the payment.

(7) If the directors act in good faith, they do not incur any liability to the holders of shares conferring preferred rights for any loss they may suffer by the lawful payment of an interim dividend on shares with deferred or non-preferred rights.

Calculation of dividends

71.—(1) Except as otherwise provided by the articles or the rights attached to shares, all dividends must be—

(a) declared and paid according to the amounts paid up on the shares on which the dividend is paid, and
(b) apportioned and paid proportionately to the amounts paid up on the

shares during any portion or portions of the period in respect of which the dividend is paid.

(2) If any share is issued on terms providing that it ranks for dividend as from a particular date, that share ranks for dividend accordingly.

(3) For the purposes of calculating dividends, no account is to be taken of any amount which has been paid up on a share in advance of the due date for payment of that amount.

Payment of dividends and other distributions

72.—(1) Where a dividend or other sum which is a distribution is payable in respect of a share, it must be paid by one or more of the following means—

(a) transfer to a bank or building society account specified by the distribution recipient either in writing or as the directors may otherwise decide;
(b) sending a cheque made payable to the distribution recipient by post to the distribution recipient at the distribution recipient's registered address (if the distribution recipient is a holder of the share), or (in any other case) to an address specified by the distribution recipient either in writing or as the directors may otherwise decide;
(c) sending a cheque made payable to such person by post to such person at such address as the distribution recipient has specified either in writing or as the directors may otherwise decide; or
(d) any other means of payment as the directors agree with the distribution recipient either in writing or by such other means as the directors decide.

(2) In the articles, "the distribution recipient" means, in respect of a share in respect of which a dividend or other sum is payable—

(a) the holder of the share; or
(b) if the share has two or more joint holders, whichever of them is named first in the register of members; or
(c) if the holder is no longer entitled to the share by reason of death or bankruptcy, or otherwise by operation of law, the transmittee.

Deductions from distributions in respect of sums owed to the company

73.—(1) If—

(a) a share is subject to the company's lien, and
(b) the directors are entitled to issue a lien enforcement notice in respect of it,

they may, instead of issuing a lien enforcement notice, deduct from any dividend or other sum payable in respect of the share any sum of money which is payable to the company in respect of that share to the extent that they are entitled to require payment under a lien enforcement notice.

(2) Money so deducted must be used to pay any of the sums payable in respect of that share.

(3) The company must notify the distribution recipient in writing of—

(a) the fact and amount of any such deduction;
(b) any non-payment of a dividend or other sum payable in respect of a share resulting from any such deduction; and
(c) how the money deducted has been applied.

No interest on distributions

74. The company may not pay interest on any dividend or other sum payable in respect of a share unless otherwise provided by—

(a) the terms on which the share was issued, or
(b) the provisions of another agreement between the holder of that share and the company.

Unclaimed distributions

75.—(1) All dividends or other sums which are—

(a) payable in respect of shares, and
(b) unclaimed after having been declared or become payable,

may be invested or otherwise made use of by the directors for the benefit of the company until claimed.

(2) The payment of any such dividend or other sum into a separate account does not make the company a trustee in respect of it.

(3) If—

(a) twelve years have passed from the date on which a dividend or other sum became due for payment, and
(b) the distribution recipient has not claimed it,

the distribution recipient is no longer entitled to that dividend or other sum and it ceases to remain owing by the company.

Non-cash distributions

76.—(1) Subject to the terms of issue of the share in question, the company may, by ordinary resolution on the recommendation of the directors, decide to pay all or part of a dividend or other distribution payable in respect of a share by transferring non-cash assets of equivalent value (including, without limitation, shares or other securities in any company).

(2) If the shares in respect of which such a non-cash distribution is paid are uncertificated, any shares in the company which are issued as a non-cash distribution in respect of them must be uncertificated.

(3) For the purposes of paying a non-cash distribution, the directors may make whatever arrangements they think fit, including, where any difficulty arises regarding the distribution—

(a) fixing the value of any assets;
(b) paying cash to any distribution recipient on the basis of that value in order to adjust the rights of recipients; and
(c) vesting any assets in trustees.

Waiver of distributions

77. Distribution recipients may waive their entitlement to a dividend or other distribution payable in respect of a share by giving the company notice in writing to that effect, but if—

(a) the share has more than one holder, or
(b) more than one person is entitled to the share, whether by reason of the death or bankruptcy of one or more joint holders, or otherwise,

the notice is not effective unless it is expressed to be given, and signed, by all the holders or persons otherwise entitled to the share.

CAPITALISATION OF PROFITS

Authority to capitalise and appropriation of capitalised sums

78.—(1) Subject to the articles, the directors may, if they are so authorised by an ordinary resolution—

(a) decide to capitalise any profits of the company (whether or not they are available for distribution) which are not required for paying a preferential dividend, or any sum standing to the credit of the company's share premium account or capital redemption reserve; and
(b) appropriate any sum which they so decide to capitalise (a "capitalised sum") to the persons who would have been entitled to it if it were distributed by way of dividend (the "persons entitled") and in the same proportions.

(2) Capitalised sums must be applied—

(a) on behalf of the persons entitled, and

(b) in the same proportions as a dividend would have been distributed to them.

(3) Any capitalised sum may be applied in paying up new shares of a nominal amount equal to the capitalised sum which are then allotted credited as fully paid to the persons entitled or as they may direct.

(4) A capitalised sum which was appropriated from profits available for distribution may be applied—

(a) in or towards paying up any amounts unpaid on existing shares held by the persons entitled, or
(b) in paying up new debentures of the company which are then allotted credited as fully paid to the persons entitled or as they may direct.

(5) Subject to the articles the directors may—

(a) apply capitalised sums in accordance with paragraphs (3) and (4) partly in one way and partly in another;
(b) make such arrangements as they think fit to deal with shares or debentures becoming distributable in fractions under this article (including the issuing of fractional certificates or the making of cash payments); and
(c) authorise any person to enter into an agreement with the company on behalf of all the persons entitled which is binding on them in respect of the allotment of shares and debentures to them under this article.

PART 5
MISCELLANEOUS PROVISIONS

COMMUNICATIONS

Means of communication to be used

79.—(1) Subject to the articles, anything sent or supplied by or to the company under the articles may be sent or supplied in any way in which the Companies Act 2006 provides for documents or information which are authorised or required by any provision of that Act to be sent or supplied by or to the company.

(2) Subject to the articles, any notice or document to be sent or supplied to a director in connection with the taking of decisions by directors may also be sent or supplied by the means by which that director has asked to be sent or supplied with such notices or documents for the time being.

(3) A director may agree with the company that notices or documents sent to that director in a particular way are to be deemed to have been received within

a specified time of their being sent, and for the specified time to be less than 48 hours.

Failure to notify contact details

80.—(1) If—

(a) the company sends two consecutive documents to a member over a period of at least 12 months, and
(b) each of those documents is returned undelivered, or the company receives notification that it has not been delivered,

that member ceases to be entitled to receive notices from the company.

(2) A member who has ceased to be entitled to receive notices from the company becomes entitled to receive such notices again by sending the company—

(a) a new address to be recorded in the register of members, or
(b) if the member has agreed that the company should use a means of communication other than sending things to such an address, the information that the company needs to use that means of communication effectively.

ADMINISTRATIVE ARRANGEMENTS

Company seals

81.—(1) Any common seal may only be used by the authority of the directors.

(2) The directors may decide by what means and in what form any common seal or securities seal is to be used.

(3) Unless otherwise decided by the directors, if the company has a common seal and it is affixed to a document, the document must also be signed by at least one authorised person in the presence of a witness who attests the signature.

(4) For the purposes of this article, an authorised person is—

(a) any director of the company;
(b) the company secretary; or
(c) any person authorised by the directors for the purpose of signing documents to which the common seal is applied.

(5) If the company has an official seal for use abroad, it may only be affixed to a document if its use on that document, or documents of a class to which it belongs, has been authorised by a decision of the directors.

(6) If the company has a securities seal, it may only be affixed to securities by

the company secretary or a person authorised to apply it to securities by the company secretary.

(7) For the purposes of the articles, references to the securities seal being affixed to any document include the reproduction of the image of that seal on or in a document by any mechanical or electronic means which has been approved by the directors in relation to that document or documents of a class to which it belongs.

Destruction of documents

82.—(1) The company is entitled to destroy—

(a) all instruments of transfer of shares which have been registered, and all other documents on the basis of which any entries are made in the register of members, from six years after the date of registration;

(b) all dividend mandates, variations or cancellations of dividend mandates, and notifications of change of address, from two years after they have been recorded;

(c) all share certificates which have been cancelled from one year after the date of the cancellation;

(d) all paid dividend warrants and cheques from one year after the date of actual payment; and

(e) all proxy notices from one year after the end of the meeting to which the proxy notice relates.

(2) If the company destroys a document in good faith, in accordance with the articles, and without notice of any claim to which that document may be relevant, it is conclusively presumed in favour of the company that—

(a) entries in the register purporting to have been made on the basis of an instrument of transfer or other document so destroyed were duly and properly made;

(b) any instrument of transfer so destroyed was a valid and effective instrument duly and properly registered;

(c) any share certificate so destroyed was a valid and effective certificate duly and properly cancelled; and

(d) any other document so destroyed was a valid and effective document in accordance with its recorded particulars in the books or records of the company.

(3) This article does not impose on the company any liability which it would not otherwise have if it destroys any document before the time at which this article permits it to do so.

(4) In this article, references to the destruction of any document include a reference to its being disposed of in any manner.

No right to inspect accounts and other records

83. Except as provided by law or authorised by the directors or an ordinary resolution of the company, no person is entitled to inspect any of the company's accounting or other records or documents merely by virtue of being a member.

Provision for employees on cessation of business

84. The directors may decide to make provision for the benefit of persons employed or formerly employed by the company or any of its subsidiaries (other than a director or former director or shadow director) in connection with the cessation or transfer to any person of the whole or part of the undertaking of the company or that subsidiary.

DIRECTORS' INDEMNITY AND INSURANCE

Indemnity

85.—(1) Subject to paragraph (2), a relevant director of the company or an associated company may be indemnified out of the company's assets against—

(a) any liability incurred by that director in connection with any negligence, default, breach of duty or breach of trust in relation to the company or an associated company,

(b) any liability incurred by that director in connection with the activities of the company or an associated company in its capacity as a trustee of an occupational pension scheme (as defined in section 235(6) of the Companies Act 2006),

(c) any other liability incurred by that director as an officer of the company or an associated company.

(2) This article does not authorise any indemnity which would be prohibited or rendered void by any provision of the Companies Acts or by any other provision of law.

(3) In this article—

(a) companies are associated if one is a subsidiary of the other or both are subsidiaries of the same body corporate, and

(b) a "relevant director" means any director or former director of the company or an associated company.

Insurance

86.—(1) The directors may decide to purchase and maintain insurance, at the expense of the company, for the benefit of any relevant director in respect of any relevant loss.

(2) In this article—

(a) a "relevant director" means any director or former director of the company or an associated company,

(b) a "relevant loss" means any loss or liability which has been or may be incurred by a relevant director in connection with that director's duties or powers in relation to the company, any associated company or any pension fund or employees' share scheme of the company or associated company, and

(c) companies are associated if one is a subsidiary of the other or both are subsidiaries of the same body corporate.

7

Checklist of procedures for amending or adopting articles

Procedural steps

1. Review articles to identify required amendments.
2. Decide whether amendment of articles or adoption of new articles is more suitable. Generally, adoption of new articles is favoured where changes are sizeable.
3. Consider form resolutions should take i.e. board meeting or written resolutions of directors and general meeting or written resolutions of members (not available for public companies).
4. Hold board meeting or get directors' written resolutions signed to recommend amendment or adoption resolutions to members and to convene general meeting or approve circulation of written resolutions to members.
5. Issue notice of general meeting. Length of notice required (21 or 14 clear days) depends on whether articles already amended to take into account reduced notice requirements of CA 2006 for special resolutions.
6. Consider whether separate class meetings required.
7. If general meeting is to be held on short notice, arrange for consent to short notice to be signed by shareholders.
8. Hold general meeting or obtain signature of written resolutions. 75 per cent majority required for resolution to be passed.
9. Send signed copy of special resolution and amended/newly adopted articles to Companies House within 15 days.

Companies Act 2006 checklist for amending articles

The tables below summarise the provisions of existing articles of association to be reviewed in light of CA 2006. For detailed commentary refer to Chapter 4.

Suggested wording for clauses that may need to be added to the articles following a review to ensure consistency with CA 2006 are included in the precedent materials.

Public companies

Subject matter	Provisions for review/amendment
Directors	Restrictions affecting appointment of directors • Directors must be at least 16 • No upper age limit may be imposed by the articles • At least one director to be a 'natural person' Indemnity provisions • Ensure provisions drafted widely to give maximum protection permitted • Funding before judgement permitted • Director of a pension trustee company may be indemnified against liability incurred in connection with company's activities as trustee of the scheme • Indemnity cannot cover liabilities to pay regulatory or criminal fines or in defending criminal proceedings if the director is convicted Conflict of interests • Permit directors to authorise actual or potential conflicts and associate provisions. Without such provisions public companies will have to seek approval from the members each time a conflict arises
Shares	Transfer of shares • Provision permitting directors to refuse to register a reason without giving any reason no longer acceptable. Reason for refusal must be given in writing within 2 months

Subject matter	Provisions for review/amendment
	Authorised capital • Remove any limit on the company's authorised capital (from October 2009) **Variation of class rights** • Provisions dealing with how class rights may be varied should be removed as proceedings and specific quorum rights for a meeting convened to vary class rights are included in CA 2006
Meetings and resolutions	**Redundant terminology** • Remove references to concepts not mentioned in CA 2006, e.g. extraordinary resolution, EGM. Use special resolution and general meeting instead **Written resolutions** • Public companies are not permitted to use members' written resolutions under CA 2006 and any procedures to the contrary contained in the articles should be removed **Notice requirements** • Special resolutions can be passed on 14 days' notice rather than 21* **Votes of members** • Under CA 2006 proxies are entitled to vote on a show of hands as well as on a poll • Weekends and bank holidays can be excluded when calculating the return deadline for proxies, which cannot be more than 48 hours before the meeting • Multiple proxies can be appointed • Change in rules on corporate representatives
Electronic and web communications	• Companies may communicate with members by electronic and/or website communication

* For fully listed companies an enabling resolution permitting this must have been passed at an AGM and a facility must be made available so that all members can vote electronically.

Private companies

Subject matter	Provisions for review/amendment
Officers	Restrictions affecting appointment of directors • Directors must be at least 16 • No upper age limit may be imposed by the articles • At least one director must be a 'natural' person Company secretary • No statutory need for the office • Articles should be checked for requirement to have a company secretary so that it can be removed if the company no longer wishes to have a company secretary Indemnity provisions • Ensure provisions drafted widely to give maximum protection permitted to directors • Funding before judgement permitted • Director of a pension trustee company may be indemnified against liability incurred in connection with company's activities as trustee of the scheme • Indemnity cannot cover liabilities to pay regulatory or criminal fines or in defending criminal proceedings if the director is convicted Conflict of interests • Permit directors to authorise actual or potential conflicts and associated provisions. Although not essential for private companies to have authority in their articles it is good practice as it is transparent
Shares	Transfer of shares • Provision permitting directors to refuse to register a reason without giving any reason no longer acceptable. Reason for refusal must be given in writing within 2 months Authorised capital • Remove any limit on the company's authorised capital (from October 2009) Variation of class rights • Provisions dealing with how class rights may be varied should be removed as proceedings and specific quorum rights for a meeting convened to vary class rights are included in CA 2006
Meetings and resolutions	Redundant terminology • Remove references to concepts not mentioned in CA 2006, e.g. extraordinary resolution, EGM. Use special resolution and general meeting instead Written resolutions • Remove any non-statutory procedures to avoid confusion.

Subject matter	Provisions for review/amendment
	Reduced requirements • Special resolutions can be passed on 14 days' notice rather than 21 • Only 90% required for consent to short notice rather than 95% **Shareholder meetings and voting** • No statutory requirement for private companies to hold AGMs – check there is no requirement in the articles which would override this • Remove provisions for directors to retire at AGM, following initial appointment or by rotation and consider whether alternative rotation mechanism is needed • Under CA 2006 proxies are entitled to vote on a show of hands as well as on a poll • Weekends and bank holidays can be excluded when calculating the return deadline for proxies, which cannot be more than 48 hours before the meeting • Multiple proxies can be appointed • Change in rules on corporate representatives
Electronic and web communications	• Companies may communicate with members by electronic and/or website communication (likely to be of less relevance unless company has a big shareholder base)

APPENDIX

9 Sensitive words

The wording below is based on guidance published by Companies House.

Appendix A

You will need the approval of the Secretary of State for Business, Enterprise & Regulatory Reform before you use any of the following words or expressions (or their plural or possessive forms) in your chosen company name.

(a) Words which imply national or international pre-eminence:

British	Great Britain	National	Wales
England	International	Scotland	Welsh
English	Ireland	Scottish	
European	Irish	United Kingdom	

(b) Words which imply business pre-eminence or representative or authoritative status:

Association	Board	Federation	Institution
Authority	Council	Institute	Society
Government	HSC (Health and Social Care)	HPSS (Health and Personal Social Services)	

(c) Words which imply specific objects or functions:

Assurance	Friendly society	Post office	Trade union
Assurer	Fund	Reassurance	Trust
Benevolent	Group	Re-assurer	
Charter	Holding	Register	
Chartered	Industrial & provident society	Registered	
Chemist	Insurance	Re-insurance	
Chemistry	Insurer	Re-insurer	
Co-operative	Patent	Sheffield	
Foundation	Patentee	Stock exchange	

Appendix B

The following words or expressions require the approval of the Secretary of State. If you want to use any of them in your company name you will need to write to the relevant body to obtain their written support to use the name. A copy of the supporting letter should be sent with your application to form a company or to change its name.

Word or Expression	Relevant Body for companies registered in England and Wales	Relevant Body for companies registered in Scotland
Charity, Charitable	Head of Status Charity Commission Woodfield House Tangier Taunton TA1 4BL	*For recognition as a Scottish charity HM Revenue & Customs (HMRC) FICO (Scotland) Trinity Park House South Trinity Road Edinburgh EH5 3SD*
Contact Lens	The Registrar General Optical Council 41 Harley Street London W1N 2DJ	As for England and Wales
Dental, Dentistry	The Registrar General Dental Council 37 Wimpole Street London W1M 8DQ	As for England and Wales
District Nurse, Health Visitor, Midwife, Midwifery, Nurse, Nursing	The Registrar & Chief Executive United Kingdom Central Council for Nursing, Midwifery and Health Visiting 23 Portland Place London W1N 3AF	As for England and Wales

Word or Expression	Relevant Body for companies registered in England and Wales	Relevant Body for companies registered in Scotland
Health Centre	Office of the Solicitor Department of Health & Social Security 48 Carey Street London WC2A 2LS	As for England and Wales
Health Service	Penny Turner Head of Branding Department of Health Room 230B Skipton House 80 London Road London SE1 6LH	As for England and Wales
NHS (National Health Service)	Mike Pattrick Office of the Solicitor Dept of Health, Room 518, New Court 48,Carey Street London WC2A 2LS Tel 0207 412 1225 Email:Mike.Pattrick@dwp.gsi.gov.uk	As for England and Wales
Police	Pauline Laybourne Briefing and Honours Team CRCSG Change and Support Unit 3rd Floor A Fry Building 2 Marsham Street London SW1P 4DF	The Scottish Ministers Police Division St Andrews House Regent Road Edinburgh EH1 3DG
Polytechnic	Department of Education and Science FHE 1B Sanctuary Buildings Great Smith Street Westminster London SW1P 3BT	As for England and Wales
Pregnancy, Termination, Abortion	Department of Health Area 423 Wellington House 133-135 Waterloo Road London SE1 8UG	As for England and Wales
Royal, Royale, Royalty, King, Queen, Prince, Princess, Windsor, Duke, His/Her Majesty	7C-018 (Post Point 7.42) 102 Petty France London SW1H 9AJ (If based in Wales) The National Assembly for Wales Crown Buildings Cathays Park Cardiff CF10 3NQ	Douglas Boyd Protocol Unit St Andrew's House Regent Road Edinburgh EH1 3DG

Word or Expression	Relevant Body for companies registered in England and Wales	Relevant Body for companies registered in Scotland
Special School	Clinton Roche Department for Education and Skills Caxton House 6-12 Tothill Street London SWIH 9NA Tel: 0870 0012345	As for England and Wales
University	Privy Council Office 2 Carlton Gardens London SW1Y 5AA	As for England and Wales

Appendix C

Certain words or expressions are covered by other legislation and their use in company names might be a criminal offence. These are listed below. If you want to use any of these words or expressions in your company name, then you should contact the relevant regulatory authority or ask Companies House for advice before proceeding. Companies House may seek independent advice from the relevant body.

Word Or Expression	Relevant Legislation	Relevant Body
Anzac	Section 1 Anzac Act 1916	Seek advice of Companies House
Architect	Section 20 Architects Registration Act 1997	Architects Registration Board 73 Hallam Street London W1N 6EE
Building Society	Building Society Act 1986	Seek advice from Building Societies Commission Victoria House 30-40 Kingsway London WC2B 6ES

Word Or Expression	Relevant Legislation	Relevant Body
Chamber(s) of Business, Chamber(s) of Commerce, Chamber(s) of Commerce and Industry, Chamber(s) of Commerce, Training and Enterprise, Chamber(s) of Enterprise, Chamber(s) of Industry Chamber(s) of Trade, Chamber(s) of Trade and Industry, Chamber(s) of Training, Chamber(s) of Training and Enterprise *or the Welsh translations of these words*	Company and Business Names (Chamber of Commerce etc.) Act 1999	Guidance is available from Companies House
Chiropodist, Dietician, Medical Laboratory, Technician, Occupational Therapist, Orthoptist, Physiotherapist, Radiographer, Remedial Gymnast	Professions Supplementary to Medicine Act 1960 if preceded by Registered, State or Registered	Mrs Joan Arnott Department of Health HRD HRB Room 2N35A Quarry House Quarry Hill Leeds LS2 7JE
Chiropractor	Chiropractors Act 1994	The Chief Executive General Chiropractic Council 44 Wicklow Street London WC1X 9HL
Credit Union	Credit Union Act 1979	The Public Records Section Financial Services Authority 25 The North Colonnade Canary Wharf London E14 5HS
Dentist, Dental Surgeon, Dental Practitioner,	Dental Act 1984	The Registrar General Dental Council 37 Wimpole Street London W1M 8DQ
Druggist, Pharmaceutical, Pharmaceutist, Pharmacist, Pharmacy	Section 78 Medicines Act 1968	The Director of Legal Services The Royal Pharmaceutical Society of Great Britain 1 Lambeth High Street London SE1 7JN **(for Scottish Registered Companies)** The Pharmaceutical Society 36 York Place Edinburgh EH13HU

Word Or Expression	Relevant Legislation	Relevant Body
Institute of Laryngology, Institute of Otology, Institute of Urology, Institute of Orthopaedics,	University College London Act 1988	Seek advice of University College London Gower Street London WC1E 6BT
Patent Office, Patent Agent	Copyright, Designs and Patents Act 1988	IPPD (Intellectual Property Policy Directorate) Room 3B38, Concept House UK Intellectual Property Office, Cardiff Road, Newport,NP10 8QQ
Olympiad, Olympiads, Olympian, Olympians, Olympic, Olympics, Paralympic, Paralympics, Paralympiad, Paralympiads, Paralympian, Paralympians, *translation of these or words so similar to these protected words*	Olympic Symbol etc. (Protection) Act 1995 (as amended)* Use of such words may infringe the rights of the British Olympic Association/British Paralympic Association. *Also protects the Olympic symbols of five interlocking rings; the Olympic motto "Citius Altius Fortius"("Faster, Higher, Stronger"); the Paralympic symbol of three "agitos"; the Paralympic motto "Spirit in Motion"; and anything so similar to them.* Following London's successful bid to host the 2012 Olympic Games, the London Olympic Games and Paralympic Games Act 2006 has been introduced. This provides further rights for the protection of Olympic words, symbols and marks relating to the Games. In addition to the protected words outlined in this booklet, the registration of a company name which includes specific words implying association with the London 2012 Games may infringe the rights of The London Organising Committee of the Olympic Games Limited (LOCOG) under this Act. For further information, please visit: www.london2012. com/about/our-brand/index.php	The London Organising Committee of the Olympic Games Limited (LOCOG) 23rd Floor 1 Churchill Place Canary Wharf London E14 5LN
Optician, Ophthalmic Optician, Dispensing Optician, Enrolled Optician, Registered Optician, Optometrist	Opticians Act 1989	The Registrar General Optical Council 41 Harley Street London W1N 2DJ

Word Or Expression	Relevant Legislation	Relevant Body
Red Cross, Geneva Cross, Red Crescent, Red Lion and Sun	Geneva Convention Act 1957	Seek advice of Companies House
Solicitor (Scotland)	S.31, Solicitors (Scotland) Act 1980	The Law Society of Scotland 26 Drumsheugh Gardens Edinburgh EH3 7YR
Veterinary Surgeon, Veterinary, Vet	Sections 19/20 Veterinary Surgeons Act 1966	The Registrar Royal College of Veterinary Surgeons 62-64 Horseferry Road London SW1P 2AF

Index